PSYCHOANALYSIS AND UNREPRESENTABLE

CW01432245

Psychoanalysis and the Unrepresentable opens a space for meaningful debate about translating psychoanalytic concepts from the work of clinicians to that of academics and back again. Focusing on the idea of the unrepresentable, this collection of essays by psychoanalysts, psychotherapists, counsellors, artists and film and literary scholars attempts to think through those things that are impossible to be thought through completely.

Offering a unique insight into areas like trauma studies, where it is difficult – if not impossible – to express one's feelings, the collection draws from psychoanalysis in its broadest sense and acts as a gesture against the fixed and the frozen. *Psychoanalysis and the Unrepresentable* is presented in six parts: Approaching trauma, Sense and gesture, Impossible poetics, Without words, Wounds and suture and Auto/Fiction. The chapters therein address topics including touch and speech, adoption, the other and grief, and examine films including Gus Van Sant's *Milk* and Michael Haneke's *Amour*. As a whole, the book brings to the fore those things which are difficult to speak about, but which must be spoken about.

The discussion in this book will be key reading for psychoanalysts, including those in training, psychotherapists and psychotherapeutically-engaged scholars, academics and students of culture studies, psychosocial studies, applied philosophy and film studies, filmmakers and artists.

Agnieszka Piotrowska, PhD, is an award winning documentary filmmaker and theorist, best known for her film *Married to the Eiffel Tower* (2009). Her new work in both practice and theory focuses on post-colonial relationships in Zimbabwe, including an internationally acclaimed documentary film *Lovers in Time or How We Didn't Get Arrested in Harare*. She is the author of *Psychoanalysis and Ethics in*

Documentary Film and the editor of *Embodied Encounters: New approaches to psychoanalysis and cinema*, both published by Routledge. Her new monograph *Black and White: Cinema, politics and the arts in Zimbabwe* (Routledge, 2016) combines practice research with theory. She is co-coordinator of the *Psychoanalysis in Our Time* research network.

Ben Tyrer teaches Film Studies at King's College London. He is the author of *Out of the Past: Lacan and film noir* (Palgrave Macmillan, 2016) and has published widely on psychoanalysis and cinema.

Piotrowska and Tyrer together run Psychoanalysis in Our Time, an international research network funded by the Nordic Summer University.

This anthology sets out to "do the impossible" in interrogating the paradoxes of unrepresentable and unspeakable experience. Drawing together an impressive array of writers from diverse fields including those of clinical practice, film and literary studies, post-colonial theory and cultural analysis, it weaves a complex matrix of ideas grounded in the work of psychoanalytic thinkers as diverse as Freud, Lacan, Bion, Malabou, Winnicott and Meltzer. The essays are lively and compelling, offering new perspectives on themes such as trauma and embodiment, silence and invisibility in the digital age of media, the psychodynamics of touch, voice, gesture, love, grief, adoption and anxiety. A wide range of textual material embracing literature, cinema, poetry, language, meta psychology and metaphysics, provides the basis for philosophical and psychological commentary that is often astute, and the daring inclusion of creative work premised on personal experience acts as an emotional *coup de foudre*. Piotrowska and Tyrer have curated a cracking compendium, one that seduces and challenges in equal measure, and one that will surely become essential reading for anyone interested in the riches of psychoanalytic enquiry.

—**Caroline Bainbridge**, Professor of Culture and Psychoanalysis, University of Roehampton, UK.

This is an important collection that speaks to contemporary events with compassion and poignancy. Piotrowska and Tyrer's *Psychoanalysis and the Unrepresentable: From culture to the clinic* is simultaneously wound and suture. It both opens and seeks to comprehend the cultural fault lines that exist around trauma, abuse, race, image and language itself. These diverse, and at times provocative, essays, allow for an outpouring of the unconscious and the experience of pain and anxiety. It is the inability to speak with the inability to be silent that suffuses this radical collection and yet it is these same tensions in this book that serve to heal the cultural body.

—**Luke Hockley**, Professor of Media Analysis, University of Bedfordshire, UK and author of *Somatic Cinema* (2014).

PSYCHOANALYSIS AND THE UNREPRESENTABLE

From culture to the clinic

Edited by Agnieszka Piotrowska and Ben Tyrer

Routledge
Taylor & Francis Group
LONDON AND NEW YORK

First published 2017
by Routledge
2 Park Square, Milton Park, Abingdon, Oxon OX14 4RN

and by Routledge
711 Third Avenue, New York, NY 10017

Routledge is an imprint of the Taylor & Francis Group, an informa business

British Library Cataloguing in Publication Data
A catalogue record for this book is available from the British Library

Library of Congress Cataloging in Publication Data
Names: Piotrowska, Agnieszka, editor. | Tyrer, Ben, editor.
Title: Psychoanalysis and the unrepresentable: from culture to the clinic /
edited by Agnieszka Piotrowska and Ben Tyrer.
Description: 1 Edition. | New York: Routledge, 2016. |
Includes bibliographical references and index.
Identifiers: LCCN 2016008666 | ISBN 9781138954977 (hardback) |
ISBN 9781138954984 (pbk.) | ISBN 9781315666655 (ebook)
Subjects: LCSH: Psychoanalysis.
Classification: LCC BF173 .P77527 2016 | DDC 150.19/5—dc23
LC record available at http://lccn.loc.gov/2016008666

ISBN: 978-1-138-95497-7 (hbk)
ISBN: 978-1-138-95498-4 (pbk)
ISBN: 978-1-315-66665-5 (ebk)

Typeset in BemboStd
by codeMantra

CONTENTS

Figures   *xi*
Contributors   *xiii*
Acknowledgements   *xvii*

Introduction: Representing the unrepresentable   1
Agnieszka Piotrowska and Ben Tyrer

PART I
Approaching trauma   **5**

1 The body locked by a lack of meaning   7
   Katrine Zeuthen and Marie Hagelskjær

2 Trauma without a subject: On Malabou,
   psychoanalysis and *Amour*   20
   Ben Tyrer

3 A possible way to represent the unrepresentable
   in clinical trauma   39
   Yaelle Sibony-Malpertu

PART II
Sense and gesture   **51**

4 (Un)Representing the real: Seeing sounds and hearing images   53
   Thomas Elsaesser

5 On touching and speaking in (post) (de) colonial
   discourse – From Lessing to Marechera and Veit-Wild   74
   Agnieszka Piotrowska

6 Pointing at the other   94
   Goran Vranešević

PART III
Impossible poetics   **109**

7 Is poetics a fiction about truth – in a poem? Some
   remarks about Paul Celan   111
   René Rasmussen

8 Presenting the unrepresentable in presentable ways   118
   Pia Hylén

9 Duras and the art of the impossible   130
   Carin Franzén

PART IV
Without words   **141**

10 Representation without language: Freud and the
   problem of the image   143
   Annie Hardy

11 Understanding without words   158
   John Miller

PART V
Wounds and suture   **169**

12 Rethinking the primal wound, trauma and the fantasy of
   completeness: Adopted women's experiences of meeting their
   biological fathers in adulthood   171
   Elizabeth Joyce

13 Embodying traumatic griefscapes   185
   Per Roar

14 Suture and Gus Van Sant's *Milk*   203
   Richard Rushton

PART VI
Auto/Fiction 217

15 Unnameable 219
    Anna Backman Rogers

16 Each day at a time – A daily intervention into loss 222
    Myna Trustram

17 The scent of philosophy 231
    Birthe Tranberg Nikolajsen

Index *237*

FIGURES

2.1 Georges and Anne at breakfast in *Amour* (2012),
    dir. Michael Haneke: Amour_michael_haneke©2012 Les
    Films Du Losange – X Filme Creative Pool – Wega Film   25

2.2 Georges' dream in *Amour* (2012), dir. Michael Haneke:
    Amour_michael_haneke©2012 Les Films Du Losange –
    X Filme Creative Pool – Wega Film   28

2.3 Georges in *Amour* (2012), dir. Michael Haneke:
    Amour_michael_haneke©2012 Les Films Du Losange –
    X Filme Creative Pool – Wega Film   31

2.4 Anne in *Amour* (2012), dir. Michael Haneke:
    Amour_michael_haneke©2012 Les Films Du Losange –
    X Filme Creative Pool – Wega Film   33

5.1 Ery Nzaramba and Sonja Wirhol from a shoot of *Flora and
    Dambudzo* (2014) Dir/Prod A.Piotrowska. DoP. Joe Njagu   87

5.2 Shooting *Flora and Dambudzo*. Agnieszka Piotrowska
    and Joe Njagu. ©Agnieszka Piotrowska   87

13.1 Audience watching. Photo by Fuco Fuoxos – Vijećnica,
    Sarajevo 2006   188

13.2 Circle. Photo by Fuco Fuoxos – Vijećnica, Sarajevo 2006 191

13.3 Crawling. Photo by Fuco Fuoxos – Vijećnica, Sarajevo 2006 196

16.1 Collection of flowers. Photographer: Mary Stark   225

CONTRIBUTORS

Anna Backman Rogers, PhD, is a Senior Lecturer in Film Studies at The University of Gothenburg, Sweden. She is the author of *American Independent Cinema: Rites of Passage and The Crisis-Image* (EUP, 2015) and the co-editor, with Laura Mulvey of *Feminisms* (AUP, 2015). She is currently writing a book on the films of Sofia Coppola entitled *The Politics of Visual Pleasure* for Berghahn.

Thomas Elsaesser, PhD, is Professor Emeritus at the Department of Media and Culture of the University of Amsterdam. From 2006 to 2012 he was Visiting Professor at Yale University and since 2013 teaches part-time at Columbia University. For more information and recent publications: www.thomas-elsaesser.com.

Carin Franzén, PhD, is Professor in Comparative Literature at Linköping University. She has published various articles and books on literature and psychoanalysis as well as on medieval and early modern literature.

Marie Hagelskjær has a MSc in Psychology and is a PhD scholar at the Department of Psychology, University of Copenhagen, Denmark. Her main area of research is infantile sexuality and prevention and assessment of child sexual abuse, where she focuses on developing and testing assessment methods.

Annie Hardy is a PhD candidate at University College London where her research interests focus on visual thought and philosophical issues in psychology and psychoanalysis. She came to the department after obtaining an MA in Philosophy from the University of Edinburgh and an Msc in Theoretical Psychoanalysis from UCL.

Pia Hylén is a psychoanalyst and a psychologist and the current Vice President of Antena do Campo Freudiano, Center of Psychoanalytic Study in Lisbon. She was educated at the University of California, Berkeley, and the University of Copenhagen. She did her psychoanalysis at École de la Cause Freudienne in Paris and has trained as a TFP therapist with Dr Kernberg at Cornell Medical Center. She has written numerous psychological and psychoanalytical articles, lately in *Drift (Journal for Psychoanalysis)* and *Afreudite (Revista Lusófona de Psicanálise Pura e Aplicada)*. She is an artist and a poet and has published *Au bord du continent*, a collection of poetry illustrated with her aquarelles and croquis. Pia Hylén is a member of AMP, EFP, NLS and CEP and has her private practice in Lisbon.

John Miller is a psychoanalyst who originally trained under people who worked with C.G. Jung but has since come to work in the post-Kleinian tradition, as a result of a long association with the late Donald Meltzer. He has a background in education, where he worked for a number of years as an Educational Psychologist. He is the author of *The Triumphant Victim* (Karnac, 2013) and *Do You Read Me?* (Karnac, 2015). He is in full-time practice in Oxford.

Agnieszka Piotrowska, PhD, is an award winning documentary filmmaker and a theorist, best known for her film *Married to the Eiffel Tower* (2009). Her new work in both practice and theory focuses on post-colonial relationships in Zimbabwe, including an internationally acclaimed documentary film *Lovers in Time or How We Didn't Get Arrested in Harare*. She is the author of *Psychoanalysis and Ethics in Documentary Film* and the editor of *Embodied Encounters: New approaches to psychoanalysis and cinema*, both published by Routledge. Her new monograph *Black and White: Cinema, politics and the arts in Zimbabwe* (Routledge, 2016) combines practice research with theory. She is co-coordinator of the *Psychoanalysis in Our Time* research network.

René Rasmussen, PhD, Associate Professor in Danish Literature at the Department of Nordic Studies and Linguistics, University of Copenhagen, and psychoanalyst. Selected publications: (2000) *Bjelke lige i øjet—om Henrik Bjelkes forfatterskab* (Bjelke Bull's-eye—on the Authorship of Henrik Bjelke), (2004) *Litteratur og repræsentation* (Literature and Representation), (2004), *Kognition—en liberalistisk ideologi* (Cognition—A Liberalistic Ideology), (2007) *Moderne litteraturteori 1–2* (Modern Theory of Literature 1–2), (2009) *Lacan, sprog og seksualitet* (Lacan, Language and Sexuality), (2010) *Psykoanalyse—et videnskabsteoretisk perspektiv* (Psychoanalysis—An Epistemological Perspective), (2012) *Angst hos Lacan og Kierkegaard og i kognitiv terapi* (Anxiety in Lacan and Kierkegaard and in Cognitive Therapy).

Per Roar, PhD, is an artist-researcher who combines choreography, social-political concerns and research. In his doctoral project 'Docudancing Griefscapes' (2015) at the University of the Arts Helsinki, he explored this contextually based approach to choreography, while drawing on his mixed background from choreography

(BA, Oslo National Academy of the Arts), dance history/-ethnology (NTNU, Trondheim), performance studies (MA, New York University) and social sciences and history (Cand. mag., University of Oslo, Corvinius University in Budapest, and Oxford University).

Richard Rushton, PhD, is Senior Lecturer in Film Studies at Lancaster University, UK. He is the author of *The Reality of Film: Theories of Filmic Reality* (Manchester University Press, 2011), *Cinema after Deleuze* (Continuum, 2012), and *The Politics of Hollywood Cinema: Popular Film and Contemporary Political Theory* (Palgrave Macmillan, 2013).

Yaelle Sibony-Malpertu has worked for 15 years as a psychologist and a psychoanalyst for the Sainte-Anne Hospital, Paris, France. She trained in philosophy at the Sorbonne and has published the monograph, *A Philosophical Relationship: Therapeutic Links between Descartes and Princess Elizabeth of Bohemia* (Stock Editions, 2012). She is finishing a PhD on psychoanalysis and intergenerational transmission of trauma at the Psychoanalysis, Medicine and Society Research Center, (EAD, 3522), Denis Diderot's University, Paris.

Birthe Tranberg Nikolajsen has a BA in Social Pedagogics 1994, MA in Education 2000 and two years full MA in Philosophy of Education, Aarhus University. Presently her research is a philosophical investigation into how psychoanalysis can function as an epistemic foundation for social pedagogics.

Myna Trustram, PhD, held curatorial and research posts in museums and galleries for many years including the Manchester Art Gallery and the People's History Museum. She currently works as a research associate at Manchester School of Art (Manchester Metropolitan University). Her work is about loss, melancholy and the abundance to be found in museum collections and is influenced by trainings from the Tavistock Institute, Tavistock Clinic and Group Analysis North. She writes academic prose but also works in other written forms that move around essay, memoir and performance.

Ben Tyrer, PhD, teaches Film Studies at King's College, London. He is the author of the monograph, *Out of the Past: Lacan and film noir* (Palgrave Macmillan, 2016), as well as articles and chapters on psychoanalysis and cinema. He is co-coordinator of the *Psychoanalysis in Our Time* research network.

Goran Vranešević is a research fellow at the Institute for Applied Research and Development in Celje, Slovenia, Coordinator of the Seminar for Political Theory at the Peace Institute in Ljubljana, Slovenia, and a member of the council of Aufhebung-International Hegelian Association. He has written articles on psychoanalysis, aesthetics, political philosophy, speculative philosophy and contemporary cultural phenomena.

Katrine Zeuthen, PhD, MSc Psychology, is an Associate Professor in Child Psychology at the Department of Psychology, University of Copenhagen, Denmark, and a Candidate in the Danish Psychoanalytic Society. In her research she focuses on infantile sexuality, child sexual abuse and sexual trauma.

ACKNOWLEDGEMENTS

This volume was inspired by the Nordic Summer University's Psychoanalysis in Our Time Symposium in Copenhagen in March 2014 organised by Anna Ioannou, René Rasmussen and Agnieszka Piotrowska. We also have included some contributions from the symposium in Tallinn in 2015 which we, the editors of this volume organised, and which was an inspirational forum for all concerned. We would like to thank Carsten Freiburg and Per Roar and the board of the NSU for their on-going support of the work of the Psychoanalysis in Our Time research group. We are grateful to our own institutions, the University of Bedfordshire and King's College London, for enabling us to carry out this work.

We would also like to express our sincerest gratitude to Michael Haneke for his permission to use images from his 2012 film, *Amour*, in this work, and to Lise Zipci and everyone at Les Films du Losange for their help in attaining this. We are also grateful to Professor Flora Veit-Wild for the comments on Chapter 5 On Touching and Speaking in (Post) (De) Colonial Discourse and the permission to use the Dambudzo Marechera poem in it. Material from *The Grass is Singing* by Doris Lessing is included here by kind permission of HarperCollins.

INTRODUCTION

Representing the unrepresentable

Agnieszka Piotrowska and Ben Tyrer

This book attempts to think through things that are impossible to be thought through. It is therefore by definition a collage, a loop, a space of discussion and reflection. It draws from psychoanalysis in its broadest sense, but it is also a political gesture against the "fixed and the frozen" as Edward Said would have it in his descriptions of patriarchal authority pronouncing on the difference of the exotic Other. That fixedness he thought un-ethical. We too believe in that. We believe that things that are hard to talk about one must talk about in order to bring them to light. The volume therefore aims to do just that and nothing much more.

As mentioned in the acknowledgements, this project began in Copenhagen at the symposium in March 2014, but at least half of the contributors are people who have joined us since. The notion that there is something difficult to express, to "represent" in language is not new and usually takes us to trauma studies – which of course one way or another do start with psychoanalysis. But this book also looks at other "unrepresentables", we write about love and loss, forbidden sexual desire, colonialism, the fear of mortality, anxiety over spiritual emptiness and a desire to connect these things in a way that would make meaning of the contemporary world, which is so fragmented and violent. We write about film and literature, psychotherapy and poetry, counseling and reconciliations, and hopes and fears.

In part the writers in this book give testimonies of the way they see the world in this difficult moment in time. We write attempting to give a voice to something that we sense might be important. We speak even though we know we are doomed to fail – as we know language does fail when we approach things to do with the Body, the Real as Lacan would have it. And yet the process of trying is a defiant move – a move against the fear and darkness of the world around us, in which innocent people are killed by terrorists only for governments to decide to kill more innocent people as a way forward. We give testimony and try and make sense of what we might know.

Some time ago and in a different context, namely that of hearing voices about concentration camps and the Nazis, Shoshana Felman's psychoanalytic collaborator Dori Laub felt that under the right circumstances, the process of giving testimony might have transformational qualities:

> It is a dialogical process of exploration and reconciliation of two worlds – the one that was brutally destroyed and the one that is – that are different and will always remain so. The testimony is inherently a process of facing loss – of going through the pain of the act of witnessing, and of the ending of the act of witnessing – which entails yet another repetition of the experience of separation and loss. It re-enacts the passage through difference in such a way, however, that it allows perhaps a certain repossession of it.
>
> *(Laub 1993: 91)*

In some way all chapters in this book deal with a process of facing loss: the loss is of a certain comfort from living in a world in which what happens next is known. We do not know what might happen next anymore. We speak from a position of complete non-knowledge, which we still hope might be generative, and this is a classically Lacanian or post-Lacanian position that we, the editors of this collection, have adopted. As a result, in this volume all the contributors abandon familiar sites and move to the new territories, where they might be curious visitors, strangers.

Dany Nobus, talking about young Jacques-Alain Miller and drawing from influences from Plato to Derrida, describes the stranger as somebody who might be the harbinger of a new and generative way of thinking:

> The stranger speaks from ignorance and thus forces his interlocutors to break the silence that governs mutual understanding and to explain at length what they think they know. Combining within his presence (…) physical proximity and social remoteness, geographical nearness and mental distance, the person of alien origin occupies a privileged position, which gives him an opportunity to cross boundaries and somehow be exonerated by reason of ignorance, and which can make him privy to *secrets that will never be revealed to any regular inhabitant of the community.*
>
> *(Nobus and Quinn 2005: 67, my emphasis)*

Almost all of the writers here venture into quite new territories for us – it is a risk, and we are taking it deliberately. In testimony, as Derrida teaches us (which I address in my chapter) in attempting to represent the unrepresentable one continuously bumps into secrets of a variety of kinds. How can we even begin to share these secrets in an ethical way? How much of ourselves can we put into our scholarly essays?

I wrote elsewhere (Piotrowska 2014) about a documentary encounter dealing with testimony and the ethical violence it might incur. Because speaking about delicate unrepresentable matters, about secrets, can be very problematic ethically, too, in sharing a secret, which has to do with truth, fiction and betrayal, we enter a difficult and dangerous territory in which theories and emotions meet, but the breaking of that boundary is often too painful to bear. And yet the non-representing is fatal too: not just to individuals but to societies. We try consciously to move into the unconscious – knowing that it is not possible and again risky. Jacques Lacan in his *Seminar XI* makes a point that "his" unconscious is different from that of Freud's, namely, he says, it "is situated at that point, where, between cause and that which it affects, there is always something wrong" (1977: 23). It is a gap that causes something to happen – neurosis that then becomes a "scar" (ibid.: 22), not of the neurosis but of the unconscious: something Lacan says, of the order of "*the non-realized*" (ibid.: 22, original emphasis). Lacan says that perhaps the analyst should "be besieged" by the zone of shades rather than bringing them to light as spelling things out can be dangerous (ibid.: 23). Lacan introduces the idea of the unconscious being in "the domain of cause, the law of the signifier, in the locus of which the gap is produced" (ibid.: 23). Here we have tried in a gesture of defiance even to our Master, to abandon the world of the shadows, believing, also after Lacan and of course Freud, that representing fundamentally might have curative effects, despite the pain.

The organisation of this book

This book is organised with the aim of bringing together interdisciplinary approaches to a particular aspect of the unrepresentable. It begins with the question of trauma, that most fundamental challenge to representability: from the complexities of fantasy and seduction in cases of sexual abuse, to the trauma of brain injury considered in filmic, scientific, philosophical and psychoanalytic contexts and the role of history in both transmitting and providing a framework for understanding personal traumas. The next section addresses what can be communicated through the senses of touch and hearing and through gesture, in encounters with the cinema screen (e.g. synaesthesia) and in post-colonial encounters where forbidden desire and historical legacy mean that, for example, voice can become violence when representation ("metaphorisation") fails and through encounters that reveal the paradoxes of pointing. The third part examines poetics and the ways in which literature of various forms can evoke impossibilities at the heart of subjective experience, while the next section considers what can be transmitted without words in terms of the metapsychology of mental images and profound transferential relationships in the clinic. The fifth section addresses wounds, sutures and recuperations in the psychosocial analysis of adoption experience, as a question of embodying national grief at a personal level, and in the socio-political realm via the cinema. The final portion of this book turns to creative writing, poetry, and auto-ethnography, which provide for our authors some means of addressing their own unrepresentable and thus bears witness to the power of that founding psychoanalytic principle of the "talking cure", of finding ways in which to put into words (or indeed images) those things that haunt us, press upon us, prevent us from going on.

We hope this collection might be an intellectual and emotional adventure for the reader and that it will invite further reflection on the position of language in our dealings with the difficult and sometimes impossible intersections of experience, history and the unconscious.

References

Lacan, J. (1977) *The Seminar of Jacques Lacan, Book XI: The Four Fundamental Concepts of Psychoanalysis*. Ed. J.-A. Miller. Trans. A. Sheridan. New York: Norton.

Laub, D. (1993) An Event without a Witness: Truth, Testimony and Survival. In S. Felman and D. Laub, *Testimony: Crises of Witnessing in Literature, Psychoanalysis and History*. New York: Routledge.

Nobus, D. and Quinn, M. (2005) *Knowing Nothing, Staying Stupid: Elements for a Psychoanalytic Epistemology*. London: Routledge.

Piotrowska, A. (2014) *Psychoanalysis and Ethics in Documentary Film*. London: Routledge.

PART I

Approaching trauma

1

THE BODY LOCKED BY A LACK OF MEANING

Katrine Zeuthen and Marie Hagelskjær

Why is Freud´s dilemma still relevant today?

The theme of this collection, "Representing the Unrepresentable", could also be the title of Freud's longstanding examination, discussion, and theory development of how sexuality and sexual trauma come – or don't come – into expression. Freud's examination began with his original scientific ambition from his *Studies on Hysteria* (Freud and Breuer 1955) of uncovering a causal relationship showing that child sexual abuse expresses itself through bodily symptoms in a significant way that can be attributed to a specific starting point, thus proving what *really* happened. Present societal as well as academic discussions of what infantile sexuality is, how it expresses itself, and how it can be understood and not least protected, seem to hold on to Freud's original ambition of finding a causal connection between an event and its expression: its symptom or its representation (see Elkovitch et al. 2009).

We still seem to be looking for a direct link between the child's expression and reality, a correlation that can free us from analyzing and thus free ourselves from participating personally in what we see, hear, feel. We want to uncover the truth; however, the manual for this does not exist. Sexual abuse doesn't express itself through unambiguous symptoms and reliable signs. On the contrary, sexual abuse challenges us and demands that we make use of some of our best abilities of discernment and interpretation: of analysis. It is therefore essential to have a theoretical model describing how infantile sexuality develops within the relationship between child and adult and what this means for the child's development: both when development is handled with care and when the child is subjected to sexual abuse. Without a theoretical frame with which to understand the development of sexuality, our ability to assess and make judgments remains in a private and diffuse sphere, making reference to our own unconscious without us being aware of it (see Zeuthen and Hagelskjær 2013).

In his article "Fear of Breakdown", Winnicott writes: "that what is not yet experienced did nevertheless happen in the past" (Winnicott 1974: 105). Something has occurred, but it has no place to be, because the child's psyche is not yet a place that is structured in such a way that it can make sense of trauma. The French psychoanalysts Botella and Botella would add that what happened is a negativity. Trauma is first and foremost an absence or the negative of what could and should have happened:

> A violent and abrupt absence of topographies and psychical dynamics, the rupture of psychic coherence and the collapse of primary and secondary processes as the ego loses its means. This brutal disorganization has its origin, not in a perception but in the absence of meaning in the violent excess of excitation and in the ego's state of distress: in the ego's incapacity to form a representation of them, to present them to consciousness.
>
> *(Botella and Botella 2005: 116)*

Freud's hysterics and the abandonment of the theory of seduction

Maybe because Freud himself was looking for a presence rather than an absence, he remained in doubt as to the origin and nature of infantile sexuality. He introduced his final seduction theory in 1896 (Freud 1962a, 1962b, 1962c), where he proclaimed that a sexual trauma could always be found as the basis for hysterical symptoms. Hysterics were suffering from memories of events that had been repressed, the brutal content of which they continued to defend against. The women had not been able to protect themselves against the sexual violations in childhood, while they were still in the process of growing up; therefore, the trauma came to delayed expression or *nachträglich* through the hysterical symptomatology.

However, Freud's search to find a universal connection between repressed events and symptoms didn't go so easily. He concluded that because his patients had registered the sexual experiences at the time they took place, even earliest childhood must contain sexual tension. In this way Freud began to allude to what would later take shape in his theory of infantile sexuality (Freud and Breuer 1955; Freud 1953). Freud's journey back into his patients' factual realities ended when he gave up the seduction theory and with it the belief that particular symptoms were always an expression of sexual abuse in childhood. Based on this finding, Freud concluded that it was not possible to determine whether the patients' memories had actually taken place in reality or they were simply expressions of their fantasies. Freud wrote to his friend Fliess that: "there are no indications of reality in the unconscious, so that one cannot distinguish between the truth and fiction that is cathected with affect" (Freud 1966b: 260). Thus he confirmed his discovery that the unconscious did not distinguish between fantasy and reality, which made it difficult or even impossible to distinguish between truth and fiction when it came to remembered experiences that had been invested with affect.

Following this discovery, his studies shifted from investigating how outer events came to be expressed in the patient's inner life to examining the significance of the patient's inner world in and of itself to psychic life. Freud began from this point on to be interested in fantasy as an expression of the psychic. Fantasies were not direct depictions of external reality; rather, they represented something internal. In this way, psychic reality rose up out of the ashes of the seduction theory and was also constructed using some of the same clinical findings made by Freud under the production of that theory. The clinical findings took on a new meaning when they were understood in the context of psychic reality, now referring to something different and more uncertain than historical reality.

These examinations led Freud to the theory of a sexuality coming from within: an infantile sexuality not yet grounded in the body as a genital and goal-directed sexuality. And thus Freud's groundbreaking *Three Essays on Sexuality* were born (Freud 1953). With his description of the psychosexual drives Freud broke from and for that matter still breaks from a more conventional view of sexuality, because he defined the sexual drive as both distinct from and also more than genital sexuality and the sexual act as such. Freud integrated the theory of psychosexual development into his metapsychology, in which he described the lack of synchronicity in development by showing that the individual is only able to understand the meaning of his own maturation retrospectively or *nachträglich*, as biology and the formation of cultural meaning do not progress at the same pace. The small child has fantasies about life's big mysteries: birth, reproduction and the difference between the sexes; but he or she does not grasp the meaning of these fantasies until later in life when he or she has reached a level of biological maturity sufficient for understanding what we might call the culture of biology (see Zeuthen, Holm Pedersen, and Gammelgaard 2010). Contemporary theorists have attempted to reinterpret Freud's essays by reading the theory of infantile sexuality as a theory about the breach that occurs between childhood and adult life at puberty, when the meaning of sexuality begins to dawn on the child. One of the most important of these theorists is the late French psychoanalyst Jean Laplanche, who rewrites Freud's seduction theory in his own theory of generalized seduction (Laplanche 1970, 1987).

What is infantile sexuality according to Laplanche?

With his theory of generalized seduction and *the sexual* (2011a) Laplanche makes it clear that the sexual emerges through the manner in which the adult meets the child's pleasure, and it is a premise of development that the child is at the mercy of the adult's interpretation of the child's needs. His theory can explain why we must give up a fruitless hunt for unambiguous symptoms of child sexual abuse, and it can sustain us in our view that it is not a question of whether a child has or has not been seduced, but rather of how and on whose premises the seduction took place.

Laplanche insists that the relationship between adults and the child must form the core of our understanding of the way in which infantile sexuality is potentially traumatizing. In his introduction to the concept of the enigmatic message, Laplanche takes up seduction as the foundation of child development in relation to the adult (1997, 1999a). The adult approaches the child with a special kind of care that is characteristic of that particular adult and which the child can sense. With the care comes a message: the adult *shares something with the child*, the meaning of which the child does not understand. The message is enigmatic. Nevertheless, the child must trustfully allow himself to be drawn in or *seduced* by the adult's care, because it is the adult that will ensure the child's survival. The child must let himself be seduced by the adult and by the meanings of the adult world, because children are dependent on adults and dependent on figuring out what is involved in relations to the adults, in order to be included and eventually to participate in the world on their own. Thus, for Laplanche seduction is a universal phenomenon based on the asymmetrical relation between adult and child: it is a fundamental anthropological situation created by the fact that the adult has a sexual unconscious and the child does not.

In this way Laplanche rereads Freud's seduction theory and his later abandonment of that theory by adding that the child always gets seduced by a specific adult and that the child registers the adult's sexuality and tries to understand its meaning (see Gammelgaard 2010). The adult meets the child's search for pleasure, consciously as well as unconsciously, in a special way connected with the specific person that he or she is. The adult's story and membership in a culture propels the child in his or her development, and in this way the child propels him- or herself from being passive and open to being actively able to close in on him or herself and create his or her own sense of meaning of the sexual. When puberty arrives and sexuality becomes genital and aim-directed, its place has already been taken:

> What is acquired through the drives *precedes* what is innate and instinctual, in such a way that, at the time it emerges, instinctual sexuality, which is adaptive, finds the "seat already taken" as it were, by infantile drives, already and always present in the unconscious.
>
> *(Laplanche 2001: 49)*

"The seat is already taken," Laplanche writes, because sexuality has already been made sense of in the relationship between the child and the adult even before the child was able to understand this. Laplanche thereby confirms the importance of how we with our care allow the child to give pleasure content and meaning in a way that makes room for the child to turn his sexuality out into the world in accordance with the child's development. It is therefore the adult's job to allow some of the space to stand open by remaining unable to provide an explanation as to the meaning of the enigmatic sexuality, so that the child in time can discover it. The way that the child up to this point has been cared for, and the way in which the sexual has at once been present, inaccessible, and enigmatic between the child and the adult, create the foundations for sexuality (see Laplanche 2011b). When we begin to fathom the meaning of sexuality, its foundation has already been laid down within us by way of relationships with caregivers: for better, but also sometimes for worse.

The pathological perverse seduction: child sexual abuse

Today, psychological assessments of children causing concern about sexual abuse are mainly done through classical psychological test-instruments, examinations of drawings, observations of doll-play, and checklists such as The Trauma Symptom Checklist for Children (Briere 1996) and Child Sexual Behaviour Inventory (Friedrich 1997) that assess different kinds of behaviors such as hyper-sexualized behavior, sexual play, etc. It is commonly acknowledged that there is no direct way to gain univocal insight into the meaning of the child's expressions, but still the aim is to get as close to the truth as possible. Furthermore great sensitivity from the psychologist is needed, as there is an ongoing preoccupation and societal expectation that the psychologist doesn't induce certain ideas, fantasies, or memories in the child by being *suggestive*. From our point of view many of the internationally used assessment methods lack the central understanding that the child's experiences and expressions are always embedded in a specific family, with specific relations and with unconscious conflicts tied to the adults that are taking care of the child. To examine the child detached from a theoretical understanding of the infantile sexual unconscious as something always developing in the relation between child and adult seems simplified and idealistic, putting the field in the same paradoxical situation as Freud experienced over a hundred years ago.

Laplanche's theory of generalized seduction expresses a continuum of seduction, from the seductive and enigmatic yet humanizing communication that takes place between every caregiver and infant to the pathological perverse situations where communication is solely on the adult's premises. Following this line of thought Laplanche divides the adult unconscious into a repressed part – what is generally known as the unconscious – and an enclaved part, an inner foreign body. The enclaved part of the unconscious is an encapsulated place where no psychic elaboration and representation can take place. According to Laplanche (2011b) the message given from the adult to the child through the sexual abuse stems from this enclaved part of the adult's unconscious, and it affects the child's psyche in a specific way. Laplanche describes sexual abuse as an intromission of messages that the child receives passively and cannot translate. The enigmatic part of the message is out of reach for the child, because for translation to take place the adult unconscious needs to be working at a level where the child can take part in the relation. The violent process of intromission creates a rupture in the child's development, as the sexual abuse isn't subjected to psychic representations and gaps of something unrepresentable, something that hasn't been subjected to any psychic elaboration is placed as a foreign body in the child's psyche. The enclaved message from the adult becomes enclaved in the child as well. This stands in contrast to the generalized seduction where the child can participate in a meaning-giving process (Laplanche 1999b). How these enclaved messages affect the development of infantile sexuality is of great interest to us and thus is a central part of our theoretically driven clinical research.

Practicing Laplanche's theory

Here we try to combine Laplanche's theory of generalized seduction, translation, and the sexual with our clinical research on childhood trauma, thus encircling the gaps of the unrepresentable: that which isn't directly approachable and yet is so present in clinical practice. In one of our current studies we make use of a psycho-analytic and projective imagery called *Play Room*, developed by Katrine Zeuthen and grounded in the psychoanalytical theory of Laplanche (Zeuthen 2013). From *Play Room* we use a selection of eight illustrations that depict everyday situations between children and adults always containing an element of conflict, emotion, and interaction. The illustrations are thematically distributed within four dualities, these being voluntariness/force, activity/passivity, fantasy/reality, and care/abuse. All four dualities have the general underlying theme of pleasure/unpleasure. The conversa-tion unfolding between the child and the psychologist is structured around four gradually more complex questions about the illustrations. The psychologist struc-turing the conversation by performing the trial with *Play Room* is well known to the child, as a good relation between the child and psychologist is a fundamental premise for the study.

The children included in the study are divided into two experimental groups: one group is made up of children whose sexual abuse has been fully or partly substantiated by a conviction or child protection services assess the sexual abuse as highly probable; one group is made up of children in psychological treatment due to parental neglect and maltreatment but there is no suspicion of sexual abuse. Furthermore, a control group of non-abused, non-neglected children has been established.

Preliminary results and how they can be interpreted in light of the presented theory

This division into the two experimental groups is easily done in principal, but in practice it is difficult or even impossible to accomplish. When doing research within the field of child sexual abuse, the categories applied – such as our two research groups – are seldom extensive enough to capture the complexities of the phenomenon. Interestingly, this problem first materialized when we tried to adapt to the quantitative empirical methodological standards that are expected and that other research projects within our field apply as a matter of fact. When we discovered how this taken-for-granted methodology became a limitation rather than a scientific objective we allowed our phenomenon in question to speak more clearly for itself. The field of child sexual abuse seems to lack a concept of the unconscious that opposes observation based on clear distinctions between categories. We have met many borderline cases where the structure and relations within a given family can be severely pathological, sexually speaking, but where no factual sexual abuse seems to be taking place. These cases are often excluded from other studies, as they do not possess the simplicity to fit in to clear categories, and in this way the severe and diffuse pathology of sexual trauma and thus *the nature of the subject* are neglected:

> I have not always been a psychotherapist. Like other neuropathologists, I was trained to employ local diagnoses and electro-prognosis, and it still strikes me myself as strange that the case histories I write should read like stories and that, as one might say, they lack the serious stamp of science, I must console myself with the reflection that the nature of the subject is evidently responsible for this, rather than any preference of my own.
>
> *(Freud and Breuer 1955: 160)*

Freud's statement maintains its importance and relevance in relation to a field such as child sexual abuse. Rather than following the methodological requirements that stem from a positivistic paradigm that more often than not restricts and edits the nature of the subject, he acknowledged the importance of letting the subject speak for itself, thus amending his methodology in accordance with its nature.

One case that insists on the importance of letting the subject speak for itself is the case of Hanna. Hanna lives with her mother, who originates from a poor European country. Hanna's mother was abused by her father throughout childhood and into adulthood and became pregnant by him. She fled her country and has no contact with him today. The rest of her family turned its back on her when she told them that the birth of Hanna was the result of the intergenerational abuse to which her father had subjected her. Hanna is not aware that the man that she knows as her father is also her grandfather. She has no regular contact with him but has tracked him down and visited him a few times without her mother's knowing. Hanna was referred for psychological treatment at 10 years of age when it was discovered that she visited her father and that she has a massive daily use of Internet pornography, an activity in which she has included other children. The psychological assessment of Hanna shows no indication that she has been subjected to factual sexual abuse. Hanna is an intelligent, chatty girl with no other scholastic or social problems.

In the case of Hanna and cases similar to hers we find it meaningful to distinguish between sexual abuse and sexual trauma. In sexual *abuse* there is a genital sexual acting out, a sexual counterpart of the unconscious and enclaved message from the adult to the child. In sexual *trauma* the enigmatic enclaved message from the adult to the child has no genital counterpart; it isn't acted out genitally. Hanna might not have been subjected to sexual abuse in the literal understanding of the word, but Hanna is born as the outcome of a massive intergenerational sexual trauma. She is included in the empirical project in the non-abused group, and so far in our analysis she doesn't exhibit the same deviant pattern as the children in the sexual abuse group. But something that is most interesting to us is that Hanna uses the whole *Play Room* trial for one thing and one thing only, namely to try to figure out what the relations between the illustrated children and adults are: "Is it a brother, a mother, a father? Sometimes you can tell by looking at the color of the hair. Are they lovers?" she often asks the psychologist.

When seeing the picture of a woman kissing a child, Hanna says that only once and only by coincidence, her mother kissed her on the mouth. "Should mothers do that more often? Or is once too much?" she thinks aloud. In light of the theory of Laplanche, one could say that Hanna has received an enigmatic message from her mother about her complicated heritage, but she has never been given any help to translate this. The general seduction has been saturated with the unspoken encapsulated trauma of her mother, a mother who has been unable to show her daughter natural signs of affection, like kissing. Hanna's emerging biological maturation and dawning ability to understand adult sexuality makes her seek out genital pornographic seduction in order to figure out how tenderness, closeness, and romantic relations can be understood outside and inside the family. She is looking for the genital counterpart of her sexual trauma in order to give it meaning.

Other preliminary research results from our study indicate that children for whom there are strong indications of factual sexual abuse have great difficulty in trying to give meaning to the illustrations in *Play Room*. This comes to expression as an over-representation of rejections of the dialogue with the psychologist, "I don't know, I don't want to answer", or only superficial, vague, and dismissive answers within the group. The sexual abuse expresses itself as an absence of creation of meaning or in the words of Botella and Botella as a negativity (see 2005). It isn't there or it has no place to be, and genital maturation has not yet set in in the child's development, withholding the child's attempts to understand *nachträglich* what happened.

In the current empirical study we also conduct structured observations of the children's verbal and non-verbal expressions during the *Play Room* trial. It seems that there is a pattern, where both experimental groups display a wide range of deviant expressions, like strong bodily restlessness, a small shivering voice, or speaking in a manic way. When confronted with illustrations that seem to have the most provocative content (i.e., bathing children and an adult man), the children within the sexual abuse group have remarkably more deviant answers with little or no relation to the specific content of the illustration. The situations in which the children in the sexual abuse group are most affected are often followed by the children's having an urgent need to eat something or drink the small juice box, calming themselves with what seemed to be instant oral pleasure in order to minimize the tension from the enclaved message coming from the outside but acting as a foreign body from within.

It seems that these children convey an absence of ability to symbolize and to create psychic representations when it comes to meaningful translations of the content of the illustrations (see Botella and Botella 2005; Brilleslijper-Kater 2004; Dalenberg 2000; Dalenberg, Hyland and Cuevas 2002; Dalenberg and Palesh 2010), as if something is blocking the way of creating the appropriate meaning or at least trying to do so in cooperation with their psychologist. We find that our psycho-analytical approach can offer a new way of uncovering that which isn't identifiable through mere observation and registration of a child's behavior and symptoms. By encircling the absence of meaning or the negativity of sexual trauma we find an alternative way of investigating and supporting the child's capacities of creating meaning and psychic representation, thereby giving room for the relational development of the encapsulated unconscious parts of the child's psyche in due time and in balance with the child's overall development.

How does infantile sexuality and sexual trauma express itself?

When working psychoanalytically with children with sexual trauma we examine how their bodily expressions are connected to their inner as well as their outer world. Our aim is to show how the body expresses that which cannot be represented, symbolized, and integrated in the psyche exactly because an original experience as such can never be situated as coming either from inside the body or from the outside (see Botella and Botella 2005; Scarfone 2001; Zeuthen and Gammelgaard 2010).

Sara was referred to us when she was six years old because, according to her parents, she has been masturbating excessively since she was a baby, something that worries them increasingly. Also, Sara finds it difficult to relate to her peers in a flexible manner, either wanting to control the game or withdrawing from it when negotiations of what to play and how become too challenging for her. Her parents describe her as a very intelligent, creative, and curious girl always seeking knowledge. They find her insatiable when searching for the right answers to her many questions. Her father especially seems to identify with her insistence and what he calls her desire to always learn more from him: he himself enjoying his ability to satisfy her thirst for knowledge and continuing to do so.

Martin is 14 years old and started therapy three and a half years ago due to an intensified and seemingly dangerous preoccupation with pornography and sexual chat sites on the Internet, as well as excessive masturbation. He was referred to us from his child psychiatrist where he received psychiatric treatment for ADHD, a diagnosis he was given when he was six years old.

How can we come to understand a child's fantasies? What is at stake motivating the child's expressions? Is it anxiety that cannot be processed in fantasy and symbolized? These children cannot find the answer in themselves and thus they act in realized ways. What are they driven by? A thing-like inaccessible entity? An absence of meaning? The negative of the trauma being: "The potentiality of an excess of energy tending to deploy itself in an unbound hallucinatory-perceptual movement, a potential effect without content?" (Botella and Botella 2005: 116). The dynamics in the children's families could qualify some of the answers to what it is that goes on in them. Sara's father is restless and anxiety ridden: the way he can relate to his daughter is by seeing himself in her, by identifying himself as a child in her image. His answers to her questions are not formulated as new questions with which she can examine her fantasies; rather, they are fixed and very detailed descriptions of an adult world full of terrifying reality. His answers intrude her like phallic but non-genital fulfillments of something she is missing and should—in time—be helped to find on a child's premises. His answers project into her an anxiety she tries to control by answering his phallic and enigmatic message with what *she herself* understands to be phallic—with her masturbation she tries to fill that lack of meaning her father does not allow to stand open with something. Thus she tries in an autoerotic way to prevent him from entering her with his meaning, with his understanding of her: that is with his mirroring of himself. The mother stands outside the relation, not being able to intervene, carefully trying not to reveal the father's approach to his daughter, it being insecure and inflexible, leaving no room for other translations of meaning than his own.

Martin's relation to his father is regressive. Every other weekend it is only the two of them: playing FIFA on the PlayStation, watching football, eating pizza, and sharing the same bed—catching up for the lost time when he was small and they were out of contact, the father says, without acknowledging the lack of a repressive barrier established by him and the lack of an awareness of a necessary asymmetry embedded in a sleeping arrangement with separate beds and bedrooms. "We need each other", Martin says. In terms of his relation to his mother, she is always looking after him, guarding him, and guiding him. She is very often in conflict with and in opposition to his surrounding relations, using his ADHD diagnosis as an exhaustive explanation for the aspects of life that are so difficult for Martin. The mother is very involved in his sexuality but it is an autoerotic sexuality she supports, making arrangements for when he may or may not masturbate, changing his sheets, and educating him to use a specific towel for the purpose, suggesting to buy him porn-magazines—to control his desire, she says—to keep it safely at home. She has encapsulated his sexuality by referring it to his diagnosis. It is an encapsulation she refuses to understand in the light of Martin's development: in the light of his relationship to her, to his father, as well as to his social world as such.

The intrusive and thing-like character of Sara's father's approach to Sara prevents her from developing her own world of fantasy and reality, of symbolization—a world where representations are created in interplay between the child's ability to create meaning and an adult world full of reality and enigmatic messages coming from the "Other". With her masturbation she tries to keep a room for herself where the father cannot intrude, but her room is without representation, and thus it is locked by the lack of meaning in her father's approach. Sara's inner world is at one and the same time emptied and filled out by her father, and her masturbation is a reaction to this that prevents her from symbolization and creation. She tries to prevent an emptiness that captures her from outside as well as from within.

Also with Martin it seems that the controlling character of his parents' relation and relating to him prevents him from developing his sexuality by means of his fantasies. He is locked in an actual, external reality, which, due to its enigmatic but at the same time untranslatable nature, remains poignant and excessive, yet real (see Stein 1998a, 1998b, 2008; Scarfone 2001). This reality lacks a repressive barrier that should have been established by his parents, a barrier that could and should have been tested in fantasy by Martin. Instead the reality becomes distorted by the timelessness of the unconscious, leading to his compulsive need to live out his unsymbolized fantasies in reality (see Zeuthen and Gammelgaard 2010).

What original scene could ever be constructed in order to understand these children's fantasies? What absence of meaning can be driving them, in fantasy as well as in reality? When will Martin or Sara run like Emma did in Freud's famous scene from *Entwurff* (Freud 1966a) or close their eyes like Oedipus did in *The Interpretation of Dreams* (Freud 1958) and leave behind an original scene of seduction, thus giving room for symbolization? When will they at one and the same time establish *nachträglich* the sexual trauma and repress the unsymbolized excessive infantile sexuality of their parents that seems to work from inside these children as an internal foreign body and from outside of them through the parent's enigmatic and perversely seductive address poignantly capturing them? We conclude that it would be just as wrong to understand these expressions of the body as exclusively representing a sexuality imposed from the outside as it would be to understand them solely as formations of fantasy. Paraphrasing Botella and Botella, the children's expressions represent the enigmatic approach of the Other as always being inside and outside: always for real and in fantasy (2005).

Listening to listening

The child senses the sexual without conceptualizing it, and the adult must be in balance with the child in this developmental limbo. The child's utterances should be understood on the basis of the actuality and insistence with which they, despite their intangible nature, make themselves known (see Scarfone 2001). Infantile sexuality is expressed in the relationship and must be understood as an inquiry and a request. The unconscious speaks through the expressions of infantile sexuality, and it speaks in a manner that requires the adult to listen openly and without prejudice. It is the adult who holds the responsibility in relation to the child, because in the sexual domain there is no symmetry or synchronicity. The child must find himself or herself in the presence of the adult (see Laplanche 2002). We support the development of infantile sexuality in the best possible way by listening to it with the same openness with which it is expressed. This is not enough; we must also listen to our own ways of listening (see Faimberg 1996). Infantile sexuality speaks, and we must listen to the drive within ourselves and within the other as testimony to that which is not directly accessible in our communications (see Gammelgaard 2010), but which nevertheless takes place between us. Thus the adult is also responsible as regards those aspects of the child's development that are not directly accessible and which awaken something in the adult's own unconscious: because infantile sexuality is never silent.

References

Botella, C. and Botella, S. (2005) *The Work of Psychic Figurability*. Hove and New York: Brunner-Routledge.

Briere, J. (1996) *Trauma Symptom Checklist for Children: Professional Manual*. Odessa, Psychological Assessment Resources, Inc.

Brilleslijper-Kater, S. N. (2004) *Beyond Words*. Amsterdam: Vrije Universiteit.

Dalenberg, C. J. (2000) *Countertransference and the Treatment of Trauma*. Washington: American Psychological Association.

Dalenberg, C. J., Hyland, K. Z., and Cuevas, C. A. (2002) Sources of Fantastic Elements in Allegations of Abuse by Adults and Children. In M. L. Eisen, J. A. Quas, and G. S. Goodman (eds.) *Memory and Suggestibility in the Forensic Interview*. Mahwah & London: Lawrence Erlbaum.

Dalenberg, C. J. and Palesh, O. G. (2010) Scientific Progress and Methodological Issues in the Study of Recovered and False Memories of Trauma. In R. A. Lanius, E. Vermetten, and C. Pain (eds.) *The Impact of Early Life Trauma on Health and Disease*. Cambridge: Cambridge University Press.

Elkovitch, N., Latzman, R. D., Hansen, D. J., and Flood, M. F. (2009) Understanding Child Sexual Behavior Problems: A Developmental Psychopathology Framework. *Clinical Psychology Review*, 29, 586–98.

Faimberg, H. (1996) Listening to Listening. *International Journal of Psychoanalysis*, 77, 667–77.

Freud, S. (1953) Three Essays on Sexuality (1905). *The Standard Edition of the Complete Psychological Works of Sigmund Freud, Volume VII (1901–1905). A Case of Hysteria, Three Essays on Sexuality and Other Works*. Ed. and trans. J. Strachey. London: Hogarth Press.

Freud S. (1958) The Interpretation of Dreams, Part 1. *SE IV (1900). The Interpretation of Dreams, Part 1*.

Freud, S. (1962a) Heredity and the Aetiology of the Neuroses (1896a). *SE III (1893–1899): Early Psycho-Analytic Publications*.

Freud, S. (1962b) Further Remarks on the Neuro-Psychosis of Defence (1896b). *SE III (1893–1899): Early Psycho-Analytic Publications*.

Freud, S. (1962c) The Aetiology of Hysteria (1896c). *SE III (1893–1899): Early Psycho-Analytic Publications*.

Freud, S. (1966a) Project for a Scientific Psychology (1895[1950]). *SE I (1886–1899): Pre-Psycho-Analytic Publications and Unpublished Drafts*.

Freud, S. (1966b) Letter 69 (1897). Extracts From the Fliess Papers (1950 [1892–1899]). *SE I (1886–1899). Pre-Psycho-Analytic Publications and Unpublished Drafts*.

Freud, S. and Breuer, J. (1955) Studies on Hysteria (1893–1895). *SE II (1893–1895)*. Ed. and trans. J. Strachey. London: Hogarth Press.

Friedrich, W. N. (1997) *Child Sexual Behavior Inventory: Professional Manual*. Odessa, Psychological Assessment Resources.

Gammelgaard, J. (2010) *Betweenity. A Discussion of the Concept of Borderline*. London: Routledge and The Institute of Psychoanalysis.

Laplanche, J. (1970) *Life and Death in Psychoanalysis*. Baltimore: Johns Hopkins University Press.

Laplanche, J. (1987) *New Foundations for Psychoanalysis*. Cambridge: Wiley Blackwell.

Laplanche, J. (1997) The Theory of Seduction and the Problem of the Other. *International Journal of Psychoanalysis* 78: 653–66.

Laplanche, J. (1999a) *Essays on Otherness*. J. Fletcher (ed.) London: Routledge.

Laplanche, J. (1999b) Implantation, Intromission. In J. Fletcher (ed.) *Essays on Otherness*, 133–37. London: Routledge.

Laplanche, J. (2001) Sexuality and Attachment in Metapsychology. In D. Widlöcher (ed.) *Infantile Sexuality and Attachment*. New York: Other Press.

Laplanche, J. (2011a) *Freud and the Sexual: Essays 2000–2006*. Ed. J. Fletcher. New York: International Psychoanalytic Books.

Laplanche, J. (2011b) Three Meanings of the Term 'Unconscious' in the Framework of the General Theory of Seduction. In J. Fletcher (ed.) *Freud and the Sexual: Essays 2000–2006*. New York: International Psychoanalytic Books.

Masson, J. M. (1985) *The Complete Letters of Sigmund Freud to Wilhelm Fliess 1887–1904*. London: The Belknap Press of Harvard University Press.

Scarfone, D. (2001) Sexual and Actual. In D. Widlöcher (ed.) *Infantile Sexuality and Attachment*. New York: Other Press.

Stein, R. (1998a) The Enigmatic Dimension of Sexual Experience. The 'Otherness' of Sexuality and Primal Seduction. *Psychoanalytic Quarterly* LXVII, 594–625.

Stein, R. (1998b) The Poignant, the Excessive and the Enigmatic in Sexuality. *International Journal of Psychoanalysis* 79, 253–68.

Stein, R. (2008). The Otherness of Sexuality: Excess. *Journal of the American Psychoanalytic Association* 56(1), 43–71.

Winnicott, D. W. (1974) Fear of Breakdown. *International Journal of Psychoanalysis*, 1, 103–107.

Zeuthen, K. (2013) *Spillerum. Et undervisningsmateriale om følelser, grænser og seksualitet. Fem temaer om lyst, aktivitet, frivillighed, fantasi og omsorg* [Play Room. An educational material about feelings, boundaries, and sexuality. Five themes about pleasure, activity, voluntariness, fantasy, and care]. Developed for the Service Agency, Ministry of Social Affairs. Second Edition.

Zeuthen, K. and Gammelgaard, J. (2010) Infantile Sexuality – The Concept, Its History and Place in Contemporary Psychoanalysis. *The Scandinavian Psychoanalytic Review* 1(33), 3–12.

Zeuthen, K. and Hagelskjær, M. (2013) Prevention of Child Sexual Abuse: Analysis and Discussion of the Field. *Journal of Child Sexual Abuse*, 26(6), 742–60.

Zeuthen, K., Holm Pedersen, S., and Gammelgaard, J. (2010) Attachment and the Driving Force of Development. A Critical Discussion of Empirical Infant Research. *International Forum of Psychoanalysis* 19(4), 230–39.

2

TRAUMA WITHOUT A SUBJECT

On Malabou, psychoanalysis and *Amour*

Ben Tyrer

The cinema of Michael Haneke is one that consistently interrogates the limits of representation. This can be discerned in the relationship between the seen and the obscene that Lisa Coulthard (2011) recognises in her investigation of violence and the depiction of sexual abuse in, for example, *The White Ribbon* (2009). It can also be found in the presence of death, as Serge Goriely identifies (2010), such as the lingering familial suicide in *The Seventh Continent* (1989). There is a recurrent concern here with what cinema can (*or should*) achieve, and what I will argue in the first instance is that this tendency already seems to suggest an encounter with the Lacanian Real and (or as) the unrepresentable.

In fact, Haneke's *Amour* (2012) is almost wholly determined by mortality, presenting its aged characters at the end of life and pursuing them into death. However, my focus in this chapter will be on *a different kind of death* the film suggests: a kind Catherine Malabou identifies as being precipitated by the radical supervention of *trauma*, a kind *where death takes a form of life*. For those subjects whom she christens the "new wounded", this is the life of a psyche that *survives its own destruction*. My aim is to investigate Malabou's theory of trauma, with *Amour*, to ask what questions they pose to each other, and – importantly – *to psychoanalysis*, as well as what perspectives psychoanalysis can offer on this dialogue. *Amour* thus takes a place in this discussion, not as "proof" of any of the realities of neuropathology – it is, as I will discuss, fiction rather than a documentary – nor simply as an *illustration* of theoretical ideas, but as a *participant* in this debate making a specific contribution *as a film* (i.e. in terms of the way in which the *formal* qualities of Haneke's work make a case for approaching neuropathology in a unique way).

Specifically, this chapter will explore the relationship between the unthinkable and the unrepresentable in *Amour* through an engagement with Malabou's dialogue with psychoanalysis in *The New Wounded* (*TNW*). There, Malabou identifies new forms of post-traumatic subjectivity that necessitate "the complete theoretical reinvention of psychopathology" (2012a: xv). I will approach this from a Lacanian orientation and consider what sort of questions Malabou's concept of "destructive plasticity" poses for psychoanalysis and wonder whether – for example – Žižek's riposte to Malabou might be sufficient to meet her challenge. My approach is equally that of a film theorist, and I will consider both the ways in which cinema can engage in this dialogue on "plasticity", and – equally – how this dialogue might help us to approach the depiction of trauma in Haneke's film. Malabou asserts an important connection between narrative and a clinic of trauma, and so this chapter will explore the possibility – through *Amour* – that the cinema could stage for the psyche a representation of the unrepresentable neurological injury. By focusing on Anne, I will attempt to explore the subjectivity of the new wounded and approach, from a Lacanian perspective, the post-traumatic subjective experience.

New wounded, new subject

I can't hope fully to convey the breadth and complexity of Malabou's analysis, particularly her close reading of Freud. Here, I will therefore constrain myself to some brief notes on several key features of her thesis. Malabou's project revolves around her conceptualisation of "plasticity", through the variant meanings of giving, receiving and – crucially – *destroying or erasing form*. She had begun to explore the neuroscientific dimensions of "plasticity" *before* coming to *TNW* – in *What Should We Do with Our Brain?* (2008) – but it was, in particular, Malabou's personal experience of her grandmother's Alzheimer's disease that, she professes, compelled a more complete orientation of her philosophy towards both neuroscience and psychoanalysis. In her dissatisfaction with the ability of either discourse (or her philosophical training) to account sufficiently for what I could refer to as *the subject of dementia*, she came to propose what she considers to be a radically new theory of psychopathology (see 2012a: xi–xiv).

Psychoanalysis, I'd argue, deals with the unsayable and the unsaid, the unrepresentable, indeed, the *un*conscious: the presence of things made visible by their very invisibility. To this, Malabou seeks to bring something – in her estimation – previously unrepresented and unthought by psychoanalysis: indeed, a new mode of the unthinkable itself in the realm of *cerebral trauma* and what she calls "destructive plasticity", the "dark double" of the constructive plasticity that moulds connections, which then makes form through the *annihilation* of form (ibid.: xix). It is a type of trauma, Malabou contends, heretofore countenanced by neither psychoanalysis nor neuroscience, but closely related to the principles of the former and fundamentally informed by the insights of the latter.

As a paradigmatic example, she refers to the famous case of Phineas Gage, a railway engineer who suffered a massive head trauma in 1848 when an explosion drove a metal rod into his brain. He survived the accident but was affected profoundly by its impact: he became utterly indifferent to those around him, and his personality altered to such an extent that, as Antonio Damsio relates, "Gage was no longer Gage" (cited in Malabou 2012a: 16). In effect, Malabou argues, this brain injury had created a "new person", a new identity unrecognisable from the old: indeed, predicated on the *destruction* of the previous one. Trauma thus supervenes as a sudden disruption of the subject, which Francois Lebigot describes as a "catastrophe" that introduces "a very radical rupture between [a] before and [an] after", and between which there can be no mediation (cited in Malabou 2012a: 15). Malabou extends the domain of this "after" to incorporate other – if not all – forms of post-traumatic subjectivity, from her grandmother's deterioration through Alzheimer's to victims of social exclusion and violence: all of whom, she suggests, present this same detachment or "coolness", this same radical alteration in the subject, severing them from their former selves and creating an "identity without precedent" (2012a: 49, 57).[1]

While Malabou claims that destructive plasticity is something that analysis simply cannot approach (see ibid.: xiii–xiv), Adrian Johnston insists that certain conditions – such as Alzheimer's – may not be *treatable* in a conventional psychoanalytic clinic, but this does not mean they cannot be *theorised* in psychoanalysis (Johnston and Malabou 2013: xii–xiii). Moreover, as my analysis of *Amour* will demonstrate, I suggest that this distinction can be compared to differing understandings of the *Lacanian Real*. Malabou seems to posit destructive plasticity as a Real conceptualised as preceding the Symbolic and thus forever excluded from it as a mystified, obscure and external realm; conversely, recognising the possibility of theorising destructive plasticity within a Lacanian framework – rendering the "unknowability" of the unknown in some way *knowable* (which isn't the same as turning the unknown itself *into* the known) – is analogous to recognising the Real-within-the-Symbolic: a gap, a lacuna that can be circumscribed, but only made "present" in or by its absence. It is such circumscription that allows us to continue to the question of *form*.

The form of form

Malabou's project allows us to begin thinking about representations of that unrepresentable and unthinkable dimension her work evokes: she insists "One does not fantasize a brain injury; one cannot even represent it" (2012a: 9). The question of *form* is, then, central to her project: plasticity is, above all, "an elaboration of form" (2012a: 20), and discovering a "form" appropriate to the new wounded is vital for her description of post-traumatic subjectivity. While cerebral trauma is for Malabou an accident that resists all hermeneutics, she notes, nonetheless, that "cases of brain damage can be written and narrated" (2012a: 53). Such case studies she refers to as "literary forms of neuropathology", which give the new wounded "their own form of narrativity" (2012a: 53). Here she refers not only to clinicians such as Alexander Luria and Oliver Sacks, whose very literary forms of case study are indebted to

Freud, but also to theatre of Samuel Beckett as a rhetorical expression proper to the "brain ache" of the new wounded (cf. 2012a: 55–56).

In this respect, it is important to note that Freud himself expressed the mechanism of psychic trauma in terms that suggest a sort of formal process:

> There is no longer any possibility of preventing the mental apparatus from being flooded with large amounts of stimulus, and another problem arises instead – the problem of mastering the amounts of stimulus which have broken in and of binding them, in the psychical sense, so that they can then be disposed of. (1955b: 34)

The influx of disturbing energy constituting trauma must be *contained* in order for mental functioning (i.e. the pleasure principle) to re-establish itself: it must be bound and rendered quiescent. Moreover, as Adam Phillips suggests, the fundamental problem posed by trauma is *how to find a form for it*, to tell a story about it; our experience is in large part a product of our annexing (or cathecting) traumas internal and external (2013). Malabou brings the very idea of *Bindung* into question (see 2012a: 194–198) – and we could perhaps consider destructive plasticity as *the trauma which finally refuses any psychic binding* – however, I would contend that the "case studies" she references could be considered a form of *conceptual binding*: giving shape to the trauma of the new wounded, finding a way to tell a story about it through theory.

Such cases then, in their literary elaboration, attempt to find a form specific to the traumas they relate. And, I suggest, Haneke's *Amour* fulfils a similar function given that it follows one of the "new wounded", as Anne suffers a series of increasingly debilitating strokes that ultimately leave her incapacitated and dependent on the care of her husband, Georges. My focus therefore will be on the way in which *Amour* presents *but doesn't represent* the unexpected, unpredictable, unthinkable moment in which the radical supervention of trauma creates *another form of form* that is elaborated as a living death. *Amour* can thus serve to establish Anne – as Malabou advocates – as a "case" in the strong sense, a paradigm, a mirror in which we learn to look at ourselves (cf. 2012a: 54). All such case studies involve, as Malabou notes, an element of *fictionality*. Sacks, for instance, compares his patients with characters in epic narratives; they are "heroes, victims, martyrs, warriors (...) travellers to unimaginable lands" (quoted in Malabou 2012a: 55). These "fictionalised" aspects allow the writer to find the form specific to the case and thus to narrate the new wounded, which, I suggest, is equally true for *Amour*.

Most importantly, what this fiction presents is what I will call "the moment of the accident". By its very nature, the unexpected, unpredictable intervention of such brain trauma would be next to impossible to record as documentary footage, except perhaps as an *accident itself* while attempting to film something else. The fictional frame of Haneke's cinematic case study therefore allows for a staging of the Malabouan trauma while retaining a fundamental unrepresentability.

The moment of the accident

The presentation of the moment of the accident in *Amour* – specifically, the first stroke that precipitates the destruction of Anne's psychic life (but also the second stroke that completes it) – is therefore particularly significant. The "moment of death" here becomes the *moment of destructive plasticity*: the point at which, Malabou might insist, Anne's psyche is "shredded" by her cerebral trauma. And, I suggest, in order to appreciate the full import of these scenes, it is worth comparing them with "death" scenes in some of Haneke's other films.

Perhaps most striking is *Benny's Video* (1992), which begins with home-movie footage of the slaughter of a pig. The textural video image shows, in a continuous take, two men trap the animal and then, in close up, apply a stunbolt gun to its head; the pig's squeals are cut short as it keels over and its body spasms. The image is then rewound, and we watch again, this time in slow motion, the moment of the pig's death. The filmic image thus presents this passage to us directly and in the most explicit way possible. Similarly, in *Caché* (2005), Majid stages his suicide both for Georges and the camera in an immediate and shockingly violent way. By contrast, much of the violence of *Funny Games* (1997) occurs off-screen. First, through extra-diegetic sound, is the dog's demise evoked as barking and howling turn to silence; then, we realise that the son has been killed off screen as his body is shown in the corner of the room; finally, the father lies just out of frame as Paul shoots him. Again, this technique of *suggesting* rather than directly *presenting* the moment of death occurs in *Benny's Video*: in contradistinction to the pig's slaughter, when Benny uses his purloined stunbolt gun to kill a young girl, her death is again obscured by framing and evoked through sound as her shouts are silenced by the stunbolt's report.

Amour thus combines both representational strategies: in one sense, we see Anne fall victim to the stroke just as clearly as Benny's pig falls victim to its own head injury – both are framed by the camera, we see their eyes, their faces, as destructive plasticity strikes – however, this irreparable damage is no more graphic (in fact, much less) than the suggestions of Paul's or Benny's murderous violence. Indeed, Anne's psychic "death" lacks even the aural dimension of the earlier films; it is marked by her profound silence alone. And like Majid, Anne is present before the camera in a precisely arranged domestic space (see Figure 2.1), but whereas he slashes at his throat with a razor, she succumbs to a blockage in that same carotid artery: blood sprays up the wall in the first instance, its circulation stalled in the second. One explicit, one obscure: both moments are, in the end, equally decisive. *Amour*, in a sense, shows us "everything" while at the same time telling us *nothing* about the violence that occurs.

FIGURE 2.1 Georges and Anne at breakfast in *Amour* (2012), dir. Michael Haneke: Amour_ michael_haneke©2012 Les Films Du Losange – X Filme Creative Pool – Wega Film.

The catastrophe in *Amour* – this event that forever changes (and ultimately *ends*) the lives of Georges and Anne – is thus presented as almost *nothing at all*. Preceded by a slight movement of Anne's leg and a tilt of her head, the accident goes entirely unnoticed by Georges – and the spectator – as it *strikes dead* his wife's present self. It is effectively imperceptible, unseen, barely "represented" at all and, in a version of Freud's *Nachträglichkeit*, can only be discerned or constituted *qua* trauma *after the fact*, once it has been diagnosed as what neurologists advocate calling a "brain attack".

Although Haneke thanks doctors from the *Salpêtrière* hospital in the credits, I'd argue that the *complete medical accuracy* of the film, and these scenes in particular, isn't necessarily what is here at stake. More important – following both Malabou *and* Freud – is the question of finding the form for this trauma, and a purely "scientific" representational strategy here would add very little. If we recall Malabou's insistence that a brain injury can't be represented, here one could well imagine, by contrast, a *CSI*-style computer animated rendering of Anne's internal organs depicting every detail of her heart and blood vessels and the flow of blood to her brain being restricted thus precipitating a stroke, but this would tell us nothing of the radical alterations Anne will undergo as a *subject*.

Haneke's cinematic case study of destructive plasticity therefore allows for a staging of the crucial, Malabouan unthinkable event, while – I suggest – retaining an element of its unrepresentability, its ephemerality, as well as its devastation. The moment of the accident is figured as a blank, an absence, an aporia of the subject itself; the film *presents* the unrepresentable – allows us, in a sense, to know its unknowability – without rendering it known. Indeed, the second – *truly decisive* – stroke that renders Anne profoundly debilitated presents itself only as a complete absence. We might infer from the morning scene in which Georges finds that she has lost control of her bladder that this stroke took place during the night, but it is again only reported after the fact in a conversation between Georges and Eva, and without making clear when or how it occurred.

Goriely suggests that death in Haneke's films is "like Medusa's head; [it] cannot be looked at directly" (2010: 121), and this is most obviously true in the cases of *Benny's Video* or *Funny Games* where we get only an indirect representation of the fatal moment. However, I'd argue – and Goriely doesn't seem to address this even though he discusses Majid's suicide – that this is no less true of those instances where we *do* seem to witness the death "itself" on screen (such as Anne's smothering). The cinema might be able to record the duration in which this instant occurs (even – or especially – in documentary), but this doesn't give us knowledge of death, of what dying means to *us*. It remains – in a Malabouan way – unthinkable, unknowable even then, and this is what *Amour* demonstrates effectively: we both see and don't see – for example – Anne's psychic death, her cerebral destruction, at the breakfast table. The moment is given to us in its fullness but it remains *absent*.

On the other hand, Anne's breakfast time fugue in particular *does* accord strikingly with the descriptions that Malabou relates as her "Psychopathological Cases": from the "absence seizures" endured by patients with epilepsy to the "akinetic muteness" (loss of speech and motion) demonstrated specifically by those suffering a stroke. In each instance is the subject's disposition characterised by a "veritable absence", a "suspension of selfhood", of being "there but not there" (2012a: 50–51). And it is precisely this utter lack of self-presence that the stasis of Emmanuelle Riva's performance evokes as she sits blankly at the table. As Georges grasps Anne's face, dabs her with cool water, she remains impassive, unmoved, *absent*. And I am tempted therefore to ask here whether we could say in fact that, "*Anne is no longer Anne*"?

This lack of self, Malabou suggests, extends to the very destruction *of* the self: a radical rupturing of identity. She insists, "A person with Alzheimer's disease, for example, is not – or not only – someone who has "changed" or been "modified," but rather *a subject who has become someone else*" (2012a: 15). Over the course of *Amour*, we bear witness to profound changes in Anne's character that would certainly serve to corroborate a Malabouan psychopathology (indeed, it is after the second stroke that we truly find Anne among *the new wounded*). However, I'd argue that it isn't enough simply for the film – any film – to illustrate the particular questions at hand (even if *Amour can* illustrate a certain impossibility when it comes to representing the traumatic event). In a film-philosophy of destructive plasticity, we must also ask in what ways does the film *contribute* to an on-going discourse here: what problems might it pose to Malabou?

Trauma – break-in

Amour begins with a break-in, as the fire-service forces open the front door of Anne and Georges' apartment. Bright light and loud noise explode the darkened image and silenced soundtrack of the film. This already suggests the classic definition of trauma as *wound*: a rupture or invasion of the body. And, moreover, it evokes Freud's memorable declaration in *Beyond the Pleasure Principle*:

> We describe as "traumatic" any excitations from outside which are powerful enough to break through the protective shield. It seems to me that the concept of trauma necessarily implies a connection of this kind with a breach in an otherwise efficacious barrier against stimuli. Such an event as an external trauma is bound to provoke a disturbance on a large scale in the functioning of the organism. (1955b: 33)

However, as Malabou would no doubt be quick to point out, in the context of *Amour*, the injury we are faced with should, in the first instance, be considered *cerebral* rather than *psychic* (or "sexual") in its eventuality (see 2012a: 39–44). Nonetheless, Freud's image remains useful: the threatening possibility of a break-in looms over the first part of *Amour*. After Anne and Georges return home from the concert, Georges inspects the front door and sees that someone has tried to force the lock with a screwdriver. He then notes that several neighbours have already been burgled, and Anne relates a story about a robbery in another building where the burglars entered the top floor through the attic, knocking a hole in the wall – that otherwise efficacious barrier – and removing valuable paintings (provoking large scale disturbance).

The domestic space of the apartment is under the threat of intrusion from the very beginning and in a Malabouan context it therefore starts to evoke a dimension of destructive plasticity where a break-in through the attic points to the "break-in" of brain trauma occasioned by Anne's stroke. Anne suggests that she would be scared to death if someone should break in during the night, while she was in her bed. And if we recall, this is precisely how the second trauma – the decisive stroke – hits her: one night in bed. The brain injury is thus an intruder in the dark that comes to take something from them (dignity, mobility, control, life).

Such an intervention, I argue, further insists upon the psychoanalytic context: it calls forth Lacan's depiction of the "irruption" of the Real, the break-in of *tuché*, that derails the smooth functioning of the Symbolic. This is how Lacan takes up Freud's theorisation of trauma and assigns it a function within his own metapsychology. For Lacan:

> The function of tuché, of the real as encounter – the encounter in so far as it may be missed, in so far as it is essentially the missed encounter – first presented itself in the history of psycho-analysis in a form that was in itself already enough to arouse our attention, that of trauma. (1977: 55)

I will return to the question of *tuché* in a moment, but what we can say first of all here is that at the origin of analytic experience, Lacan notes, the Real presents itself "in the form of that which is *unassimilable* in it – in the form of trauma" (ibid.). Trauma-*qua*-Real is the intrusion of an impossible event, an unthinkable wound that resists symbolisation, a shock (or fright, Freud's *Schreck*) in the face of which the signifier stutters and fails. It is only this very *failure* that the Symbolic can circumscribe, without ever signifying its traumatic core. It could then provide fertile ground for a theorisation of the new wounded: as I have noted, the way in which *Amour* depicts Anne's injuries through absence and blankness does suggest the impossible presence of the Real of her trauma. However, Malabou is more sceptical, even closed to this possibility of thinking together *tuché* and destructive plasticity.

Traum/a – dream

Amour addresses such trauma – its absent presence – in various ways at the formal and diegetic levels, and in this context a particularly significant form here is in *dreams*. In a striking sequence, we bear witness to one of Georges' dreams – his nightmare – which returns us, first of all, to the traumatic break-in/intruder motif: the sound of a doorbell draws him into the hallway and he stumbles into ankle-deep water. The film cuts to a close-up of his face: *suddenly* a hand reaches impossibly from behind his head and clasps his mouth before an equally sudden cut to black (see Figure 2.2). Georges' waking screams form a sound bridge across these images, which then reveal him nightmare-stricken in bed next to Anne. This dream, then, suggests a terrible, unacknowledgeable truth for Georges: something impossible or unthinkable directly, a trauma that finds only indirect expression through the dreamwork. The horror of Anne's illness, her degeneration; the promise he made never to take her back to hospital; the proximity of his own mortality: all this is condensed into a dream-image of unbearable intensity.

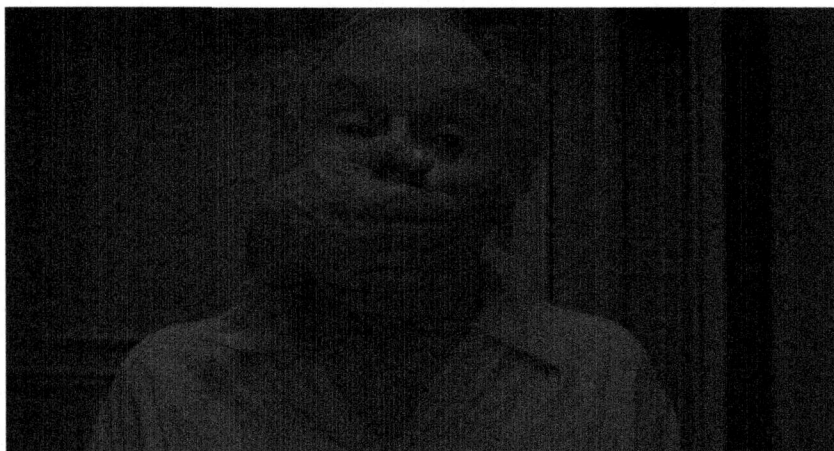

FIGURE 2.2 Georges' dream in *Amour* (2012), dir. Michael Haneke: Amour_michael_haneke©2012 Les Films Du Losange – X Filme Creative Pool – Wega Film.

Similarly, this is how to interpret the famous dream of the burning child, which Freud related in *The Interpretation of Dreams*: a trauma given shape only indirectly through the nightmare. A father sleeps, while in the next room an overturned candle sets alight the body of his dead son; in his dream, the father is confronted by the son, who reproaches him, "*Father, don't you see I'm burning?*" (1958: 509). Here we can detect the Real, as Lacan puts it, only "in what the dream has enveloped, hidden from us, behind the lack or representation of which there can be only one representative" (1977: 60). The terrible image is not, therefore, a direct encounter with or access to the Real but a representation of its traumatic impact, which, as Bruce Fink explains, is at the level of the "unthinkable, unnameable, unspeakable" (1995: 227).

Again, I'd contend that, in the context of the new wounded and a destructive plasticity that resists all hermeneutics, this could put us on the track of a psychoanalytic theorisation, following Malabou's insistence that we can, nonetheless, find a form for this trauma with our case studies, and even *narrate*, to some extent, this post-traumatic subjectivity. For example, Georges' nightmare seems to narrate (or prefigure) aspects of the central trauma of *Amour*: the suffocating hand over his mouth perhaps suggesting his unconscious knowledge of, even his plan for, what is to come and his sheer terror in the face of both this realisation and Anne's decline.

Malabou, however, rejects any psychoanalytic rapport. She addresses Lacan's theory of "*tuché* and *automaton*" in chapter seven of *TNW* but instead of finding scope for productive dialogue, Malabou deems the theory to be as inadequate as the rest of psychoanalysis. First, she performs a predictable – but nonetheless interesting – deconstructionist gesture by returning the Greek terms to their origin in order to demonstrate how *tuché* and *automaton* can be shown to mean their opposites: contingency becoming necessity, and vice versa (2012a: 136). It's a nice move, and for Malabou enough to suggest that psychoanalysis once again must fall silent when faced with unthinkable trauma. Nonetheless, it doesn't change the fact that this is precisely what Lacan *is* attempting to conceptualise.

Lacan is clear from the outset that he is taking Aristotle's terms and translating (even redefining) them into his metapsychology.[2] Thus an appeal to etymology will only get us so far: for Malabou, *tuché* and *automaton* might signify differently for the language of Aristotle, but Lacan is forging here his own language in attempting to think the unthinkable, represent the unrepresentable, through psychoanalysis. Moreover, Malabou's transposition of these two terms in her approach to Lacan seems to result in a curious reading of the burning child dream, where – again – I suggest that Lacan can be understood as being much closer to Malabou. In German, of course, a dream is "*ein Traum*" and, as I have shown, both *Amour* and Freud understand well the intimate relation between *der Traum* and *das Trauma* – one effectively contained within the other – and by going into the dream again here I will attempt to circumscribe the locus of Malabou's *missed encounter* with Lacan.

Malabou returns to the question of *tuché* and *automaton* in an essay titled, "Post-Trauma", where she offers a sustained reading of the dream, and it is here, I suggest, that her particular (mis)interpretation of Lacan becomes most clear. In her commentary on *Seminar XI*, she states:

> Obviously, what belongs to tuché is the falling of the candle and the burning of the child's arm. This is the reality, Lacan says, but not the real. The Real is the unreal "resurrection" of the child and the words "Father, can't you see I am burning?" And here, Lacan starts to analyze tuché as a secondary kind of causality or of reality. The child's burnt arm is not the real accident in this dream, it is not the Real. The Real comes with the speech, the son's address to his father. Tuché has no autonomy, it is in fact only a means for the Real or the automaton to emerge. There would only be one mode of happening, that of automaton, with a disguised version of it, a mask, tuché. (2012c: 231)

And in this passage, I suggest, we can see how Malabou's transposition of Lacan's terms causes a confusion in her reading of the dream and the place of the Real. The *tuché* is not, as Malabou suggests, the falling candle; the latter is certainly an *accident* that is woven into the fabric of the dream, but it isn't the traumatic encounter. The Real is indeed in the child's reproach, but it isn't literally "in" the words: they only indicate its presence indirectly. Moreover, this doesn't mean that *tuché* has no autonomy, being *only a means for the Real or automaton to emerge*: it *is* that very Real, its traumatic irruption in the father's psyche, the disruption of automaton.

His trauma isn't in the burnt arm (or the letter of the words themselves) but in the devastating guilt over his son's death that resurrects him in the dream and burns in the address, *Father, don't you see I'm burning*; and it is from *this* encounter that he wakes *in order to escape into reality*. That Malabou seems to treat "Real" and "automaton" as somehow equivalent here further suggests the confusion of terms that originated in *TNW* and by the end of the passage quoted above, *tuché* and *automaton* have once again exchanged conceptual places: *tuché* is not, as Malabou asserts, the "mask" of automaton but its *cause*. This doesn't mean that trauma is effective only to the extent that it resonates with some previous experience (as in the classic Freudian version); it is an external shock precisely conceptualised by psychoanalysis. *Tuché* is, like destructive plasticity or Freud's *Schreck*, a violent, unanticipatable catastrophe that *disrupts* the subject; what Malabou theorises (perhaps beyond Lacan) is thus a type of *tuché* that doesn't simply *disturb automaton* but irrevocably damages (or destroys) it.[3]

Georges' dream in *Amour* is thus a disturbance according to a similar principle: it isn't some noise outside the apartment that gives rise to his nightmare. It isn't the quotidian anxiety about intruders or burglars in the building, but what – as I have already suggested – these interlopers could represent. Here, an arm appears in the dream – impossibly reaching into the image with irruptive force – but it serves the same function as the child's words: indicating the traumatic Real that lies beyond it. His *automaton* thus masks the truth of *tuché* and the impossibility of Anne's destruction.

No subject

To address this destruction, I will return, for the last time, to the moment of the accident. What I want to suggest is that Haneke's staging of the kitchen scene in particular emphasises something that comes through again and again in Malabou's discussion of the new wounded, which is to say the fundamentally *intersubjective* nature of this trauma. As I described, the scene begins in the recognisably observational, Haneke style: deep focus photography and slight reframings to follow Anne as she prepares breakfast. It is also at this distance that we see, or rather don't really see, Anne suffer the stroke. However, as Georges begins to realise that something has happened, the film switches to more intimate close-ups and – importantly – a clearer orientation towards not Anne's but *his* experience of the accident. Aside from those striking shots where Anne stares blankly and Georges clasps her face, the camera focuses mainly on Georges and allows Jean-Louis Trintignant's performance to convey the combination of confusion and horror that the subject of the accident presents to the other. The camera follows Georges to the sink and back, and as he wets his wife's forehead: and almost throughout our perspective is simply the back of Anne's head (see Figure 2.3). Moreover, the camera follows Georges into the bedroom as he dresses himself to leave for help, and so even Anne's return to self-presence – signified obliquely by the extra-diegetic sound of the running tap being turned off in the kitchen – is presented from *his* perspective rather than hers.

This depersonalised image of Anne certainly evokes that loss of self that Malabou identifies, and prepares us for the creation – through her destruction – of a "new" Anne. However, as the concomitant focus on *Georges* in this instance must insist, when – as Malabou suggests – "neurologists speak of a person becoming unrecognizable" (2012a: 19), the question begs itself: "unrecognisable" to whom?

FIGURE 2.3 Georges in *Amour* (2012), dir. Michael Haneke: Amour_michael_haneke©2012 Les Films Du Losange – X Filme Creative Pool – Wega Film.

In this context, it makes little sense to suggest "to herself" because – if we follow Malabou – that (former) "self" no longer exists. It is only for Georges that "Anne is no longer Anne": the identity "no longer Anne" cannot serve as a point of reference for *her* because of this traumatic supervention.

While, in *The Ontology of the Accident*, Malabou asserts that "All of a sudden these people become strangers to themselves" (2012b: 13), this isn't congruent with her wider conceptualisation of the new wounded. If it is the case that "When damage occurs, it is another self who is affected, a new self, unrecognizable" (2012a: 141), as she states in *TNW*, then there cannot be the requisite distance between two senses of "self" for such dissonance; if Malabou's conjecture is correct – that destructive plasticity brings forth a radically new form of subjectivity – then the "new self" would be unable to "compare itself" with any sense of former identity. They are, then, only strangers to *themselves* in a metaphorical way; the new wounded are more literally strangers to those around them. Indeed, Malabou herself even describes this at certain points in *TNW*: she explains, "What people with brain damage have in common are changes in personality that are serious enough to lead their family and friends to conclude that they have metamorphosed into another person" (ibid.: 48).

It is for family and friends, *for others*, that the transformation occurs. And this is in fact reiterated in *Amour*: when Eva comes to visit her parents after the second stroke, she is disturbed by her mother's decline and exclaims that she is *unrecognisable*, which is to say that the daughter no longer recognises Anne as the mother she knew. I will return to this point below, but what I want to emphasise here, in the first instance, is that Malabou's formulation of destructive plasticity seems to present, then, a *trauma without a subject*: because the subject is simply not present at the site of her own destruction. It is an event that erases its subject, while at the same time preserving its form: *psychic death as a form of life*.

In light of this, Žižek offers an intriguing attempt to rehabilitate the Freudian notion of present trauma's resonance with past experience, arguing that destructive plasticity "repeats" the founding gesture of the subject as such: the traumatic separation from substance that constitutes subjectivity. He asserts that "the subject is the survivor of its own death" and this is why Lacan's matheme for the subject is the barred $\$$: the subject as void, divided or alienated from itself (2010: 307). Apropos of Malabou, then, it isn't a question for Žižek of whether Lacanian psychoanalysis is capable of thinking a new subject, a form of subjectivity that survives its own death, because – for Lacan – this is the form of the subject *as such*: the "surviving form of the loss of its substance" (ibid.). What results, Žižek argues, after the violent intrusion of trauma – the destructive plasticity that "erases all substantial content" – is nothing but "the pure *form* of subjectivity, a form which must have already been there" (ibid.: 312, emphasis added). This does not entail, as Malabou suggests apropos of Freud, a return of or to the "child" as the "imperishable" form of the subject (see Malabou 2012a: 58–59), but of the emergence/persistence of form as such, of the subject *qua* form (there is no "permanent" form except the form of form itself, i.e. *plasticity*). It is therefore a bold speculative redemption of psychoanalysis that

Žižek proposes, and it is – I contend – by recognising what he describes as this "zero-level" form of the subject without content that we can proceed in an interrogation of both Malabou and *Amour*.

As I have suggested, the film charts Anne's disintegration as a result of her disease, but what remains perhaps the most striking and certainly most significant image of Anne *qua* new wounded is her blankness at the breakfast table: her absent, staring face clasped in Georges' hands (see Figure 2.4). Haneke's screenplay describes her staring into the void (see 2012); however, I'd contend that it isn't only *she* but also *we* who stare into the void in this moment, as we lock eyes with her. This could well invoke that most famous of Žižekian reference points, that "empty nothing" of Hegel's "night of the world". As Georges gazes helplessly at Anne, this much-quoted passage might resonate with our experience: "One catches sight of this night when one looks human beings in the eye – into a night that becomes awful" (quoted in Žižek 1999: 30). And in keeping with Žižek's thesis that the new wounded constitute a formal exemplar of subjectivity as such, we could similarly consider the "night" in Anne's eyes as that of the "pure self" of every human, reduced *in extremis* to pain and horror.

However, Žižek frames this *night* – via Schelling and Hegel – as a "passage through madness" (1999: 34), while Malabou insists that "The brain injured are not mad; they abandon even madness" (2012b: 24), and "madness" does not seem here the appropriate paradigm. Instead, I'd suggest that Žižek himself offers a more apt image where, in his response to Malabou, he reframes this look in terms of the uncanny experience of "encountering nothing when we expected to see something" (2010: 313). Where we expected to find a subject (Anne), we instead encounter a complete absence: the pure void of subjectivity itself, which Žižek suggests gives us the sense of an "empty house where 'no one is home'" (ibid.).

FIGURE 2.4 Anne in *Amour* (2012), dir. Michael Haneke: Amour_michael_ haneke©2012 Les Films Du Losange – X Filme Creative Pool – Wega Film.

And here again we return to the space of the apartment in *Amour*: when the fire brigade breaks down their door, Georges and Anne are "there" but they are no longer "home".

The new blessed ones?

It is, moreover, this uncanny coincidence of presence and absence in *Amour* that is so unsettling: as I suggested, we "recognise" Anne but at the same time, *she is no longer Anne*. As Žižek notes of the new wounded in general, there is in fact a double lack here: there is no recognition *in* us, no chance of empathy, and at the same time there is no recognition *of* us as a partner in communication (2010: 300). For Lacanian psychoanalysis, *identity as such* depends upon the Other, arising initially from the imaginary dyad and developing into a relation to the trans-individual unconscious, where desire is inscribed in the Other. Here, I'd argue, this dialectic of identity is wholly suspended: as Malabou suggests, the subject becomes "intransitive (he or she is not the other of someone)" (2012b: 24). I'd add, then, that *Amour* can reveal instead only the point at which a *trauma* is inscribed *in* an other: there is no *Nachträlichkeit* for Anne (*qua* subject) so "we" have to do it, to experience it as trauma "ourselves".

Indeed, the genesis of Malabou's project begins with such intersubjective connection: recall that it is *her* experience of her grandmother's Alzheimer's disease and *her* speculation on the states of trauma involved that occasioned *TNW*. When faced with this degeneration, she concluded that "this absence, this disaffection, this strangeness to oneself, were, without any possible doubt, the paradoxical signs of profound pain" and that only further exploration of neuroscience, philosophy and psychoanalysis could help her to comprehend this malady (2012a: xii). Equally, as Haneke explains, was the motivation behind *Amour* the question of dealing with the pain of another, the pain of one that we love. This, he suggests, is more unbearable than suffering the disease oneself – to watch another stricken by illness – and it was this feeling that motivated the writing of the film.[4]

This insight into both projects – and the proximity of intentions – is vital, but it also raises important questions. Žižek captures something of this when he asks, in a typically provocative manner, whether "*les nouveaux blessés*" couldn't be understood as "the new blessed ones": their trauma only experienced as such from within the horizon of meaning, while they themselves remain indifferent (2010: 299). Predictably, for him this becomes a version of the tasteless joke, "the bad news is you have Alzheimer's, the good news is you will forget this by the time you get home". But Žižek's contention – that when we approach such "trauma" we might forget to include ourselves, to take into account our own desire in the observed phenomenon – is a crucial point for understanding destructive plasticity: one that is equally emphasised by *Amour* in what I have identified as the presentation of Anne's trauma from Georges' perspective.

Malabou claims that we live "in the epoch of the end of transference" because a "deserted, emotionally disaffected, indifferent psyche" no longer has this capacity (2012a: 214), and this is borne out in *Amour* by the blockage of intersubjective connection caused by Anne's blankness. Moreover, Malabou proposes that our task in this light is – following Françoise Davoine and Jean-Max Gaudillière – one of "becoming subject to the other's suffering, especially when this other is unable to feel anything" (quoted in 2012a: 214). And we can equally see both *TNW* and *Amour* as gestures towards this, as the comments above from Malabou and Haneke attest. Nonetheless, a nagging question persists, and this is where (in their very proximity) the distance between the two projects – as well as the necessity of a Lacanian perspective – becomes apparent.

Malabou further states that, "Between psychoanalysis and neurology, it is precisely the sense of 'the other' that is displaced" because of the need that she sees for welcoming a conceptual alterity (i.e. destructive plasticity) (2012a: 215). To this I'd add that there is also a need for Malabou to recognise the place of the other *for* the new wounded. Her book ends where it began, with "a patient with Alzheimer's", but we should recognise that *TNW* is not so much "about" a grandmother as it is about a granddaughter's *response to* this patient. This response is certainly a reparative gesture, to "gather the other's pain" not to take his or her place "but to restore it to [her]" (2012a: 215); however, this proposition raises a number of questions.

Like Georges, we can become subject to the other's suffering, but – in the Malabouan paradigm – is there a "subject" there to suffer in the first place? Žižek wonders, again provocatively, how we can be sure of the way in which this affects the patient: "does it do them any good whatsoever?" and, more radically, "how can we be sure that it is really the patient's suffering we are assembling?" (2010: 297). It is at this point, I contend, that Malabou's attempt to think the limit of thought (i.e. destructive plasticity) reaches its own limit. Malabou attempts to conceptualise a trauma beyond the horizon of all meaning, but this conceptualisation itself must remain *en-deçà, on this side* of the horizon. As Žižek observes, the traumatic intervention of which Malabou speaks is only experienced *qua* trauma from *our perspective* because we encounter the absence of a meaningful Self: "when the patient's old personality is destroyed, the very measure of their suffering also disappears" (2010: 300). Whether blessed indifference or unbearable suffering, we are unable to determine and this, for us (the other), is indeed *traumatic*.

The point here, I'd insist, is not that Žižek is right (they really are "blessed") or Malabou is wrong, *per se*, but that within this framework any answer is *unknowable*. However, where the Žižekian paradigm *does* come forward, I suggest, is in the necessity of understanding this as not an *epistemological* question but an *ontological* one: "the gaps and voids in our knowledge of reality are simultaneously the gaps and voids in the 'real' ontological edifice itself" (1999: 55). And nowhere is this more apparent than when we are dealing with the *Real* – the aporia of the Lacanian Real-within-the-Symbolic – of destructive plasticity. Moreover, it is this unknowability that Haneke's representational strategy in *Amour* preserves: showing everything can tell us only that *we do not know*, even while this unknown is circumscribed and given form.

Representing the unthinkable, thinking the unrepresentable

To conclude, then: where Malabou argues of destructive plasticity – "We know it, but the psyche cannot stage this knowledge for itself" (2012a: 9) – I'd argue, first of all, that a film like *Amour*, *as a film*, can further help us to "know it" through the immediacy of its cinematic depiction. But, importantly, the *cinematic form of neuropathology* that Haneke presents can serve to stage, to evoke, for the psyche this unknowable, unthinkable event while at the same time retaining an element of its fundamentally unrepresentable nature. The film thus demonstrates that – *pace* Malabou – Lacanian psychoanalysis *can* theorise such an aporia, and bringing both together can help us to think this unrepresentable.

Indeed, the question of *representation* comes to the fore as Malabou brings her own project towards its conclusion. In the last section of *TNW*, she turns her attention to the death drive. Freud, she argues, doesn't accord the death drive its own form. He could not find its "representative" in the way that Eros functions for the life drives; it is always given form *by the "life drives"* (e.g. the "example" of sadism/masochism). The question thus becomes, as Malabou summarises, "How does one render the death drive visible?" (2012b: 18). Sadism/masochism can't account for the new wounded *qua* "living figures of death" (2012a: 198), but destructive plasticity *can*: these figures thus become, as Žižek notes, "the pure subjects of the death drive" (2010: 305) and – Malabou contends – destructive plasticity therefore gives the death drive its own particular form.

Her development of psychoanalysis here is compelling; nonetheless, in this context I can't help but detect – in Malabou's phrase *living figures of death* – a summoning of the figure of the *undead*, evoked from Freud to Lacan to Žižek. Freud might not have found a representative of the death drive in *Beyond the Pleasure Principle*, but he had already done so in his essay on *The Uncanny* (1955a), where the return of the dead constitutes an avatar of *das Unheimliche* (and thus, retroactively, a rendering visible of the death drive). And in *The Parallax View*, Žižek renders this image even more explicit: anticipating his subsequent description of the new wounded, he connects this "zero-level" of the subject with the death drive and the space of the death drive with "the 'living dead' (the monstrous life-substance which persists in the Real outside the Symbolic)" (2006: 210, 121). This is not to say that we should consider Anne and her company as "zombies"; rather, it is to insist that the horrifying persistence of "life after death" in the new wounded has indeed been theorised by psychoanalysis. It is therefore true that, as Malabou proposes, "a new chapter in the history of the death drive (*Todestrieb, pulsion de mort*) writes itself" (2013: 224), but at the same time – I would add – this chapter, Malabou's project, is not *without precedent*.

Notes

1 This is a particular bone of contention between Malabou and not only psychoanalysis but also neuroscience: a point raised by Dr Diana Caine of the National Hospital for Neurology and Neurosurgery, London, in an intervention at the Psychoanalysis and Science conference, University of Tallinn, 15 March 2015. She noted that many neurological disorders do not present such radical disconnection from the patient's past (e.g. Caine 2009).

2 "First, the *tuché*, which we have borrowed (…) from Aristotle, who uses it in his search for cause. We have translated it as the *encounter with the real*" (1977: 53).

3 Johnston makes a comparable point when he connects *tuché* and *automaton* to Lacan's coin toss game in the Postface to the "Seminar on 'The Purloined Letter'" to suggest that Malabou's model points to an instance where the coin is lost or destroyed, leaving the subject without "enough coin for analysis" but which does not mean the "complete bankruptcy of analysis" (2014: 290).

4 See *The Making of Amour* (Montmayeur, 2012).

References

Caine, D. (2009) Reflecting on Mirror Self-Misrecognition. *Neuropsychoanalysis* 11(2): 211–26.

Coulthard, L. (2011) Interrogating the Obscene: Extremism and Michael Haneke. In T. Horeck and T. Kendall (eds.) *The New Extremism in Cinema: From France to Europe.* Edinburgh: EUP.

Fink, B. (1995) The Real Cause of Repetition. In R. Feldstein, B. Fink, and M. Jaanus (eds.) *Reading Seminar XI: Lacan's Four Fundamental Concepts of Psychoanalysis.* Albany: SUNY Press.

Freud, S. (1955a) The Uncanny (1919). *The Standard Edition of the Complete Psychological Works of Sigmund Freud, Volume XVII (1917–1919): An Infantile Neurosis and Other Works.* Ed. and trans. James Strachey. London: Hogarth.

Freud, S. (1955b) Beyond the Pleasure Principle (1920). *SE XVIII (1920–1922): Group Psychology and Other Works.*

Freud, S. (1958) *SE V (1900): The Interpretation of Dreams (Second Part) and On Dreams.*

Goriely, S. (2010) Pieces of Truth for Moments of Death in Michael Haneke's Cinema. In A. Ornella and S. Klauss (eds.) *Fascinatingly Disturbing: Interdisciplinary Perspectives on Michael Haneke's Cinema.* Eugene: Wipf and Stock.

Haneke, M. (2012) *Amour.* Available from: www.sonyclassics.com/awards-information/amour_screenplay.pdf. [Accessed 10 March 2014].

Johnston, A. (2014) *Adventures in Transcendental Materialism: Dialogues with Contemporary Thinkers.* Edinburgh: EUP.

Johnston, A. and Malabou, C. (2013) *Self and Emotional Life: Philosophy, Psychoanalysis and Neuroscience.* New York: Columbia UP.

Lacan, J. (1977) *The Seminar of Jacques Lacan, Book XI: The Four Fundamental Concepts of Psychoanalysis.* Ed. J-A Miller. Trans. A. Sheridan. New York: Norton.

Malabou, C. (2008) *What Should We Do with Our Brain?* Trans. S. Rand. New York: Fordham UP.

Malabou, C. (2012a) *The New Wounded: From Neurosis to Brain Damage.* Trans. S. Miller. New York: Fordham UP.

Malabou, C. (2012b) *The Ontology of the Accident: An Essay on Destructive Plasticity.* Trans. C. Shread. Cambridge: Polity.

Malabou, C. (2012c) Post-Trauma: Towards a New Definition? In T. Cohen (ed.) *Telemorphosis: Essays in the Era of Climate Change, Volume 1*. Ann Arbor: Open Humanities Press.

Phillips, A. (2013) Seminar on *Beyond the Pleasure Principle*. University of York. 14 February.

Žižek, S. (1999) *The Ticklish Subject: The Absent Centre of Political Ontology*. London: Verso.

Žižek, S. (2006) *The Parallax View*. London, Verso.

Žižek, S. (2010) *Living in the End Times*. London: Verso.

Filmography

Amour (2012) Directed by Michael Haneke. France/Germany/Austria: Les Films du Losange.

Caché (2005) Directed by Michael Haneke. France/Austria/Germany/Italy: Les Films du Losange.

Benny's Video (1992) Directed by Michael Haneke. Austria/Switzerland: Bernard Lang.

Funny Games (1997) Directed by Michael Haneke. Austria: Wega.

The Making of Amour (2012) Directed by Yves Montmayeur. France/Germany/Austria: Les Films du Losange.

The Seventh Continent (1989) Directed by Michael Haneke. Austria: Wega.

The White Ribbon (2009) Directed by Michael Haneke. Germany/Austria/France/Italy: Les Films du Losange.

3

A POSSIBLE WAY TO REPRESENT THE UNREPRESENTABLE IN CLINICAL TRAUMA

Yaelle Sibony-Malpertu

On fascination with a traumatic event: A psychoanalytic psychodynamic approach

I will not talk here about the "unrepresentable" in just any representation: that is to say, the constitutive gap between the word and the object, between the word and its referent. These are important issues but not within the specific terms of my approach, which concerns clinical trauma. Nor will I discuss the trauma of birth, but rather psychological trauma related to specific traumatic events, here linked to murder or attempted murder.

Civility and politeness in an individual accused of a crime against humanity never cease to amaze, as if an assassin were supposed to be always busy killing and murdering. One remains surprised that a criminal can sometimes be gentle and considerate, yet it is perhaps one of the criminal's most powerful weapons that he or she does not always act in a destructive manner. Articles from newspapers, born from this fascination of intermittently monstrous criminals, can for example talk of the "tender hubby" that a war criminal could be with his wife or with his children. It seems that those articles do not so much reflect the complexity of murder as mitigate our indignation, presenting this data as if it were an unsurpassable finding. These images represent the intrinsically fascinating dimension of a traumatic real. It has a dreadful ability to spread by creating disarray in our ethical landscape: it seems to suggest to people, because he seemed to be a good husband, that reciprocally, any good husband could once resemble him.[1]

On the contrary, clinical trauma forces us to break this fascination with trauma: not only is fascination incompatible with any therapeutic work, but also, it regularly threatens therapeutic work itself. Thus, the ethic underlying this kind of clinical approach starts from similar observations to those of the articles, but brings about almost opposite conclusions. In my opinion, Hannah Arendt's thesis can help to encourage vigilance against the fascination with the "banality of evil" (2005) and, at the same time, warns us not to overlook the significant number of people who suffer from psychological trauma. One of Arendt's goals can be to prevent society (which here mainly means potential bystanders and witnesses of traumatic events) from falling into routine and insensitivity to this kind of banality of evil, thus contributing to it. Otherwise, we return to the previous situation in which fascination prevails. There, the risk of being locked, in spite of oneself, in "doublethink" is very high. Described by George Orwell in *1984* (1949), and omnipresent in totalitarian systems, it is not foreign to the cleaved reasoning of a man who is a father at home and commits crimes against other children out of his home.

This said, I will talk about people having experienced traumatic events, manifesting more or less decipherable symptoms, acting out what they fail to say and showing what they cannot think. I will try to delve into the available clinical resources, to see whether the unrepresentable is definitively so for everyone, or whether it is possible to move towards some kind of representation. This will allow me to point out how the unrepresentable can find a mode of representation initiating self-reconstruction after psychological trauma.

On the representable and unrepresentable

The unrepresentable, whose presence does not refer to any link with anything, refers to absolute inadequacy and questions the limits of language and words that reach it neither literally nor metaphorically. Words and things are *de facto* disconnected. Thus, it consists in an active obstacle, preventing word and thing from being linked or existing for one another. There is no immediate equivalent between what is representable and what is unrepresentable. What kind of links can be made between representation and what is unrepresentable? Indeed, the problem would seem to be: how to move from the traumatic real to a symbolic register? Therefore, we can assert first that the unrepresentable is what can only be shown without being seen, what can be said without being clearly understood.[2]

A survivor of a massacre or ruthless fighting might say, while still alive: "I'm not alive", "I am no longer myself", "I am dead". What did Wilfred Ruprecht Bion – who received the *Distinguished Service Order* after World War I – mean when he said he had "died – on August 8th 1918" (1982: 265)? Was it "just a metaphor", a "figure of speech"? A sentence pronounced by a war survivor such as, "I could never flame with life again after James, Ernest, Charles and I were extinguished at Cambrai" (Bion 1991: 150), indeed talks about the violent death of his fallen comrades, whom he could not protect, who could not survive.

These words also introduce us to the ghostly omnipresence of dead people, haunting their survivors. In other words, Bion partly lives in a world he shares with dead people. How can anyone still be alive *and also* have died on certain days, at certain places? This sentence says something "impossible", and thus refers to something unrepresentable. These words mean and express that the universal law separating dead and living humans in ordinary life has been warped and destroyed by a "massive psychic trauma" (Laub and Auerhahn, 1993). It is possible, drawing on the reflexes of our defense mechanisms, to look for a metaphor. But broadly speaking, wouldn't it express an unconscious attempt to preserve our selves from the events signified by the violence of the terms used, hence abandoning a listening position, and by extension, our position as a therapist? Dori Laub warns us against the professional reflex of listening to a patient's speech as if he were always talking about his fantasy; it "is effective when applied to non-victims, but disastrous with victims who can neither use trauma defensively nor playfully" (ibid.: 300).

Clinical trauma

Description without any affects

For the first time during a therapy session, a man refers to having been hit by a car and left for dead in the street. He talks without any apparent emotion or affect and indeed describes his problem as feeling nothing and wanting nothing. He seems very detached from this traumatic event, as if it had happened to someone else. He is the survivor of an attempted homicide, first involuntary (the drunk driver had not planned to run over him) which then became voluntary (after having been dragged several meters, he was abandoned on the road). At this early stage of his therapy, he can only talk about the events without feeling any affect, with a distance that, all things considered, preserves both the patient and the therapist (see Searles 1981: 69). This distance shows the "frozen reality" of trauma (Laub and Auerhahn 1993: 295) in its space and time dimensions.

Here, we can see that the therapeutic starting point for clinical trauma is something that exceeds speech – something that cannot be represented – because the trauma is, by definition, not immediately in the sphere of representation but in the sphere of presentation.

"Remember your dead"

A woman came to see me because her nephew, whom she saw as a surrogate son, had died from a medication overdose. There had been no investigation concerning his demise, which was of a kind that could happen after decades of heavy treatment, though not to a young man in his early twenties. To this patient, a crime of medication overdose had been committed and had remained unpunished. In the course of our sessions, she repeatedly brought up the mistakes and inconsistencies of the doctors she consulted for various symptoms, which they never succeeding in curing.

She was very upset because of their contradictory diagnoses and prescriptions, and she suffered from multiple side effects caused by medication. Pharmacists also had once delivered medications other than those specified; their subsequent apologies meant nothing to her.

After a few sessions, I realized that the woman was wearing one watch on each wrist; I then learned that she owned a lot of watches. "I don't know why," she just said, however pointing out that some of them sounded the hours, and others didn't. I felt that the nature of this "not knowing" needed to be elucidated (cf. Laub and Auerhahn 1993); that is to say, they both needed to understand to which "un-presentable" what was shown needed to be attached. My remark concerning the watches was soon followed by the story of the murder of the woman's grandfather.

This woman had lived in Paris for decades but didn't feel Parisian "at all". She only came to find work. Nevertheless, she had remained; although she hadn't worked for several years. She much preferred the city where she grew up. Her parents came from an Eastern country. She then tells me that her grandfather died there under dramatic circumstances. She recounts the death of her grandfather, who belonged to a religious minority and was beaten to death one evening as he was closing his shop. Her parents had left the country a few months earlier, shortly after her birth. She explained, however, that the reason for their emigration had been a transfer obtained by her father at that time. The family knew very little about France. The mother never spoke to her children about her own father's violent death. No story had ever been told, and neither had there been any reference to the grandfather's life, as if this man had never existed at all. It was her grandmother (the murdered man's widow) who spoke to the patient one day, when she was a teenager, without any preparation. "What good is it to talk about it? It is in the past", said the patient once.

It was the beginning of a process whereby the watches seemed to be used as indicators of a time that does not pass, or more precisely could only pass when a "catastrophic area" (Davoine and Gaudillière 2004: 29), cut off from any given time and place, was identified and would start having an assigned time and place. Broadly speaking, the proliferation of watches shown in the sessions,[3] constituted a link between "presentation" and something "unrepresentable". It presented a frozen moment in time: the time of a murder she only managed to evoke 50 years after it had occurred. Obviously, the family trauma had remained intact; it had never been possible to talk about it within the family.

Yet, justice has not been done; the murder was still unpunished, as this sort of thing *could happen* in that country, at that time. According to the grandmother, the mother's relation to the grandfather had been warm. The patient, then, started to put into words what, *for the mother*, had been unrepresentable. She needed to dis-"encapsulate" certain inherited traumas:[4] that is to say, to explore in therapy its effects on her own life, in order to recover from her depression, which had become chronic. She started looking for scattered clues and gathered them with me. We built together a specific story, which was a testimony of traumatic events and of a distress not immediately attached to it, but to which it nevertheless belonged. In this research, I had a more active position, which differed from benevolent neutrality. In this case, such neutrality would have been inadvisable because it would create a loneliness, which could have echoed the absolute loneliness felt by the patient facing the psychic traumas she had inherited (see Danieli 1984; Herman 1992).

This kind of clinical work brings us to the waves of violence and killings that the community to which the patient belongs had been exposed in her home country. I have been explicitly sensitive to the gravity of the situation and wish to express to her clearly my disapproval of such abuses.[5] I named things bluntly: for instance, using the word "assassination" instead of "death". In other words, I felt involved with her, not through an empathy that is so often reduced to over-sentimental compassion, but as a person fighting for the recognition of certain facts and the ability to feel adequate affects (of rebellion, anger, sadness, for instance) that are linked to crime.[6] According to Françoise Davoine and Jean-Max Gaudillière, this is the attitude of person they call a "therapôn" (2004: 249), someone who agrees to second another in a specific fight, which is therapeutic.[7]

It turns out that, like a lot of therapists, I have many books in my office. Among them there are history books that relate the histories of different countries, including those from where some of my patients come, and of course including some that concern the countries of my own origins. I started to read these kinds of books after taking the measure of the impact of history on individual history. I was then more able to analyze the traumatic heritage that I was carrying. It had, over the years, been underestimated in the same way as Arthur Blank explains it, saying to Cathy Caruth: "I went over it in detail – with non emotion, with no affect. And the analyst, bless his heart, who was a wonderful person, didn't know any better. – So you let it go. – And he let it go. And I let it go. And we went on by" (Caruth 2014: 279). Some clinical and historical books did explain it and give useful therapeutical directions. For example, in *History Beyond Trauma*, Françoise Davoine and Jean-Max Gaudillière gave clinical examples of the transmission of trauma through silence. They showed the great importance it had for their patients: to know more about the way their history had been penetrated, without their awareness, by a war in which their grandparents were involved, or by a political event that had happened in their birth country, etc. (2004: 47). In other terms, they showed how helpful it was to acknowledge the official information history books could give. Indeed, it constituted a precious, further matter for consideration, which would have been missed, leaving instead a painful lack. Broadly speaking, I realized that history could give shape to something that was shapeless and open a space where subjectivity could better reappear.

In *Lost in Transmission* (Gerard Fromm, 2012), Dori Laub explained how his own analyst told him something about reactions of denial in concentration camp inmates: something, that, at this period of time, he didn't himself know. Because he was Swedish, he "taught" him something concerning what "he knew" of concentration camp experiences:

> I have to tell you something. It was the Swedish Red Cross that liberated Theresienstadt and took depositions from women inmates in the camp. Under oath, some of these women declared that conditions in the camp were so good that they received each morning breakfast in bed brought by SS officers.
>
> *(Laub 2005: 51)*

Thanks to that, Laub could think further in his own therapy. He gave him the ability to leave a position of denial. Due to this specific involvement of his own psychoanalyst, Laub was able to work through his psychoanalysis, including his own massive psychic traumas. He then shows us how it is also necessary, in clinical trauma, to become more involved – accepting the need to speak, ask, express the feelings that you feel – in order to give back to the patient that which he himself is not able to tell, to think, to feel, because of traumatic experiences: experiences that they first have to approach together.

Returning to the clinical situation of the woman mentioned above, why did I take from my library the history book about the historical context of this patient's family? This patient was born in the same area as some of my ancestors. I "knew" that this minority group underestimated, in conversations, the traumatic impact of the persecution they had suffered and of the exile into which they had been forced, and I had started to learn more about it. Concerning my patient, I learned how historians had retraced a pogrom she had told me about – in vague terms, almost unreal – and in which her grandparents were involved. During the next session, I talked to her about what I had read, reading to her some parts of this book. This investment enabled her to find more pride in what she had started to tell me, and also to realize that "even" historians had related the violence to which her community had been exposed, including the pogrom her grandparents had survived. This official recognition made a great and encouraging impression on her: she was no longer the only depositary of an "isolated" family disaster. Other people also knew something about these traumatic events and had described them in uncompromising terms. This book symbolized the evidence that non-hostile third parties actually existed. For someone who had always read many books, trying to find answers to questions she could only sense but not enunciate with words, the existence of this specific book was very important. She bought this history book about her birth country and told me she had talked about it with her mother.

This patient had also bought a book I had written (I hadn't mentioned to her I had written a book) and started to use it as a sort of transitional object, with therapeutic value, which permitted her to project and develop some psychic issues.[8] It talks about the impact that the Thirty Years' War (1618–1648) had on Elizabeth Princess Palatine, and how Rene Descartes, with therapeutic concepts, like "body and soul union" and "contentment", helped her to heal her somatizations. She wondered how, "with all that she had suffered", the Princess philosopher could pull through. She was wondering, while reading it, if Elizabeth would be cured or not. I simultaneously heard a questioning about her own chances to get better.

Returning to the patient's watches, she told me, as if it were obvious, that she had stored some of the watches in drawers; in sessions, she was now wearing a single watch.[9] For the therapist, that was an indication that some of the events had found their right place and time. The watches no longer needed to exhibit the "pieces of time" hitherto hidden in their semblance of an indefinite present, as she had now found an appropriate time and place for those "pieces". Historical facts opened a space for dialogue, where an aspect of the "unrepresentable" could be described. Henceforth, an official recognition existed of the murders of and riots against this religious minority, of the bullying and the oppression that they suffered as second-class citizens. In an interesting manner, a book containing facts, "real" events, was helping a deep process of symbolization. Until then, third parties who had witnessed these traumatic events have been active accomplices or tacitly endorsed them with their passive neutrality.

The patient's description of her mother's overprotection and of her father, worrying if she came home from school just a little later than expected, could be seen in a new light. She admitted her parents never left their two children alone and had stayed too close to them, even after their adolescence. She was then able to sense a link between the murder, the psychic trauma passed from one generation to another, and the possible consequences of this murder in their everyday lives, starting with her mother's constant worrying.

In a nutshell, this patient needed to grasp the impact of her grandfather's murder, after having spent years without "knowing" it, without thinking about the impact it had left on both generations. Involved in this research, I held a specific position. I was brought to ask questions that the patient couldn't ask herself and sometimes to express feelings the patient couldn't feel (see Davoine 1994). I behaved this way in order to "empower" this woman to ask questions and to feel these kinds of emotions, this time, in a safe environment (Herman 1992: 133). A silent position would have duplicated the feeling of absolute loneliness felt when facing the inherited psychic trauma. As Judith Lewis Herman notes, "The moral stance of the therapist is therefore of enormous importance. It is not enough for the therapist to be 'neutral' or 'nonjudgmental'. The patient challenges the therapist to share her own struggles with this immense philosophical question" (ibid.: 178). One of the purposes of this part of the therapy we described was to decipher the trauma of the murder and to produce a less fragmented narrative of it. The accumulation of watches was significant as the accumulation of time: that is to say, the compactness of the time of the trauma, which accumulated the unrepresentable in a silent transmission over the generations. They seemed to mean: "remember your dead".

Technical aspects of this clinical trauma and the representation of the unrepresentable

The unrepresentable is what can be shown without knowing to what it refers. It is a presence to be found in reality, indicating the failure of identification and sending patient and therapist on a quest for meaning. In this chapter, we have presented a piece of therapeutic work on the traumatic real. In a repetition that doesn't "know" what it represents, its traumatic content "doesn't stop not being written" (Lacan 1998: 94). This work is done in a specific way, and we need to specify its formalization.

In the context of psychoanalytic psychotherapy of clinical trauma, we have to take into account the fact that knowing some precise information may be useful and important. Faced with traumatic reality, one needs to find a way to build images, to follow its course to symbolization, which means acquiring the ability to move slowly out from the absolute loneliness experienced during the trauma. Herman states that it is important to find as much information as possible about how a traumatic event took place, and simultaneously, on how each element was experienced, precisely in order *not* to project the therapist's own fantasies on what the patient has lived and therefore miss the specificity of what he experienced.[10]

With the help of historical research, re-placing the existence of a traumatic event in its specific context may better allow us to take into account its specificity. Both the therapist and the patient can take some objective information that is shared with society, which is to say with other people, who may or may not have lived the same traumatic events. Subjectivity and personal fantasy can then appear instead of the unrepresentable of the trauma, which was formerly expressed only by a threatening feeling of emptiness. The question must be asked, however: Is the disposition to take into consideration the family's historical context and the intergenerational transmission of trauma only a rationalist reflex? I hope I have shown that in a first step, it is not a matter of rationalization. The information gathered by such consideration can initiate an active position for those who were devastated by psychic traumas. It can contribute to the emergence of words and the ability, to use an orientation shared by Hannah Arendt, "to tell a story about them" (1998: 175).

In this kind of therapeutic context, in which a traumatic transference occurs, the therapist has to listen to her traumatic countertransference (see Herman 1992; Searles 1981). Of course, the therapist needs to know more about her therapeutic investment so that it does not impede the progress of the patient's train of thought. But not only this: she also must go further in deciphering this countertransference. In Bionian terms, the therapist may be led to recognize "a thought without a thinker" (1997: 27), to think this thought-without-a-thinker in order to find to whom and to what it is linked. People working on clinical trauma frequently speak of this particular commitment, even in spite of themselves. They discover more about the traumatic experience that has led them to hear the psychic trauma of their patient, in order to work *with it*, and not *in spite of it*. Broadly speaking, patients often ask: "Who are you to listen to my traumatic experience?", or "Who are you to help me think about traumatic experiences I couldn't reach?" If Bion had "died in 1918" during World War I, then he *also* listened to catastrophic experiences because of this war experience from which he never hid himself. Davoine's parents were involved in Resistance; she grew up feeling the great risks that they undertook. She never tried to put this experience aside, but to use it as an enlightening point. She understood that she could better work on traumatic experiences with her patients if she used it as a therapeutic resource because she had succeeded in thinking and symbolizing it.

As we see, patients and therapist are led to think together. Furthermore, the therapist can be led – occasionally – to submit hypotheses that put the patient in a position to think more deeply and to gain a sense of "empowerment" over what has happened. This main therapeutic principle helps the survivor to regain his active subject position. Otherwise, the therapist may indeed repeat, involuntarily and discreetly, what aggressors and murderers accomplished by seeing their victim and descendants as objects undergoing inner destruction, leaving them alone with their trauma.[11] Then, if a patient says: "I had never thought of it that way", it doesn't necessarily mean that the therapist wants to influence him in a specific way. Wouldn't it be possible to consider it as a hypothesis that the patient can accept or not, without feeling threatened if he refuses it, but which, at this point in time, he couldn't find himself because of traumatic symptoms? The patient can be, as Bion said, a "thinker" who has no access to specific "thoughts" but that he nonetheless tries to find some. The patient can live "without" the thought that he needs to think, because his thoughts have been frozen on a specific level. But the therapist – thanks to her analysis of the transference and the countertransference – can, at that moment, be the depositary of a "thinking without a thinker" that needs to be returned.[12] Then, a patient adds: "things seen in this light are more understandable", "I realize now how important it was". And he also adds, almost for the first time, a free association he hadn't been capable of before.

These clarifications require a final one, which is always present when considering any evolution and change in relation to clinical trauma. Important therapeutic moments are not isolated, unique. On the contrary, symbols need to be built after having been destroyed: thus, repetition of some communications needs to be repeated and repeated. To put it all in a nutshell, my patient – the woman whose grandfather was murdered – didn't think the conclusions that she had reached after having read the history book, "once and for all". Therapeutic evolutions are only possible because we are able to think about them several times.

Notes

1 See, for example, reactions concerning Heinrich Himmler and his wife's correspondence (Wildt 2014).
2 In French, we can refer to the word "*monstration*", an action to show something, which is etymologically linked to the "monsters" ("*monstres*", in French, which were "shown", "*monstrés*", in the *foires*).
3 In French, the language this patient speaks during the sessions, there is a homonymy between a watch, "*une montre*", and to show, "*montrer*".
4 See Dori Laub and Nanette Auerhahn (1993: 289).
5 Such an intervention doesn't mean that one abandons a therapeutic position, but precisely succeeds in keeping it.
6 See also Lionel Bailly (1996). If a therapist avoids this kind of explicit ethical involvement, she may come across as indifferent, and the patient may just stop the therapy. When a patient stops therapy, we can say that the transference wasn't there, but this isn't the only reason.
7 See also Gregory Nagy's *The Best of the Achaeans*, where he defines the word "therapon" (1979: 32–33). I also use this concept in my book about Rene Descartes and Elizabeth, Princess Palatine (2012: 22).
8 The book is Yaelle Sibony-Malpertu, *Une liaison philosophique* (2012).
9 Cf. Joël Pommerat's *Cendrillon* (2013). This piece of theatre helped us understand the link between mourning and the tyrannical use and place of a watch: as Cendrier (Cendrillon) fears forgetting her dead mother, she sets an alarm clock in order to think about her.
10 Judith Lewis Herman explains that, "As the therapist listens, she must constantly remind herself to make no assumptions about either the facts of the meaning of the trauma to the patient. If she fails to ask detailed questions, she risks superimposing her own feelings and her own interpretation onto the patient story. What seems like a minor detail to the therapist may be the post important aspect of the story to the patient" (1992: 179).
11 As Judith Lewis Herman states, "Recovery can take place only within the context of relationships (…) The first principle of recovery is the empowerment of the patient. She must be the author and arbiter of her own recovery" (1992: 133).
12 W. R. Bion: "If a thought without a thinker comes along, it may be what is a 'stray thought', or it could be a thought with the owner's name and address upon it, or it could be a 'wild thought'. The problem, should such a thought come along, is what to do with it … What I am concerned with at the moment is the wild thoughts that turn up and for which there is no possibility of being able to trace immediately any kind of ownership or even any sort of way of being aware of the genealogy of that particular thought. First of all, it seems to me to be simplest to try to tackle the problem by considering what this strange thought is. We might get a clue to it by wondering in what frame of mind of in what conditions this wild thought turned up and became enmeshed in our method of thinking" (1997: 27).

References

Arendt, H. (1998) *The Human Condition (1958)*. Chicago: Chicago UP.

Arendt, H. (2005) *Eichmann in Jerusalem*. London: Penguin Classics.

Bailly, L. (1996) *Les catastrophes et leurs conséquences psycho-traumatiques chez l'enfant. Descriptions cliniques et traitements*. Paris: ESF éditeur.

Bion, W. R. (1985) *The Long Week-End, 1897–1919: Part of a Life*. Abingdon: Fleetwood Press.

Bion, W. R. (1991) *A Memoir of the Future*. London: Karnac Books.

Bion, W. R. (1997) *Taming Wild Thoughts*. Ed. F. Bion. London: Karnac.

Caruth, C. (2014) *Listening to Trauma: Conversations with Leaders in the Theory and Treatment of Catastrophic Experience*. Baltimore: JHU Press.

Danieli, Y. (1984) Psychotherapists' Participation in the Conspiracy of Silence about the Holocaust. *Psychoanalytic Psychology* 1 (1): 23–42.

Davoine, F. (1994) *La folie Wittgenstein*. Paris: E.P.E.L.

Davoine, F. and Gaudillière, J.-M. (2004) *History Beyond Trauma*. Trans. S. Fairfield. New York: Other Press.

Fromm, G. (2012) *Lost in Transmission*. London: Karnac.

Gampel, Y. (2005) *Ces parents qui vivent à travers moi, Les enfants des guerres*. Paris: Fayard.

Herman, J. (1992) *Trauma and Recovery: From Domestic Abuse to Political Terror*. London: Pandora.

Lacan, J. (1998) *The Seminar of Jacques Lacan, Book XX: Encore, 1972–1973*. Ed. J-A. Miller. Trans. B. Fink. New York: Norton.

Laub, D. (2005) Traumatic Shutdown of Narrative and Symbolization: A Death Instinct Derivative. *Contemporary Psychoanalysis* 41 (2): 307–26.

Laub, D. and Auerhahn, N. (1993) Knowing and Not Knowing – Forms of Traumatic Memory. *International Journal of Psycho-Analysis* 74: 287–302.

Nagy, G. (1979) *The Best of the Achaeans*. Baltimore: Johns Hopkins University Press.

Orwell, G. (1949) *1984*. Oxford: Clarendon Press.

Pommerat, J. (2013) *Cendrillon*. Paris: Actes Sud, Babel.

Searles, H. (1981) *Le Contre-transfert*. Trans. B. Bost. Paris: Gallimard.

Sibony-Malpertu, Y. (2012) *Une liaison philosophique*. Paris: Stock.

Wildt, M. (ed.) (2014) *Himmler privat. Briefe eines Massenmörders*. München: Piper.

PART II
Sense and gesture

4

(UN)REPRESENTING THE REAL

Seeing sounds and hearing images

Thomas Elsaesser

Digital cinema, sound and embodiment: A paradigm shift in the film experience?

Lacanian film theory of the 1970s limited itself to vision and based itself primarily on the specular relation of the imaginary to subjectivity as, famously, illustrated and enacted by the mirror stage. This theory, in conjunction with the Renaissance perspectival image, constructed the look as all-powerful, conferring upon the (implicitly male) film spectator an all-perceiving/not perceived (that is, voyeuristic) status. Yet, this initial theory of the look (as a function of the imaginary) already by the time it became widely discussed and applied in film theory, had been superseded in Lacanian psychoanalysis (specifically, with *Seminar XI*) by the theory of the gaze, the gaze as *objet petit a*. As Lacan stated, "The *objet a* in the field of the visible is the gaze" (1977: 105)[1] and as Todd McGowan reminds us:

> The *objet petit a* is (…) a lost object, an object that the subject separates itself from in order to constitute itself as a desiring subject. It is the loss of the object that inaugurates the process of desiring, and the subject desires on the basis of this loss. The subject is incomplete or lacking because it doesn't have this object, though the object only exists insofar as it is missing. (2007: 6)

To the extent that it is constituted by desire – a desire, ultimately, for the lost object – vision is not all-perceiving but is deficient, for it is (like all symbolic systems) based on lack; the object resists mastery; it is unachievable. Whereas the imaginary look seemingly conferred visual mastery on the perceiving subject by making everything visible, the gaze (as what is lacking in the image, as *objet petit a*) introduces the unseen into the field of vision. McGowan again: "The gaze compels our look because it appears to offer access to the unseen, to the reverse side of the visible. It promises the subject the secret of the Other, but this secret exists only insofar as it remains hidden" (ibid.). The gaze is constituted on the invisible, or, more accurately, the unrepresentable, which exists in the realm of the Real. It is what the symbolic is structured around, without being able to represent.

The voice, like the visual, is similarly structured around desire: and therefore lack and unrepresentable. Traditionally conceived in psychoanalysis as "full speech", the voice is the realm through which the analyst gains access to and therefore mastery over the patient's symptoms (psychoanalysis as the talking cure). But Lacan dismissed this theory of the voice and reconceived it, too, as *objet petit a*. Just as the gaze is structured around what cannot be seen, the voice is structured around what cannot be said. In other words, vision is constituted on the invisible, and voice is constituted on silence. Psychoanalytic theories of cinematic voice and vision need to begin not with full speech and the omnipotent look, but with silence and the invisible.

Such apparent contradictions are common in critical theory quite generally, and they only seem to proliferate in cinema's digital age. Anyone who pursues the question, "what has changed with the introduction of digital production methods in film and the widespread acceptance of the digital media?" should be prepared for some contradictory answers.[2] I single out just one such contradiction, namely, that, since the arrival of digital code for image, sound and text, there has been a remarkable turn towards the body and the senses. It is tempting to suggest that the more abstract the code, the more sensuous the experience will be. The contradiction is only apparently resolved if we assume that the increasing abstraction – think of the mathematical basis for generating images and sound – has induced a kind of compensatory counter reaction, as if we intuitively sensed something uncanny about these abstractions and therefore sought closer contact: significantly, however, not with what is being depicted or represented, but rather with the process of self-reference, in other words, with ourselves as recipients, as if – in the face of the digital – we felt we had to reassure ourselves that we still possess a body: a body now conceived as a total perceptual surface. As we shall see below, this something uncanny is itself an effect of the *objet petit a*. The "loss of reality" (reference, indexicality) associated with the digital must register on a different plane, and this different plane happens to be our own bodies. The paradox here is that the digital medium – in the broadest sense of the term – seems particularly apt to invoke physical embodiment or at any rate to generate effects of "bodiliness". A further consequence of this contradiction would be the question whether the cinema allows us to experience this sense of bodily presence because it is essentially a medium of emulation, of mimicry and simulation (i.e. functions as the Lacanian "mirror"), and thus has always serviced the needs and desires that the cinema itself has awakened, or whether its ability to engender a phantom body intensifies tendencies that have always been latent within the technical media and digital cinema has merely brought to the fore.

Both possibilities raise a further question: why has attention in film studies and among filmmakers shifted in recent decades towards the tactile, the skin and the sense of touch and also, to an equally great extent, towards the ear and sound? Why are these "turns" in turn representative of the trend of placing "embodiment" at centre stage for the cinema experience in general, and how does it not only reference the psychic relation between body and voice/silence, but how does it also shift the balance between visible and invisible, the represented and the unrepresentable? Voice and gaze as *objet petit a*, signifying a loss of mastery and control over vision and voice, it would seem, play a determining role in both these "turns".

While it is a truism that cinema always involves more than one sense at a time, the exact function of the individual senses and their interaction or "division of labour" relative to one another within the cinema experience remain controversial. This no doubt also underlies the subtitle of this chapter "Seeing sounds and hearing images", which refers not only to the potential reversibility of the relationship between sound and image; it also suggests that there are certain hierarchies of our perceptual senses – for example, the culturally conditioned prioritisation of the sense of distance, i.e. the eye over the sense of closeness, such as the hand – of which we are not always aware. These hierarchies, identified, for instance, by Norbert Elias as part of the "civilization process" (2000),[3] would seem to have entered, with the digital turn, into a process of reversal or a re-orientation, in which the ear plays something like a mediating role.

It would of course be possible to argue in the opposite direction: why has our watching of films been dominated for so long by the eye and vision, to the exclusion of all the other properties, agencies and effects inherent in the moving image? Without going into this question in detail – there are specific historical reasons relating to film theory and its institutional legitimacy (film semiotics, psychoanalysis, gender studies, the idea of the cinema as an instantiation of Plato's Cave) – it is worth recalling at least one historical factor: the *eye–vision* paradigm was dominant for such a long time because, from the turn of the 20th century, the cinema has opened to the eye previously unknown or unattainable worlds and has done so by offering a single point of view. Cinema made sight mobile and canny, prying and penetrating, as the camera permitted the viewer to break and enter into prohibited or closed worlds. In other words, the original "attraction" of the cinema was indeed varied and polymorphous and could not even then be reduced to one sense alone, given that the silent cinema was rarely silent and that attention in dimly lit halls (prior to wholly blacked-out theatres) was free to wander and stray, yet it was nonetheless very much about a field of action for the eye, i.e. about visual pleasure in and for itself, across the mastery of the camera (at once summoned and deconstructed in Dziga Vertov's *Man with a Movie Camera* [1929]).

There is a second point worth recalling. Even if it is true that in its early days cinema was first experienced as a stage, as a special kind of interaction or exchange between the physically present auditorium space and the imaginary screen space (the two had not yet merged into one another as they would in classical "illusionist" cinema), the turn to linear narrative and suspenseful storytelling soon transformed this stage into a window on the world and a door into the lives of others. The fact that art cinema in Europe after WWII tended to render this transparency opaque and reflexive, turning the screen into a sometimes baleful and lugubrious mirror of the existential self, did little to disrupt this primacy of the eye.

Causes for the paradigm shift

The paradigm shift – if this is what it is – away from the eye and towards the other sense organs and the body should therefore be considered in a broader context, of which the rapid implementation of digital technologies is a factor, but one with implications that go beyond the usual argument about loss of indexicality, and also concerns the psychoanalytic dimension of vision and hearing and in particular of the senses in relation to partial objects:

1. To recapitulate the case concerning *indexicality*: In the transition from the analogue medium of photography to the digital post-photographic image, it is said that there has been a *loss of indexicality*, meaning that the physical bond that exists between the image and that of which it is an image is no longer given. Indexicality is based on physical light passing through an optical lens, transforming a light-sensitive surface, which is then chemically developed. In digital cinematography, the light is transformed into pixels, a digital code that can be manipulated, as well as used to simulate. That is, to generate a photorealistic image one does not require an original source of light passing through a lens: the digital image can simulate the visual-optical-chemical relationship, thereby losing part of the truth claim on which almost all theories of realism are based. Such a loss of evidence, which is both technologically guaranteed and ontologically anchored, clearly constitutes a crucial turn, especially with regard to the ethics and aesthetics of the documentary film. No longer anchored to its referent, the digital image can circulate as a signifier in different contexts, where it signifies a multitude of connotative meanings: each of which can make truth claims. But such claims about the reality, authenticity and truth of the photographic image are associated at least as much with convention, with rhetoric and performance, as with the "ontology of the photographic image".[4] The resulting loss of faith in indexicality (however problematic this term ultimately is) conjures up the gaze as *objet petit a*, i.e. the desire for the lost referent, while the simulated photorealism can conjure up the opposite; it can produce an uncanny effect by claiming truth and authenticity for something that does not exist (such as the digital dinosaurs in Spielberg's *Jurassic Park* movies).[5]

2. The digital camera is *more hand than eye*. First, the way digitally produced films often seem closer to the object creates an impression of *touch*. Second, as depth of field and close-up can be combined in a single image, and as the digital image

can, in general, present visual surfaces and pictorial compositions in appearances that are unfamiliar to the human eye, the brain must process this ambiguous visual information either according to familiar templates (and thus reduce the pleasure of unfamiliar sensations) or switch to a different sense, in order to attune itself and dis-ambiguate the resulting perceptual-cognitive uncertainties. For instance, the once again popular concept of "haptic seeing", the interest in empathy and synaesthesia, or the concept of "the skin of the film", can also be explained with reference to the different distribution of sensory signals generated by the digital image.

At the same time, our idea of what a screen is has changed. On one hand, the size of screens has increased, extending beyond the human field of vision, as in the case of IMAX, to create a feeling of immersion and envelopment. On the other hand, screens are now also monitors and user interfaces, small enough and mobile enough to no longer be located in front of the user's field of vision but in our hands and controlled with our fingers. A *touch-screen* requires *tapping*, *pinching* and *spreading*. The image comes towards me, I grasp it; I no longer immerse myself in it or allow it to wash over me.

This also relates to an anthropologically significant change observable through-out the 20th century. Put far too briefly, one could argue that during the first half of the last century, the muscle strength of the body was gradually replaced in the industrial production processes by machines, which in turn had to be closely observed by the eye, making the body obsolete for social production: to the point where sports and fitness began to re-fetishise first the male and then the female body, with the gym almost literally mimicking the factory floor. By the end of the second half of the century, however, it was the eye that was beginning to become obsolete, reduced to monitoring and surveillance functions in front of a screen, with the machines themselves supervised and guided by computer programs. At the same time, new uses were being opened up for the hand via keyboard and mouse, touch screens and texting. The films of German director Harun Farocki (*As You See* [1986], *Eye/Machine* [2000], *Serious Games* [2010]) have been documenting this process as it affects piece work on the assembly line and is reflected in weapons technology,[6] but obviously such momentous changes in human motor coordina-tion also have an unconscious dimension with respect to the subject's self-image, i.e. ego's relation to its ideal ego and ego ideal.

3. The digital image gives rise to a new *concept of the moving image* especially because we are no longer dealing with a *succession* of individual images, but rather the *refreshing* (and re-arrangement) of a single surface and frame. In principle, this already applies to the video image and was anticipated long ago in the history of art. One need only think of Conceptual Art, Pop Art or Minimalism: all of which challenged (or played with) the finally artificial convention of an image having to mimic an aperture in the wall, such as a window. But the idea that an image is no longer primarily a framed view or prospect has gathered momentum only in recent decades; instead, we now have a much broader concept of what an image is.[7]

This means that our ideas of what an image can be have changed to such an extent that it is no longer defined by framing or even by a frontal, upright orientation of the spectator. The concept of the image as "an open window" – with the dominant direction of view from inside to outside, arranged according to the principles of the central perspective to create the illusion of a three-dimensional representation on a two-dimensional surface, which has predominated since the Italian Renaissance – no longer sets the norm. A completely different feeling of space applies, where the image can surround us, but where it can also even look at us (as Lacan famously pointed out, when distinguishing the look from the gaze), or where it becomes a pure surface or is encountered in three-dimensional depth, as in installation art.

Because this window metaphor of the image was transferred more or less seamlessly to cinema – at least to classical narrative cinema – thus reinforcing the notion of the viewer as a voyeur, these changes in the nature of the image will also affect psychoanalytical theories of the cinema, so strongly predicated on fetishism and the look, on suture and disavowal.

Setting the tone with sound

Voice and the gaze are linked to the extent that each is an *objet petit a*; they cannot be mastered or appropriated by the subject and are predicated on lack, and therefore instigate desire. The voice as *objet petit a* means that it "is part neither of language nor of the body" (Dolar 2006: 73). The voice, which points to but does not disclose a bodily interior, is not coterminous with articulated language, but neither is it pure sound emanating from a physical body. The voice is *in between* abstract signification and physical sound. Mladen Dolar argues that the voice conceived as *objet petit a* does not coincide with the voice that is heard; it is aphonic. The voice is therefore uncanny because it is both familiar and unfamiliar, existing somewhere between the known symbolic structures and the unknown Real.

But where does the broader category of *sound* enter into this discussion of the aphonic voice as *objet petit a*? First, sound (including the voice) cannot be contained in the way that space is contained in a frame. Second, sound cannot be eliminated as easily as light: one cannot close one's ears to sound the same way we close our eyes to light. Yet the reason for sound having become the critical tone-determining factor in cinema may not, in the first instance, be due to the psychic make-up of its spectators. It is to be located primarily outside the cinema and in fact also outside the world of images per se. As Emily Thompson shows in her study, *The Soundscape of Modernity* (2003), sound concerns the day-to-day experience of our environment in itself and has a social as well as a psychic dimension, which can now be seen as symptomatic for a certain concept of urban modernity itself, in contrast to Benjamin's ocular-centric notion of the metropolis. One of the features of modernity, then – according to Thompson's argument – is the degree to which sound, noises and background noise decisively shape our life-world. People did not try to escape from this stress on the ears by insulating their walls with cork panels like Marcel Proust or by retreating to the silence of the forest. Instead, we have been surrounding ourselves increasingly with music, that is, sound articulated (composed and designed), which is to say, with an attempt to tame the unrepresentable real, by taking it into the register of the symbolic, the imaginary and the social. Whether in the concert hall, at home with the radio and gramophone or in the cinema, the response to sound throughout the 20th century has been *more sound*, not less. Sound in the cinema is therefore revealed in all its contradictoriness. On the one hand, the realism claim of the motion picture demands a carpet of sound that corresponds to lived reality filled as it is with noises and sounds – even silence in a film must be signalled by ambient sound – yet on the other hand, the film theatre is like the concert hall to the extent that both promise the spectator a filtered, orchestrated and carefully modulated counter-sound, known either as "music" or as "sound design".

Since the invention of the Walkman (personal stereo) and especially since the introduction of the miniaturised, ultra-portable digital MP3 player, our visual environment is accessible to us not only through a technologically generated sound space; it has become an individually programmed environment. The so-called "auditory experience of self and place" associated with the personal stereo involves a visual field that is always already experienced together with an auditory space, into which are projected the associated affective, cultural and psychic associations, in a kind of montage effect that can be either wholly enveloping, soothing and calming or borderline schizophrenic. At any rate, it is highly a-social, as the beat between my ears translates itself into body, gesture and motor-mimicry. Thus, even before Wi-Fi hotspots and interactive buildings we have been inhabiting an "augmented reality", in which internal and external space are combined and synchronised with one another differently than was the case when street noise and concert hall, or muzak and a film's sound design functioned as each other's rival, complement or compensation.

Traditional limits around identity, as psychoanalysis reminds us, such as the boundaries between inside and outside, active and passive, centre and periphery, private domain and public domain, are questioned if not entirely obliterated by the MP3 player.[8] Sound has become something we produce in our own heads, because, through the mobile sound medium, we become the (acoustic) centre-point of the world, however peripherally we might be positioned geographically or even socially. This entails a kind of personal *empowerment*, an augmentation of self-esteem and reflexive self-reassurance, but also a level of aggression that feeds directly into youthful rebellion or outsider anomie.

Given this different "sound mix of subjectivity", every perception tends to become an "image" that, in turn, makes the expanded idea of the image (already mentioned in relation to video and digital images, conceptual art and IMAX screens) mutually reinforcing through sound and thus also anthropologically plausible. To cite media commentator Dieter Wenk:

> Paradoxically, with the video sphere [a term coined by Regis Debray], we experience the primacy of hearing. (…) [I]t is sound, ambience, the environmental, in short, the end of the contemplative, the distanced, which has led and continues to lead to the realisation that we now no longer live in a "society of the spectacle". (2003)

Wenk elaborates:

> Vision has become an appendage, a modality of hearing, "the sound of the eyes". (…) Now that we have come to the end of the subject-object divide, perhaps it is the video sphere that returns us to the feedback loop of sound, in which the embryo feels so comfortably protected. (ibid.)

A similar observation is made by the musicologist Michael Schmidt, who asks if the media-driven ubiquity of music – as a "murmuring drone" – in everyday life means that:

> music [is] once again close to the murmuring of water and wind, those omnipresent sounds of nature? Or is it rather that the media has made music a part of the noise characteristic of our technical world, whose ubiquitous acoustic signals drown out nature altogether, making it inaudible? (2015)

Could it be that a kind of handover has taken place, from the metropolitan experience of modernity, which for Walter Benjamin was centred on vision and the eye to a more general, and effectively *electronic* experience of (post)modernity focused on the ear? At approximately the same time as Benjamin formulated his shock-and-trauma theory of the eye, Paul Valéry noted "the ear is the preferred sense of attention. It watches at the frontier, beyond which the eye no longer sees" (1974: 934). But if, instead of the built city, we now imagine our own urban environment and even our private homes as one big data-space of flows, it would stand to reason that the register of sound is a more fitting metaphor for these flows than even the moving image including in Hans Belting's anthropological sense of "picture, medium, body"? The relation of the visible to the invisible is then not simply a question of presence and absence in the field of vision and not even about hearing in itself, but rather about a different modality of seeing and being. That is, through listening, it is possible to map one's spatio-temporal co-ordinates, and thus experience self-presence without this being anchored in sight (with all the miscognition and asymmetrical power-relations this implies, according to Lacan and Michel Foucault). Media theorist Friedrich Kittler has traced the logic of this shift away from the eye to hearing all the way back to the Greeks (2015: 3–20), and if we follow what architect Rem Koolhaas has to say, we do indeed need a non-visual vocabulary in order to describe the contemporary urban environment, which he calls the *generic city*, that is, typified by shopping centres, airports, industrial zones, overpasses and tenement housing, for which he prefers to use the metaphors of *scratch-video* and *sampling*, drawn, that is, from DJ practice, and hip-hop music (2001).

It suggests that we now live in a world of continuous becomings: a world of *liquidity* (Zygmunt Bauman), of *viscosity* (Jean Paul Sartre), of the *informe* (Georges Bataille) and the *abject* (Julia Kristeva). Each of these terms refer us back to Lacan's notion of the Real; the eye cannot keep pace, is overstretched, so that the ephemeral, volatile sound of our current way of living is in fact what "grounds" us, which is to say, what provides the fantasy frame that situates us in the Imaginary. In other words, sound now epitomises our affective and psychic relation to each other, but also determines our sense of being in the world. Sound – the muzak of the supermarket, the beat in the fashion boutique, the TV on all day as audio wallpaper, the car stereo, the MP3 player – all of them separate and together have become the social glue that binds us together even as it isolates us in bubbles or burbles of an auditory amniotic fluid. Could it therefore be the case that the paradigm shift reversing the image-sound hierarchy in favour of the latter, often noted for contemporary cinema, is merely catching up, mimicking or tracking these changes in everyday life?

As it happens, these observations, namely that "vision is a modality of hearing" and, in the case of Rem Koolhaas, that "sound is a modality of seeing", can also be found in contemporary film theory and resonate with the history of cinema. Three aspects, which relate to the spatial dimension, the somatic-subjective dimension and the material dimension of the cinema experience, are worth highlighting in this context. First, a general proposition: central for the role of sound in film is the capability for (three-dimensional) sound to give a body to (two-dimensional) image. This fact was familiar even in silent film, which, as already mentioned, was never really silent. Before the advent of synchronised sound in the late 1920s, the cinema was characterised by an enormous diversity of tonal materials and variations: from film lecturer to symphony orchestra, from cinema organ to sound-effects artist. However, these were often present in the mode of *counterpoint* or separate *commentary*, because the individual film as a self-contained sense unit (that is, as "text" or a narrative, with a beginning, middle and end) was less stable until the general introduction of the sound film after 1927–28 and because the accompanying sound always promised or threatened to give another meaning to the image.[9] Image and sound were not only independent from each other at source, but they also occupied two quite different types of space.

The source of sound emanated from and was physically present in the auditorium, i.e. in the same space as the audience; the image emanated from and was contained within the imaginary space of the screen. Only with synchronised sound film did both sound and image seem to come from the screen, creating the illusion of "full bodies" so to speak, an impression reinforced by the emerging techniques of cinematic storytelling, with shot-reverse shots, eye-line matches and cuts on action: all of the techniques aimed at "suturing" the spectator into the image-flow and carrying him/her along in a linear direction. Furthermore, the result of synchro-nised sound was to supplement the pyramid of light emanating from the projector (located behind the audience) with an inversely oriented auditory cone (located in the front of the audience).

Looking at the history and even pre-history of cinema, one notes that there were countless attempts at synchronising recorded sound and moving image well before 1927.[10] Thomas Alva Edison, whose Kinetoscope is considered a precursor of the Lumière Brothers cinematograph, originally developed his invention as a supple-ment to his phonograph. His claim that the Kinetoscope was designed "to do for the eye what the phonograph does for the ear" has become legendary. Thus, even at the very beginning of a media-history of film, we find the idea that sound sup-plements the image, and even more strongly that the image is merely a supplement to the sound, and not vice versa. In a sense, it was only with the emergence of the Hollywood feature film in its "classical" form, from around 1917 onwards, that the image was deemed to "lead" the sound, so that the rule and very soon the norm became that the sound asked the question "where" and the image answered "here". Hierarchy and delay remind us of Echo and Narcissus, with all the mythological, as well as psychoanalytical and gender-specific ramifications that these two figures imply. Furthermore, as already mentioned, this principle of spatialised or delayed synchronisation is generally optimised in Hollywood in order to facilitate narrative progress and intelligibility.

With the massive improvements of sound technology in the 1970s, Hollywood began rethinking image-sound relationships. Earlier, I argued that this ran in paral-lel to the sound revolution initiated by the personal stereo and that Hollywood was merely catching up with societal developments at large, which created entirely new kinds of subjectivity whose imaginary ground was in sound rather than vision. However, such an argument would seriously underestimate both the changes and the challenges faced by Hollywood feature films in the 1970s. Movies like *Nashville* (1975, Robert Altman), *Jaws* (1975, Steven Spielberg), *Star Wars* (1977, George Lucas) or *Apocalypse Now* (1979, Francis Ford Coppola) not only managed to libe-rate themselves from the traditional hierarchies of giving the image the lead over sound. These four films are in fact a turning point in film history, because each tried in its own way to bring about radical change in the cinema experience by means of new sound-recording, sound-spaces and sound-playback techniques.

Yet their techniques, aesthetics and effects on the audience experience and ulti-mately also their influence on the direction taken by film history could not have been more different. Altman, for instance, multiplied the sound sources – as in the documentary film – with clip-on microphones and portable Nagra equipment and, instead of separating them and hierarchising them in postproduction, superposed them and allowed them to overlap, so that viewers almost had to lean forward and push themselves into the sound, in order to follow the dialogue. By contrast, Lucas concentrated on redefining the auditorium space, using Dolby technology (an electronic noise-reduction system) in order to redesign, almost from scratch, the viewers' audio experience, as if he were returning to the days of the early cinema, now supercharged with directional loudspeakers and amplifiers borrowed from rock concerts; on the other hand, of course, he was connecting the imaginary image space of the big screen even more closely with the newly equipped auditorium. Retaining the classical separation of different sounds, but developing further the multi-layering and differentiation of soundtracks, Lucas' surround-cinema achieved a plasticity, directional specificity and spatial fullness of sound hitherto unknown. The loudspeakers, placed strategically in the cinema auditorium and playing back different soundtracks, help to transcend the screen, so that the film no longer unfolds exclusively on the screen but spreads into the auditorium. As Barbara Flückiger remarked "the complete liberation of the screen through the surround technique released a suggestive effect (…) Orientation within the room, which had previously been transparent because of the coherence of screen and sound source, was now dissolved. Sounds piled in on the viewer from all sides simultaneously" (2001: 56). Via the ear, the spatial structure of the film experience, which had previously been oriented forwards towards the filmic image, as with a peephole camera, supported by a single sound source located in the same position, had been radically changed: casting doubt on (if not challenging altogether) the psychoanalytic theory of the voyeuristic look developed that same year by Laura Mulvey (1975).

In *Apocalypse Now*, Coppola adopted a similar approach – who can forget the helicopters in the opening scene, which hover to and fro directly above us? But he placed more emphasis on the idea that, through sound, we should experience the interior world of the protagonists as an exterior world or that, through the level of sound, the exterior world immediately has a subjective, hallucinatory or nightmarish presence, which, to some extent, imports the Walkman experience into the cinema auditorium and produces it as a collective experience to be shared: the iconic *bad acid trip*, which has come to symbolise not only the portrayal of the Vietnam War, but probably also our image of every modern war. The key person for *Apocalypse Now* in this respect was Walter Murch, perhaps the single most important figure in bringing about the transformation of film sound in contemporary cinema.[11]

A striking confirmation would come some 30 years later, with *Waltz with Bashir* (2008, Ari Folman), where the nightmare of war, with its constant fear of death, aggravated by an invisible enemy, is doubled by the trauma of (perpetrators') guilt: all of it in large part generated by a sound design that, while strikingly original in its own terms, was nonetheless evidently inspired by *Apocalypse Now*. Designated an animated documentary, *Waltz with Bashir* begins with a scene in which a subjective camera is pursued by a pack of bloodthirsty dogs, but the camera runs with the pack like another "dog". Only later does it become apparent that this was a dream sequence, which a man in a bar recounts to the director. The uncertainty about whether this relates to an external action or a purely internal experience depends critically on the music and the soundtrack, in which hyper-realistic animal sounds are underscored with electronic music and a strong beat (which it is tempting to describe as a disco beat). As Ari Folman explains:

> one of the basic ways I envisage it [the war in the film] is as a bad acid trip. (…) Everyone talks about visions when they talk about LSD, but really it's more about sound, and rarely do you see that truth expressed in filmmaking.
> *(Gullen 2009)*

Folman elaborates:

> In the 10–12 minute Mardi Gras scene in *Easy Rider* (…) it's all about sound, nothing about visuals. I felt that I had to take the audience immediately into that dimension, to strike them with the opening sequence, shock them, and then let them fly into the film. (ibid.)

Sound in *Waltz with Bashir* – at once disorienting and re-focusing the viewer – has strongly psychoanalytic connotations, not only by shocking the spectator into being him/herself traumatised by the aural assault doubled by those fearsome-looking dogs, but by mimicking the trauma-logic of dissociation and psychic fugue, combining an insistent sense of presence with the terror of not being able to locate oneself. This is further underscored by Max Richter, a composer from the school of Philip Glass and Steve Reich, whom Folman hired precisely to create the kind of repetition compulsion we associate with trauma, guilt and obsessive behaviour. Folman even claimed to have listened to Richter's music while he was writing the script, which shows how powerfully even a documentary film can be shaped by the primacy of sound: at every level, from conception to production to reception.[12]

Body and voice: the acousmêtre and the ventriloquist

The primacy of sound has both an ontogenetic and a phylogenetic dimension. From an ontogenetic perspective, for example, hearing is more primary than seeing for our orientation and stabilisation in space, and this also applies in the physiological sense. Our first contact with the world takes place through sound, as the embryo grows surrounded by the body and voice of the mother. Sound is our primary medium, and for quite some time even after birth, all the horrors of life, such as dependency, abandonment and helplessness, but also all the pleasures of immersion and nurture are associated with sound. Walter Murch himself pointed out that the resonating enclosure of the womb (through the mother's voice, breathing and heartbeat) is the environment in which we develop before birth. "We begin to hear before we are born, four and a half months after conception. From then on we develop in a continuous and luxurious bath of sounds. (…) Throughout the second four-and-a-half months, sound rules as solitary queen of our senses" (1994: vii). It is the memory of this wholeness, of this nurturing but also hermetically enclosed environment, that accompanies us for the rest of our lives.

The phylogenetic, evolutionary aspects of sound are also significant. At the most basic level, as already mentioned, we cannot close our ears the way we close our eyes. Our ears "watch" over our sleep and they do this for sound [sic] survival reasons:

> Animism and paranoia have more survival value than equanimity. Of the two creatures who might have wondered whether that low rumbling they just heard was really the growl of a tiger or just distant thunder, the one disposed to hear the noise as an animal voice is more likely still to be among us than the one displaying a more relaxed and philosophical attitude.
>
> *(Connor 2014: 8)*

Therefore, the regressive-immersive aspects of sound stand in some tension to the active stance of listening, but both raise the question of agency with respect to sound. Because sound is usually thought of as active, as a transmitter, even the person making sound might under certain circumstances be thought of as a mere instrument of transmission. Sound emanates from an object, it has an origin, and this in contrast to colour, for instance, which we imagine to be the property of an object and associated with its substance. In the case of sound, we always try to locate a provenance, a place of origin, a source, because we experience it as travelling, as on the move.

In other words, we regard sound as a force, a power or a special carrier of authority, and this is the presupposition upon which French musicologist and film theorist Michel Chion bases his theory of the "acousmêtre", his term for the disembodied voices in cinema, which apparently have no origin but are omnipresent. Chion derives the neologism from acousmatic and être, where the first part refers to something that is heard but whose origin is not seen, while the second part means "master" (maître), "measure" (metre) as well as the infinitive of the verb "to be" (être). Chion uses this idea to show that sound is ontologically tied to being and existence, that it has the power of agency and that it is not just a volatile breath that can be blown away by the wind.[13] The power of the acousmêtre resides in its apparent omnipresence, omniscience and invisibility, in other words, its origin is to be found neither within the film nor outside of it, but in the dimension or space where omnipresence joins invisibility, a point where the Real, the Symbolic and the Imaginary intersect: the realm of the Almighty Himself, as Chion also implied.[14]

Hence the acousmêtre, the master (-signifier). The most famous examples of the acousmêtre cited by Chion are the wizard in *The Wizard of Oz* (1939, Victor Fleming), the mother in *Psycho* (1960, Alfred Hitchcock), the computer voice Hal in *2001:*

A Space Odyssey (1968, Stanley Kubrick) and Mabuse in *The Testament of Dr Mabuse* (1933, Fritz Lang). In all four films, the power of these uncanny voices must be tracked down, exposed and broken at the end, in order to restore the (world-) order they threaten, yet once uncovered, they reveal themselves as shams, empty shells or mere mechanical contraptions, thus keeping intact, as it were, the imaginary dimension that lent them their power in the first place. But one can also find examples for the power of the acousmêtre from the daily news: some time ago when celebrated golfer Tiger Woods had receded into the twilight because of his extramarital activities, his sponsors at Nike believed that he could prove his readiness to show remorse through a TV spot in which his (deceased) father appeals to his conscience.[15]

It could be a scene out of a David Lynch film, for this director's entire oeuvre presents extreme and extremely unsettling cases of the acousmêtre as the source of power, in situations where the imaginary encounters the real without any mediation by the symbolic.[16] Think, for instance, of *Lost Highway* (1997) and the scene of the Mystery Man face to face in physical space, while his voice is present at the other end of a mobile phone call. Even as we watch what appears to be a tense, but ordinary encounter, some ontological ground gives way right under our feet (or seats). Lynch demonstrates what Rudolf Arnheim had already remarked in the 1930s, namely, that, on the one hand, the sound gives the film a "body" by creating a third dimension, but, on the other hand, it always also threatens the integrity of the body.[17] Lynch takes us back to the very origins of synchronised sound and the psychoanalytically very intriguing sleight of hand on which it is based. Being a technical operation that matches a separate image with a separate sound, synchronisation acquires its added value of "realism" and of the third dimension at a price: the fusion, blend or alloy of the two is basically unstable and can be rent apart at any moment. And since we expect sound to emanate from an object, and a voice from a body, disembodied sound or a voice without its appropriate body instantly evokes an entire array of negative emotions of dread and danger. It lets surface the uncanny nature of all cinematic representation, over which hovers the anxiety of a breakdown of its fragile amalgam of heterogeneous elements.

These deep-rooted anxieties over the integrity of the body and voice, whose sources in repression and disavowal Lacan was at pains to analyse, are most vividly mobilised by instances of ventriloquism, whether in real life or on film. When a voice emerges not from the face or mouth but apparently from a different part of the body, or when a wooden doll takes on a life of its own, we feel the cold chill of death brush over us. Such is the case in *Dead of Night* (1945, Alberto Cavalcanti and Charles Crichton), where the dummy functions as the acousmêtre of repressed feelings and of murderous intent, and likewise, in *The Exorcist* (1973, William Friedkin), the words in the young girl's mouth are not hers but those of the devil.[18]

Lynch's *Mulholland Drive* (2001) contains several scenes in which voice and body lead their own separate lives, reinforcing the basic conceit of the film, namely the arbitrarily interchangeable identities and infinitely pliable personalities of the two female protagonists. Not least thanks to the film's soundscape, the viewer becomes attuned to the perceptual oscillations in the image, while trying to find his/her bearing within the multiple time-frames and layered narrative spaces. With a director like Lynch one can cope with a considerable amount of disorientation in the image, mainly because the sound is so precise and hard and feels so solid. It acts as an anchor, becoming a mediator between space (general) and place (local). But it would not be Lynch if such assurance did not itself prove deceptive. Most famous among such scenes (suggesting the solidity of sound only to whisk away the ground) is the visit of the two women to Club Silencio, where a singer by the name Rebekah gives a rendition of Roy Orbison's "Only the Lonely" in Spanish, during which she faints and collapses into a lifeless doll, while her voice – and the song – carry on, revealing the mechanical sound system beneath the passionate and plaintive voice, once more demonstrating the uncanny power of the acousmêtre – here the "master" of ceremonies – over life and the machines, but especially over the life of women, treated as machines.

In *The Pervert's Guide to Cinema* (2006) Slavoj Žižek briefly discusses the scene, arguing that here we "confront [in the female voice] this nightmarish dimension of an autonomous partial object". It turns the Club Silencio performance into an allegorical mirror, held up to the two women, so desperate to believe in the reality of their imagined Hollywood stardom. To them apply the MC's words: "there is no band; there is no music", even though we hear it and may even be moved to tears by it, as are the women. The voice as "partial object" i.e. as *objet petit a* here stands once more for the unobtainable object of desire, a narcissistic desire directed at the self or that version of the self that each of the women wants to become, in relation to the men whom they imagine hold the key to their success as stars. The collapsed body of the singer is then a kind of "fainting into reality", turning the sustaining fantasy frame of the women into nothing but a "recording", the mechanic rehearsal of a predefined role: with the typical Lynchean twist that such knowledge in no way destroys the fascination emanating from the spectacle of Club Silencio, where the Imaginary encounters the Real on the empty stage of the Symbolic.

Rarely has a filmmaker let us see so clearly how the power and impotence of sound are the recto and verso of each other, as if Lynch wanted to prove that the Hollywood hierarchy, where sound finds itself subordinated to image, is not a sign of sound's weakness as a signifier, but on the contrary, its subordination was so strictly enforced during the classical period, because it has always been a matter of taming sound's disruptive power and keeping it under control.

Aural objects and the materiality of sound

On the one hand, sound possesses tactile and haptic qualities, because sound is a phenomenon of waves and therefore of movement. In order to generate and propagate a sound, an object must be touched (the string of an instrument, the human vocal cords, the wind in the trees), while in turn, sound puts a body into oscillation, makes it vibrate, including the fact that it touches, envelopes and agitates the viewer's body. Sound acts on the medium (air), which it requires for its transmission and thereby gives it body and presence. When powerful bass notes are resounding, we can feel the draft of air from the deep notes on our bodies. It is the same with high-hats, which set the rhythm. We also think that a sound fills a space like water fills a glass. Along with the feeling of centeredness already discussed, according to which we immerse and surround ourselves with sound in order to imagine ourselves to be in the centre of it, sound also makes us feel our body mass as "gravity" and our body surface as "skin".

On the other hand, as already suggested, sound (and especially the voice) is also something volatile, fluid and transparent and therefore escapes the urge to hold it. Sound eludes the sense organ that tries to fix or freeze it, making it the partial object at once necessary for our identity as subjects and frustrating that identity by slipping from our grasp. If it is possible to reproduce the traditional film image via stills or frame enlargements, sound – even when recorded – can only be reproduced in time and not condensed or compressed into the moment. Sound, therefore, invariably reminds us of the irreversibility of time, it is an index of loss and a messenger of transience: another reason for sound being charged with fear and associated with mortality – the dying fall.

If sound is therefore a prominent part within today's cinema experience, it is not only because our everyday lives have become more and more filled with noise, to which we respond with more music and more sound, but also because of sound's inherently ambiguous status in the cinema, with its multiple valences as signifier of both embodiment and disembodiment, as both tactile and invisible, resolved in the digital era by making sure that a film is an audio event before it is a visual event. Especially in action movies – a genre that relies strongly on the material properties of bodies and the weight of objects – movements and gestures, say, a push, a shove, a collision or a body walking, an object falling, are communicated primarily via sound. The post-apocalyptic landscape at the beginning of James Cameron's *Terminator II* (1991), for instance, is given contour and shape through the sound of crunching under the terminator's boots. It is the sound that causes something that looks like dusty rubble to be experienced as human skulls or as Chion remarked, explaining his term synchresis: "it's the ear that makes the skulls visible" (2012), once more confirming that the subordinate or supplemental position of sound effectively determines the visibility of the image, while adding a new materiality to the (digital) image. For Chion, the idea of the "rendu" (in the sense of both "rendered" and "applied") becomes one of the key features of digital sound, because (like the digital image itself) it is perceived as a "substance", perhaps like a filling compound or clay, which must be formed, contoured or kneaded into shape.[19]

Sound: signifying loss or compensating for loss?

This pseudo-materiality of the acoustic helps the impression of "seeing with the ear", as if today it required a medium of "invisibility" to make the world (once more) "visible". It suggests a possibility with which I want to end: If indeed there is a sense that sound can compensate for our loss of faith in the image and the power of vision in the digital age (for the many different reasons I have discussed above), does this signifier of loss and transience nonetheless – inadvertently, and for the viewer unconsciously – serve as the paradoxical "anchor"? The digital image, so the argument would go, needs sound in order to lend it the discernible truth of the trace and the ontological bond of the index. Sound surrounds us and its material waves physically "touch" us in the enclosed space of the movie theatre, so perhaps the vivid clarity and mastery once enjoyed by the eye transfers itself to the body itself, now experienced as a total perceptual surface and organ.

However, if the "loss of indexicality" means we can no longer trust the image and our eyes (if ever we could), why should we have any greater confidence in sound and our ears (surely even more easily deceived by special effects than the eye)? The fact is, we ought not to need to trust either eye or ear, since the very notion of trust in this context (as a pledge to truth, reference and evidence) is probably misconceived. Rather, it is obvious that we need both, image and sound: not to synchronise each other, or each to verify and testify for the other so that together they can project the phantasm of the body whole (as in classical cinema) and also not to counterpoint and war with each other (as in avant-garde films of the 1970s), but to mutually dis-orient each other, in the sense of generating an oscillation that directs our attention to and fro, making us experience a cognitive-dissonant mode of reception as the default value of the new "realism".

This would be an appropriate note to end on, were it not for a small, but significant, detail: in psychoanalytic terms, "seeing with our ears" does not stand in exact mirror relation to "hearing with our eyes". For instance, Slavoj Žižek – who agrees with Chion that, as a partial object, voice (and by extension sound) has little to do with "hearing" and nothing to do with listening – nonetheless maintains that the relationships seeing/ear and hearing/eye are not equivalent but asymmetric. Discussing their dynamics in the films of Hitchcock, Kieslowski and Lynch, Žižek maintains that "seeing with our ears" refers to the enlivening curiosity of the "look", while "hearing with our eyes" refers to the mortifying power of the Lacanian "gaze".[20]

Assuming that Žižek is right, he is so only within the particular paradigm of Lacan's theory of the gaze, which, as pointed out in the beginning, is still heavily dependent on the Euclidean geometry of representation, typified by the double cone, with which Lacan diagrammatically represents the place of look and gaze, as well as the dynamics of the *objet petit a*. It has been one of the purposes of this chapter to challenge, via the discussion of the relation between sound and image, the invisible and the visible precisely this geometry and its projective mechanism, as also embodied in Renaissance perspective. If in the traditional Hollywood hierarchy of subordination, sound supported the image as the stabiliser for our sense of balance, it did so also in order to further reposition and re-centre vision within the geometry of perspectival space. However, as also argued in the introduction, this pictorial space of Renaissance perspective now exists only as the memory of its former normative self-evidence; thanks to the MP3 players, touchscreens and mobile phones that have become the supplements of the body (and in typical supplement fashion, have taken over the body that they were meant to supplement), both sound and image now contribute to the perpetual mobilisation of our senses, while we nonetheless remain subject to the irreversible arrow of transient time. "Seeing with our ears" and "hearing with our eyes" together do form the new coordinates of our reconfigured self-presence, making us the protagonists of a new drama: at one and the same time active and passive, central and peripheral, exalted and mortified, we are fated to experience with our bodies and expose to our senses the intensities but also the agonies of the world once more remade: in the "image" (and thus also sound) of our technological supplements.

Notes

1 In English there is a potential confusion about the distinction between look and gaze, insofar as "the male gaze" is the term used by Laura Mulvey to describe what in Lacan would be the (imaginary) "look" rather than the "gaze", which – as argued below – is situated between the symbolic and the real and therefore can function outside the realm of the visible (and thus be associated with hearing, i.e. with sound and voice).
2 See Elsaesser (2013), 13–44.
3 Originally published in German in 1939, *The Civilizing Process* tries to chart structural changes in Western societies by focusing on the consequences of the division of labour, the resulting specialisation of tasks and the increased mutual dependence in Western societies of members on each other. The psychological implications are increased self-restraint and self-control, which in Freudian terms would explain the formation of the modern "Super-Ego", as well as a redistribution of functions among the senses.
4 For an inspired commentary on Bazin's essay, "Ontology of the Photographic Image", within a film challenging this ontology, see Richard Linklater's *Waking Life* and in particular, the scene with Caveh Zahedi, called *The Holy Moment* (https://vimeo.com/56075178).
5 See Buckland (1999).
6 See Elsaesser (2004).
7 See Belting (2014).
8 The Walkman was the harbinger of a development that has continued through MP3 players, mobile telephones, laptops, W-LAN and other innovations: the increasing mobilisation of the media experience, which is associated with an opening of the private sphere into public space. It has had countless intended and unintended consequences, relating to the status of work or the meaning of intimacy.
9 See Abel and Altman (2001) and Altman (2004).
10 The German scholar Michael Wedel has written a 476-page book on sound, music and synchronisation, of which more than half is about sound before sound film (2007).

11 The term "sound designer" originated in the 1970s as a job description that replaced that of "sound engineer". Walter Murch, who also worked as a cutter, is certainly the key figure here: for *Apocalypse Now* he was first honoured with the term "sound design" and named in the credits before the film. For an informative discussion, see Ondaatje (2002).

12 Together with Aviv Aldema, who was also nominated for an Academy Award, Max Richter became for Folman what Walter Murch was for Coppola, namely the maestro of Sound Design, a job description that hardly even existed before Murch, at least not in such a prominent position in the nominations or as a winner of an Oscar.

13 For a very suggestive anthropological analysis of the relation of recorded sound, invisibility and mastery, see Michael Taussig's chapter on "His Master's Voice" (1993), 212–235.

14 It may be worth pointing out that in Lacan's version of the Borromean knot, the point where the three rings of the Symbolic, the Real and the Imaginary intersect is also where Lacan puts the *objet petit a*.

15 See http://skew.dailyskew.com/2010/04/tiger-woods-nike-commercial-tigers-dead-father-speaks.html.

16 In this context, it is not surprising that both Chion (1995) and Žižek (2000) have written on Lynch.

17 "The acoustic supplements the illusion in such a manner that it becomes complete. And immediately, the edge of the image ceases to be a frame, but becomes the boundary of a hole. (…) However, one of the special attractions of film is that a film scene is always a competition between subdivision of image and two-dimensional movement on one hand, and plastic embodiment and movement in three-dimensional space on the other. Audio film eliminates this aesthetically important double-play almost without trace" (Arnheim 2004: 68).

18 On a slightly lighter note, the accepted form of ventriloquism in many countries is dubbing, a habit so repugnant to me that I cannot actually watch a post-synchronised film, because it turns even a comedy into a horror film.

19 A homology in German is thus particularly suggestive: the word for clay (*Ton*) is the same as the word for sound (*Ton*).

20 "An image can emerge as the placeholder for a sound that doesn't yet resonate but remains stuck in the throat. Munch's *Scream*, for example, is by definition silent: in front of this painting, we 'hear (the scream) with our eyes.' However, the parallel is here by no means perfect: to see what one cannot hear is not the same as to hear what one cannot see. Voice and gaze relate to each other as life and death: voice vivifies, whereas gaze mortifies" (Žižek 1996: 93–94).

References

Abel, R. and Altman, R. (eds.) (2001) *The Sounds of Early Cinema*. Bloomington: Indiana University Press.

Altman, R. (2004) *Silent Film Sound*. New York: Columbia University Press.

Arnheim, R. (2004) *Die Seele in der Silberschicht. Medientheoretische Texte. Photographie – Film – Rundfunk*. Ed. H. Diederichs. Frankfurt/Main: Suhrkamp 2004.

Belting, H. (2014) *An Anthropology of Images: Picture, Medium, Body*. Princeton: Princeton University Press.

Buckland, W. (1999) Between Science Fact and Science Fiction: Spielberg's Digital Dinosaurs, Possible Worlds, and the New Aesthetic Realism. *Screen* 40(2): 177–92.

Chion, M. (1995) *David Lynch*. London: BFI.

Chion, M. (2012) Graduate and Faculty Seminar on Sound. IKKM Weimar. May.

Dolar, M. (2006) *A Voice and Nothing More.* Cambridge: MIT Press.

Elias, N. (2000) *The Civilizing Process – Sociogenetic and Psychogenetic Investigations.* Oxford: Blackwell Publishing.

Elsaesser, T. (ed.) (2004) *Harun Farocki: Working on the Sightlines.* Amsterdam: Amsterdam University Press.

Elsaesser, T. (2013) Digital Cinema – Convergence or Contradiction? In C. Vernallis and A. Herzog (eds.) *The Oxford Handbook of Digital Media, Vol. 2: Sound.* Oxford: Oxford University Press.

Flückiger, B. (2001) *Sound Design. Die virtuelle Klangwelt des Films.* Marburg: Schüren.

Gullen, M. (2009) Waltz With Bashir – Interview With Ari Folman. *Twitch.* Available: http://twitchfilm.com/2009/01/waltz-with-bashirinterview-with-ari-folmon.html. [Accessed 23 October 2015].

Kittler, F. (2015) The God of Ears. In S. Sale and L. Salisbury (eds.) *Kittler Now.* London: Polity Press.

Koolhaas, R. (2001) *Junkspace.* Available: http://www.cavvia.net/junkspace/. [Accessed 23 October 2015].

Lacan, J. (1977) *The Seminar of Jacques Lacan, Book XI: The Four Fundamental Concepts of Psychoanalysis.* Ed. J-A Miller. Trans. A. Sheridan. New York: Norton.

McGowan, T. (2006) *The Real Gaze: Film Theory after Lacan.* Albany: SUNY Press.

Mulvey, L. (1975) Visual Pleasure and Narrative Cinema. *Screen* 16(3): 6–18.

Murch, M. (1994) Foreword. In M. Chion, *Audiovision: Sound on Screen.* New York: Columbia University Press.

Ondaatje, M. (2002) *Die Kunst des Filmschnitts – Gespräche mit Walter Murch.* München, Wien: Carl Hanser Verlag.

Schmidt, M. (2015) Biography. Available: http://www.egs.edu/faculty/michael-schmidt/biography/. [Accessed 23 October 2015].

Taussig, M. (1993) *Mimesis and Alterity.* New York: Routledge.

Thompson, E. (2003) *The Soundscape of Modernity: Architectural Acoustics and the Culture of Listening in America, 1900–1933.* Cambridge: MIT Press.

Valery, P. (1974) *Cahiers*, vol II. Paris: Gallimard.

Wedel, M. (2007) *Der deutsche Musikfilm: Archäologie eines Genres 1914–1945.* Munich: edition text + kritik.

Wenk, D. (2003) Rückkopplungs-Stadien [review of Regis Debray, *Vie et Mort de l'Image*]. *Textem.* Available: http://www.textem.de/index.php?id=251. [Accessed 23 October 2015].

Žižek, S. (1996) I Hear You with My Eyes, or The Invisible Master. In R. Salecl and S. Žižek (eds.) *Gaze and Voice as Love Objects.* Durham: Duke University Press.

Žižek, S. (2000) *The Art of the Ridiculous Sublime: On David Lynch's Lost Highway.* Seattle: Walter Chapin Centre for the Humanities.

Filmography

2001: A Space Odyssey (1968) Directed by Stanley Kubrick. USA/UK: MGM.

Apocalypse Now (1979) Directed by Francis Ford Coppola. USA: Zoetrope Studios.

Dead of Night (1945) Directed by Alberto Cavalcanti and Charles Crichton. UK: Ealing Studios.

The Exorcist (1973) Directed by William Friedkin. USA: Warner Bros.

Jaws (1975) Directed by Steven Spielberg. USA: Universal Pictures.

Lost Highway (1997) Directed by David Lynch. France/USA: October Films.

Mulholland Drive (2001) Directed by David Lynch. France/USA: Canal+.

Nashville (1975) Directed by Robert Altman. USA: Paramount Pictures.

The Pervert's Guide to Cinema (2006) Directed by Sophie Fiennes. UK/Austria/Netherlands: Amoeba Films.

Psycho (1960) Directed by Alfred Hitchcock. USA: Shamley Productions.

Star Wars (1977) Directed by George Lucas. USA: Lucasfilm.

Terminator 2: Judgement Day (1991) Directed by James Cameron. USA/France: Carolco Pictures.

The Testament of Dr Mabuse (1933) Directed by Fritz Lang. Germany: Nero-Film AG.

Waltz with Bashir (2008) Directed by Ari Folman. Israel/France/Germany/USA/Finland/Switzerland/Belgium/Australia: Bridgit Folman Film Gang.

The Wizard of Oz (1939) Directed by Victor Fleming. USA: MGM.

5

ON TOUCHING AND SPEAKING IN (POST) (DE) COLONIAL DISCOURSE – FROM LESSING TO MARECHERA AND VEIT-WILD

Agnieszka Piotrowska

Introduction

Jean-Luc Nancy in his seminal book on the body and its significance in history of philosophy *Corpus* makes a point that the body and the discussions about it ought to be open. He says that in reflecting on it he did not want to:

> produce the effect of a closed or finite thing, because when we talk about the body we talk about something entirely opposed to the closed and the finite. With the body, we speak about something open and infinite, about the opening of closure itself, the infinite of the finite itself. (2008: 122)

This particular reflection came upon him whilst walking through the streets of Paris to give a lecture on the body. Suddenly, he heard about the atrocities in Bosnia and felt compelled to abandon his well-prepared talk and instead find an open space to talk about the links between the body, the soul and our place in the world. He says in his book, "Body is certitude shattered and blown to bits" (ibid.: 3), a phrase that in the age of terrorist attacks sounds particularly ominous.

In this chapter I will focus on voice and touch in colonial and post-colonial encounters as a site of loss, representing the unrepresentable collapse of ordinary human communications, reclaimed gradually in the de-colonial period. The work discussed in this chapter is "touching" something that is indeed very difficult, if possible at all, to talk about. This chapter is by no means anything definitive: as our world is continuously finding that its post-coloniality is not a history lesson but rather a living daily occurrence, sometimes painfully violent, the connections of the body, the language and the touching are worth considering from a different perspective.

Here I will look at Doris Lessing's seminal novel *The Grass Is Singing* (1950) and Dambudzo Marechera's excerpt from a larger work called *Choreodrama*, entitled *The Portrait of a Back Artist in London* (1980) (and published for the first time in Veit-Wild's Sourcebook in 1992). These read together, as if speaking to each other, thus form another "body" of work. Their work boldly addresses a painful legacy of colonialism through fiction and not a factual report. They offer a rare insight into the trauma involved in emerging from colonialism and finding a voice with which to express the pain.

It is worth recalling here Jacques Derrida's essay *"Demeure"*: attending to "the context of relations between fiction and truth which is also to say, between literature and death" (Blanchot and Derrida 2000[1994]: 15). In it he reminds us that it is often *only* through fictional stories, which offer a distance to the unrepresentable pain, that we can express the essence of the matter in an ethical way.[1] Derrida echoes here Jacques Lacan's notion of truth having a structure of fiction (2006: 684); it is often simply too painful and impossible to deal with facts just as sheer facts. In order to avoid the "ethical violence" that accompanies any attempt at "giving an account of oneself" to the Other (Butler 2005), it is sometimes necessary to fictionalise that account to make it "representable" at all, however imperfectly. This is what I believe takes place in Marechera's and Lessing's pieces of literature: they represent something that still remains largely unspeakable in the (de) colonial context: namely (non) touching and (non) speaking with the Other. I will also in connection with this briefly mention here Flora Veit-Wild and Dambudzo Marechera's personal relationship and her unexpected confession of the nature of this relationship, which took place in early 1980s but was only accounted for in 2012; I will return to this below.

Testimony and the academy

The word *"demeure"*, which means "remains" (but also in fact "home"), and its various derivations and forms dominate Derrida's whole essay: to give a testimony of one's experience of unbearable suffering is also in some way to want to combat it, to defy death itself and to "remain" against the inevitability of time. In order to be able to attempt that at all, one has to find a voice the Other can hear – and Derrida despaired due to the unknowability of the response of the Other to one's pronouncements elsewhere, in particular in *The Ear of the Other* (1982).

Derrida, himself a victim and triumphant survivor of colonialism (he was born Jewish Algerian in French Algiers, discriminated against both there and later in France)[2] was a proponent of the personal and "high theory" in one space. In his controversial statement below Derrida asks for greater freedom in the academy, precisely in order to be able to approach the "unrepresentable". In his provocative lectures and seminars in Montreal more than 30 years ago (1982) Derrida focused on the connection between one's experience and one's work. To put it differently,

Derrida enters a difficult place in which "the scholarly" might need to share space with "the emotional": an almost prohibited move in the academy even today. That means an acceptance of a certain sense of fragmentation of the presentation. This is what Derrida says:

> I would like to spare you the tedium, the waste of time, and the subservience that always accompany the classic pedagogical procedures of forging links, referring back to prior premises or arguments, justifying one's trajectory, method, system, and more or less skillful transitions, reestablishing continuity, and so on. These are but some of the imperatives of classical pedagogy with which, to be sure, one can never break once and for all. Yet, if you were to submit to them rigorously, they would very soon reduce you to silence, tautology, and tiresome repetition. (1988: 3–4)[3]

This chapter, as with most of my other work, attempts to enter such an open space in which the scholarly and the emotional co-exist, even if I accept that some links will have to be forged and some references to premises and arguments made.

I start by presenting a psychoanalytical reading of Lessing's the novel which is in some way in the opposition to interpretations advanced over the last 20 years by literary scholars. In particular I take issue with some of the notions presented by Joy Wang (2009) in her article "White Postcolonial Guilt", which also sums up a number of other scholarly interpretations. The paper offers Mary's complex relationship with Moses as a classic "interracial romance" and a kind of reparation, putting *The Grass Is Singing* in the same context as a number of other seminal, post-colonial works, thereby framing Mary's desire as "abject" within the colonial discourse. Here is what Wang says:

> This historical portrayal of white female desire for the black man as an abject and indirect form of apology is entrenched within landmark texts such as E. M. Forster's *A Passage to India* (1924), Paul Scott's depiction of Daphne Manners in *The Raj Quartet* (1966–73) and J. M. Coetzee's character Lucy in *Disgrace* (1999).
>
> If abjection can be broadly defined, as Anne McClintock argues, as an act of *expulsion, casting away, and social exclusion,* then these relationships were, for white women in Lessing's apartheid South Africa, descriptively to be labelled as abject simply by virtue of their social unacceptability. (2009: 38; my emphasis)

I take issue with interpreting Mary's drama as a form of abjection and suggest here instead that it might be more productive to reflect on the issues of touching and the voice in the novel and the (linguistic, political, affective) limits within which Lessing's unreliable narrator is capable of addressing these issues. In other words, the pain and trauma and desire felt by the protagonists remain "unsymbolised": "unrepresented" and therefore doomed. The violence that follows fits in well with Ranjana Khanna's contention that *unsymbolised* loss will lead to violence (2003):[4] in a post-colonial context in particular but also in any other traumatic situation.[5] I will return to this later in this chapter.

The issue of symbolisation and representation can perhaps offer a response to various critics' confusion over Moses's murder of Mary. Having been told repeatedly "don't speak English to me" (ibid.: 41) Moses is banned from "metaphorisation", a ban especially fraught as Lessing's narrator actually has no idea what it is that he might want to say: "what thoughts of regret, or pity, or perhaps even wounded human affection were compounded with the satisfaction of his completed revenge, it is impossible to say" (ibid.: 206).

There is something else here too, though. Derrida in his discussion of Nancy's work called *Corpus* makes some important points regarding touching in Descartes' Six Meditations, in which Derrida stresses the point that to touch means "to tamper with, to change, to displace, to call into question; thus it is invariably a setting in motion, a kinetic experience" (Derrida 2000: 25). This is in direct and hard opposition to the colonial and post-colonial notions of ideas being set in stone, what Edward Said in his discussions of colonialism called "frozen, fixed" (2006 [1978]: 27) and deeply patriarchal and conservative. The touching, Derrida reminds us here, is a harbinger of change: it can be a good change or bad, but it's a movement, and when it is accompanied by a voice and language it can become explosive and revolutionary. It is for these reasons that it is prohibited in any situations in which difference is a marker of danger: as it is in the contemporary world today, too. To define a female desire in this context as "abjection" is to miss its political dimension; it is a big move away from a separatedness always evoked by the patriarchal authority.

Here in Lessing's novel the touching takes place, and silent in its threat. Taking this voicelessness and the power-relations it signifies as a point of departure, I am interested here in reading Marechera's work in the context of searching and finding the voice that Moses, the black protagonist of the novel, never has. To oversimplify my project here, if Moses could express his rage in Lessing's novel, might he not say what Marechera says in his poem? Could one therefore read the two pieces of work as entering into dialogue with each other, a dialogue the apparent impossibility of which still haunts the contemporary relations between races and genders in Southern Africa?

The novel

To repeat then: *The Grass Is Singing* deals with colonial relationships in Rhodesia in the late 1940s. As a direct result of the absence of either means or ability to articulate pain by the white woman and the black man at the heart of the story, violence ensues. That absence is clearly created by the systematic abuses of colonialism, but the incident is still a local and private matter: Mary, the white woman, is murdered by Moses, the black man. Instead of exploring the incident's evident political significance I will reflect here on the implicit and actual prohibition of touching in colonial times as evoking desire and despair. Derrida and more recently Emma Wilson (2012) have spoken, in their reflections on the image and absence, about a longing for the embodied presence of the beloved Other who is no more. Derrida again talks movingly about any desire aroused by absence, and I am borrowing the quote from him:

> The desire to touch, the tactile effect or affect, is violently summoned by its very frustration, summoned to come back [*appelé à revenir*], like a ghost [*un revenant*], in the places haunted by its absence.
>
> *(Derrida and Stiegler 2002: 115)*

Wilson too talks about "images yielding a trace of embodied experience, of sensuousness, of engagement with the world, up to and beyond death (…). I look at the ways in which the dead still touch us and the ways in which we may respond to their demands with love" (2012: 6). If we read Lessing's and Marechera's works in this context, namely the context of longing, loss and melancholia rather than abjection and guilt, the readings might lead to more conciliatory outcomes, both in the academy and elsewhere. Lessing and Marechera in their fiction evoke images of desire and despair over the absence of embodied encounters in colonial and post-colonial Zimbabwe: an absence aggravated or perhaps even created by the absence of actual physical touching as well as verbal communications.

Lessing was a white Zimbabwean, or rather a white Rhodesian, as Zimbabwe only gained independence in 1980. I suggest here that this absence of a clear voice on the part of the protagonists in her novel is connected to the issue of "mourning and melancholia" and trauma linked to the period of colonialism, on the part of the white and black participants of the era alike. The physicality of an encounter with the Other and an actual prohibition of engaging with that Other was thrown into sharp focus during pre-independence times in almost all countries subjected to colonisation. As my field work in recent times has been taking place in Southern Africa and particularly in Zimbabwe, my experience of its legacy is both first hand and in some ways unexpectedly painful: touching is still an awkward thing in contemporary Zimbabwe. In my documentary film *Lovers in Time or How We Didn't Get Arrested in Harare* (2015), my lead actor Michael Kudawashe admitted in an interview that the touching in public, an innocent touching, was still an area of contention.

In former Rhodesia prior to independence, a physical encounter with the black Other was a taboo that was heavily sexualised, but it was also illegal and used as a way of discouraging any physical contact, however casual or innocent, with the indigenous population: touch, just ordinary touch between members of different races, was discouraged, even if it was not per se against the law. I will first briefly recall here the notion of touch as connected to voice and its importance in Judeo-Christian art and literature. It is from that tradition I argue that the prohibition of touch in colonialism comes, closely linked to the missionary work with the so-called "savage" populations.

Touching and not touching

In an episode of BBC Radio 4's *Point of View,* British novelist Will Self speaks about the importance of touch in human relationships (2015): here he focuses on the topic in connection with our contemporary over-reliance on technology and its emphasis on a disembodied means of communications, through social media such as Facebook, Twitter or WhatsApp. He evokes Isaac Asimov's science fiction novel from 1957 *The Naked Sun* in which, in a world entitled Solaria, all human contact is mediated through technology and any form of touching or embodied encounter is forbidden: people are not allowed to be in one room together for the fear of what might ensue. Touching is dangerous as it invites proximity the consequences of which are not clear to envisage or control.

Self reminds us that in Christianity the dualism of body and soul over the centuries had been translated in the Middle Ages into a reticence over a physical touch, in case that might turn into a dangerous sexualised encounter leading in its turn to Sin. Self evokes in his article the phrase "*Noli me tangere*" – Latin for "don't touch me" or "don't tread on me" – the words attributed to Christ in St John's Gospel when Mary Magdalene recognises him after the resurrection and wants to touch him. Christ is delighted that she can *see* him but doesn't let her touch him: "*Noli me tangere*" i.e. "don't touch me for I am not of this world any more, I am just a briefly embodied spirit – already assigned for greater travel".

In the Gospel Christ's bodily existence is already over but the "don't touch" as a dictum became an important way of living in medieval times – one could argue also in some way affecting and affected by two dimensional art, which avoided representing the body as it actually was – a state of affairs only changed in the Renaissance with its return to the celebration of human form coming from antiquity and therefore a different approach to touching. It is worth, however, recalling that touching and voice also in fact have a vital role in Christ's life according to the Gospels: he touches those who need healing (in Mark we have a clear evocation of this: "lay hands on the sick and they shall recover" [Mark 16: 18]); he touches Lazarus and tells him to "rise" and of course he famously defends Mary Magdalene ("May he who is without sin cast the first stone" [John 8: 7]) before letting her touch him quite intimately in fact – namely washing his feet (Luke 7: 36–50). The "don't touch me" dictum only comes when Christ's bodily existence is in fact over.

That touch, the healing mysterious touch, was in the Middle Ages reserved for those who assumed the roles of representatives of God on earth, such as the

Pope and the royalty: in more contemporary times famously John Paul II would physically lift people from the ground when they kneeled in front of him, also saying to them "do not be afraid!"[6] Princess Diana too in her work drew from the notion that a touch can have a divine healing power, including working with AIDS victims and the underprivileged in the developing world.[7]

In contemporary society the divine power of touch has lost some of its significance because of the overwhelming power of technology that attempts to replace it. Self's reflection interrogates the contemporary position of communicating through machines rather than embodied encounters. There is something curiously attractive in the contemporary detachment from the actual troublesome Other. Self goes on to say:

> Mass industrialised society developed, in part, by inculcating us with rigid taboos - not only "noli me tangere", but also "don't talk to me, jostle me, or even acknowledge my physical presence". (2015)

In other words, Self argues that we have fallen into our relationships with machines so very easily because we are culturally very familiar with the non-touching relationships and the safety they might offer. However, despite our near obsession with it, technology does not satisfy our actual deep need to be with another human being in an embodied fashion.

It is in this context that Self suggests further that sometimes the desire to touch and inability to do so can spill over into violence of various kinds in which one touches the other in a violent gesture – when men wrestle and tug in order to get close – he suggests, as, for instance, in a rugby match:

> I sometimes wonder if what a rugby forward is really seeking, as he pushes his head between the straining haunches of his teammates, is not some abstract notion of excellence or achievement, but the very concrete experience of another man's being. (2015)

In the biblical story recounted above, Christ of course uses language to stop Mary Magdalene from touching him but he speaks to her kindly. We must bear in mind that Mary Magdalene is traumatised by Christ's crucifixion and the loss of her beloved mentor, and so the vision of Christ apparently alive and speaking must offer a great relief. They don't touch physically but he does *touch* her through his address to her, which one can interpret also as a plea for patience and peace and not just a prohibition: the time for bodily contact and indeed bodily sacrifice is over; the time for communicating through voice and language is upon us.

In a post-colonial context the issue of voice, language and also the desire to touch clearly is deeply complicated as it evokes the legacy of colonial prohibitions regarding bodily encounters brought in by the missionaries and the secular administrators of the provinces. Khanna in her influential book *Dark Continents* uses the psychoanalytical term "melancholia" to describe "colonial melancholy" as a mechanism dealing with a profound sense of loss – here a loss of independence, identity, sense of national belonging, innocence and freedom – on the part of the colonised subject (2003: 21). Khanna evokes Freud's *Mourning and Melancholia* and Abraham and Torok's reworking of it as two different "responses to a loss": a mourning constitutes a state of "natural" sadness over the loss of a loved object, which will abate with time. Melancholia, on the other hand, can be a paralysing state that lasts. Khanna stresses that "what distinguishes melancholia is a state of dejection, and a form of critical agency that is directed toward the self" (ibid.). She also reminds us of the difference between mourning as "assimilating [the lost object] – and melancholia – swallowing the lost object as whole" (ibid.). And as I have mentioned elsewhere (Piotrowska 2014a), it is important to bear in mind the recent research (e.g. Straker 2013), which points to the sense of loss of the part of the white and black population alike, for a number of different reasons: the whites mourn their dominance and the blacks their pre-colonial sense of identity, never to be re-gained.

Khanna borrows Freud's concept of the critical agency in melancholia and uses the term in particular to denote "forms of critical nationalism that emerge as melancholic remainders"; she says, "And if Freud would eventually transfer the critical agency found in melancholia into the normalizing function of the superego, I would salvage it, putting the melancholic's manic *critical agency* into the unworking of conformity, and into the critique of status quo" (Khanna 2003: 21–22, my emphasis).[8]

Khanna further advances that, drawing from the work of Abraham and Torok, "demetaphorization" is often a symptom of melancholia: always induced by a loss but also by some kind of pain and trauma. In essence, this "demetaphorization" is an inability to symbolise, that is indeed to "represent", suffering and anger through language. Khanna ventures that this kind of "demetaphorization" can be a particular problem in post-colonial encounters and can lead to violence: in her work she focuses on those who have been colonised, but the sense of loss and alienation might also be present in those who have inherited both the guilt, on the one hand, and a sense of loss of their power, on the other. Khanna stresses the notion of a *secret* loss that is in some way "unrepresentable": "For Abraham and Torok the cause of melancholia is an underlying secret carried by the analysand from previous generations" (ibid.: 25). Khanna's crucial move here is to think of the critical agency of melancholia as engendering actions and not just passivity. If you cannot represent your pain through language or creativity or embodied encounter with the other that will offer comfort, you might become violent. I argue that it is indeed what takes place between Mary and Moses in Lessing's novel and that the notion of mourning the loss on both sides works better here than the concept of the abject, which in the end does not explain the violence that concludes the book. I will return to it later in the essay.

It is not completely obvious perhaps to connect the an inability to "metaphorise" to actual physical violence and that, in its turn, to a sense of loss and mourning over a *desire* to touch the other, and yet, on the other hand, it is also not that hard to see the connections: the notion of a sexual closeness with a black person was before independence not only against the law but also a matter of shame and despair on the part of the white colonisers (and one could argue that Christianity was very much a part of the project of keeping the races apart, through the introduction of the notion of obedience in the missionary teachings). A physical closeness between people of different races and cultures therefore was an important political gesture and perhaps still is. It represented something not just unrepresentable but actually deeply frightening, i.e. a possibility of change.

Let me repeat then: the touching – any touching – was pretty much forbidden in colonial countries in order to avoid the temptation of the prohibited sexual encounter. And that prohibition, however much dressed up as a moral and Christian stance vis-à-vis the world, was also simply connected to a desire to keep the white race *white*[9]. Conversely, Frantz Fanon, in his seminal *Black Skins, White Masks*, controversially writes about the black man's unconscious desire to have sex with a white woman as representing an unconscious (and sometimes conscious) wish to become empowered by her whiteness and perhaps to begin to create "whiter" offspring (Fanon 1975: 63) As with many other rules and prohibitions, it was simply easiest for the missionaries to say, as they did in the Middle Ages in Europe, "do not touch" each other, do not get close, just in case your desire to get close to the Other will transform itself into a dangerous actual bodily connection in which two people become one.

Desire and lack in *The Grass Is Singing*

The Grass Is Singing depicts life in the rural countryside of then Rhodesia. The novel's main character, Mary Turner, is enslaved by the system she lives in as well as her own prejudice and inability to withstand the pressures of the narrow-minded white community of which she is a part. She finds herself an outsider also because of her inability to form lasting bonds with women. Lessing draws Mary's childhood as a deeply traumatic experience with her alcoholic father who, we discover later in the novel, may have actually sexually abused her. Her mother struggled to hold on to a semblance of normality against the background of deeply perverse and dysfunctional race relations in South Africa in the 1930s and 1940s in which black people were treated as sub-human and referred to by a number of abusive terms, "the native" being the least demeaning (but because of its historical connotations is deeply despised now in southern Africa). Mary is able to escape her family life and achieve a limited independence through her secretarial education, which enables her to get an office job. Lessing points out that Mary could have gotten a flat but chooses not to: she lives in a hostel for unmarried young women until she is 30.

It is then that she overhears her friends commenting that "there is something missing" in Mary; she probably will never marry, they say, because "she is not like that" (Lessing 2013: 40). The phrase "not like that", which is neither completely explained nor spelled out at the time or later in the book, is nonetheless an important indicator as it signifies Mary's lack — perceived and actual — of sexual potency. Lessing describes Mary's revulsion at her first fiancé's attempt at physical contact, which resulted in the engagement being broken off: "Next morning, she was horrified at her behaviour; she, who was always in command of herself, and who dreaded nothing more than scenes and ambiguity. She apologized to him, but that was the end of it" (ibid.: 42). But marry she must as convention demands, her sexuality, though, remains locked up entirely: "if a man kissed her (…) she was revolted" (ibid.: 44).

Isolated through her unthought-through marriage, precipitated by social convention and the demands it put on her, Mary ends up with an unsuccessful if honest farmer, Dick, her agency and life itself slowly stripped away from her. In terms of Lacanian "don't give up on your desire", this is a tragic example of a compromise stifling a development of an awareness of that desire. But, in addition, Mary lives in a patriarchal, racist society in which one's embodiment forever defines one's *ate* — destiny — as Lacan would say in *Seminar VII* after Sophocles.[10]

Mary is almost literally gagged, bound and tied down by her own inability to question the white male supremacy, despite knowing that it is wrong. If the black workers have no voice, she too has none. She questions the detail of it (why is her husband unsuccessful? why couldn't they farm tobacco? why can't she have a ceiling in her house?) without challenging the systematic issue with the society in which she lives. I argue that her voice is in fact never heard until the black houseboy, Moses, listens to her plea. The very white men she wants to imbue with power and authority are impotent in their inability to offer her solace, never mind *jouissance.* Her own unspoken desire for the exotic Other is rising at the same time that anger and a sense of hopelessness over the rigidity of her situation set in. Unfortunately for her, and for Moses — although in some way unavoidably because of her limited education and the systematic ideological brainwashing — Mary is also a racist.

Mary's contact with black people is very limited, but Lessing makes sure the reader realises that on a conscious level Mary has never questioned the systematic racism that surrounds her, mixed with limited Christian religiosity that controls "the natives" on a most basic level, attempting to regulate their desire, including a desire to question authority, and repressing their sexuality. Perhaps her refusal to see the black "natives" as people also offers her the safety of a boundary, defining who she could be but also fending off her sense of fear of her own unconscious sexual desire. The colonial "de-metaphorization" is in full swing here; nobody is able to express anything that actually might matter and would get close to expressing pain and inexpressible trauma. Nobody touches each other physically either: it is prohibited. Except Mary and Moses do, eventually, in fear and despair, with no words to accompany this touching as to give it meaning. This touching — the absence of and dread of it, as well as the inexpressible longing for it – drives Lessing's novel. This, then, (the touching and the lack of speech to frame it) I argue, is ultimately the source of Mary's death, and that of Moses, too.

What happens between Mary and Moses is unclear, perhaps "unrepresentable": there is a suggestion that Mary's slow descent into insanity is accompanied by her physical relationship with Moses. It is crucial to remember that their first bodily contact begins with an act of violence on the part of Mary: she hits Moses across the face with a whip, drawing his blood, for no reason at all (ibid.:119). It is worth pausing to see why she hit him: he asked for water in English. In a passage just a couple of pages earlier Lessing describes Mary's fury at the black workers' conversations in the local language she could not understand. Now she hits Moses for speaking the language she could understand: "Don't speak English" she says (ibid.: 119), meaning do not make me hear your pain, your need or your desire. The gesture of hitting Moses with a whip creates not just a moment of actual physical pain inflicted on the young man, but also offers a point of reference in terms of power structures echoing the colonial legacy: given that at the time of the incident it was already illegal to use a whip in labour relations in Rhodesia, her transgression is a critical moment in their relationship. She hits him, and his body is hurt. He does not complain; he contains her anger. He does not respond in violence then either, although she is afraid he might. But that whip and that hurt are between them forever.

The asymmetrical power relationship so characteristic of colonial relations is therefore reversed in the novel. There comes a point where power rests with the black man and not the white boss, for Moses is the holder of secret knowledge, one that is often also present in melancholia: he knows the lady of the house, Mary, is needy and not powerful, just like the master of the house, the utterly hopeless Dick. He knows Mary wants him and not her husband, and he knows they tolerate his power silently as if to admit and anticipate an inevitable change in the political structures of the land. Initially, Moses does not abuse this power, or rather he uses it to enter into a human relationship with Mary, which we do know involves touching and perhaps more. Mary is distraught by her own desire, cannot accept it, even in dreams; Moses is forever the Other, desirable in a way that is threatening, not ever comforting. In reality Moses tries to help her and her husband when Dick gets sick. He takes over the care of them both, including encouraging her to drink more water. He tells her to drink it and then suggests she lie down. When she fails to move, "He put out his hand reluctantly, loathe *to touch her*, the sacrosanct white woman …" (ibid.: 211). Allowing herself to be touched and "propelled across the room toward the bedroom," Mary feels she is living a nightmare "where one is powerless against horror: *the touch* of this black man's hand on her shoulder filled her with nausea; she had never, not once in her whole life, touched the flesh of a native" (ibid.: 211, *my emphasis*). He touches her, things change, bearing in mind Nancy's and Derrida's points made earlier: the touching changes everything, it always does, which is why it is frightening.

I venture that what happens in between Mary's whipping of Moses and Moses's killing of Mary is an attempt to communicate – mostly through non-verbal gestures – through touching and possibly through an actual physical intimate encounter: "possibly" as this is never spelled out. Arguably, it is this humanity of the black man – his powerful beauty embodied – against her faltering whiteness that is a contributing factor to her breakdown. She wants him too much to be able to resist it, but she is not able to "metaphorise" that either. Nobody talks about feelings, desires and fears: they remain a forbidden topic. Mary realises they must talk – too late – just before he kills her with a sharp blade, repeating her initial act of violence against him: with the intimacy "in between" these acts of violence forgotten, as not underscored by the words, and therefore losing its healing power. In part, Moses kills because he is jealous – but it is a complete tragic Lacanian "misrecognition": in truth he has nothing to be jealous of. The famous passage where Mary wants to talk to Moses just before he kills her but is still unable to enunciate the words is painful to read, even more than 65 years after they were written and 35 years after Zimbabwe's independence:

> She could see his great shoulders, the shape of his head, the glistening of his eyes. And, at the sight of him, her emotions unexpectedly shifted, to create in her an extraordinary feeling of guilt, but towards him, to whom she had been disloyal, and at the bidding of the Englishman. She felt she had only to move forward, *to explain, to appeal, and the terror would be dissolved.* (ibid.: 204, my emphasis)

To my mind, this passage, more than any other, confirms the notion of the inability to metaphorise (to represent the pain in words) spilling into violence: they cannot speak, they cannot communicate and so their final touch is a violent embrace. Incidentally, the drama of the book is totally internalised, and its translation to the film would have been very difficult in any event. Michael Raeburn is a white Zimbabwean now living mostly in Europe attempted it immediately after independence; his adaptation of the film (1982) is interesting because of the decisions he made, filling the gaps by attempting to "flesh out" Moses and "clarify" what goes on, by writing more lines for him to enunciate. In other words, he tries to give Moses more of a voice. To my mind this strategy fails completely as it also takes away that space of the uncanny mystery in which the viewer can herself symbolise the unrepresentable. Possibly inadvertently, the attempt to resolve the ambiguities ends up being more patronising to all involved. Mostly though, Raeburn is in no position to speak on Moses's behalf: he is a white Zimbabwean man, and however "nice" and liberal he might be, it can never be his place to write Moses's lines. He cannot find his voice for him. The voice has to be found in a different way.

Dambudzo Marechera

What would Moses sound like if he could express himself in Lessing's novel? It is of course a provocative question: nonetheless, the quest for the voice in post (de-) colonial literature has been an overwhelming consideration for scholars as well as artists. Gayatri Spivak famously framed it in terms of structures and systems in which the subaltern is allowed to speak (1988). This is not the place to discuss it in detail, but the systematic restraints notwithstanding, the role and place of an individual voice is what is at stake here. One could argue, as I have done, that in part Lessing's novel is an example of how a system gags individuals. How then in due course will the previously gagged individual find a voice with which to express the anger and trauma of her/his colonial loss and melancholia?

Iconic Zimbabwean writer and poet Dambudzo Marechera was born a couple of years after *The Grass Is Singing* was written, and one could argue that his whole oeuvre was engaged in just that: looking for the voice, finding it, struggling with its legacy, developing a way of expressing the pain. Some of his important books were published before Zimbabwe became independent in 1980 and many after that. He died too young in 1987. In contemporary Zimbabwe, Marechera is not taught at schools, despite his stature amongst scholars of the post (de-) colonial literature as well as the youngsters of the country who see him as a symbol of freedom and radical thinking. He is still considered too dangerous perhaps, too outrageous. Marechera's English is difficult, angry, violent, often obscene. It upset Zimbabwean and international readers alike at the time of publication and still does. However, its quality is also unassailable. Marechera became the first black author to receive the prestigious Guardian prize for literature in 1979.

He was, and arguably still is, the most important voice of his generation. I suggest that he fits into the category of Deleuzian "minor literature" (Deleuze and Guattari 1986), in which a writer – coming from a colonised context, like Kafka in the Deleuzian essay – chooses to write in the language of the coloniser in order to make it his own and in order to begin to come to terms with multiple traumas.

Marechera spent his short life advocating for the European literary traditions to be embraced by the African writers, rather then rejected:

> From early in my life I have viewed literature as a unique universe that has no internal divisions. I do not pigeon-hole it by race or language or nation (…) That Europe had, to say the least, a head start in written literature is an advantage for the African writer: he does not have to solve many problems of structure – the have already been solved. (…) The writer is a vampire, drinking blood – his own blood – a winged creature who flies by night, writing his books.
> *(Marechera in Veit-Wild [1992] 2004: 366–367)*

But he too was painfully aware of the physical non-touching legacy of the colonial times as well as the issue of which language one was allowed to speak and what

FIGURE 5.1 Ery Nzaramba and Sonja Wirhol from a shoot of *Flora and Dambudzo* (2014) Dir/Prod A.Piotrowska. DoP. Joe Njagu.

FIGURE 5.2 Shooting *Flora and Dambudzo*. Agnieszka Piotrowska and Joe Njagu. ©Agnieszka Piotrowska.

was allowed to be said at all. As discussed, in *The Grass Is Singing* Moses's attempts at speaking to Mary are thwarted by her: his using her language, English, is perceived as invasive, penetrating. "Don't speak English," she says to him repeatedly, which amounts to telling him not to speak at all.

In Marechera's work, in the poem below as much as in his prose, the taboo against speaking English is manifest by its inversion: a veritable cascade of words – poetic and obscene, slangy and literary – opens the floodgates, but their very force and urgency are powerful signs of the dam they first had to break. It is interesting here to consider that Marechera is attempting to overthrow the colonial legacy of "don't touch!" through the very means mentioned by Self and Khanna: by violence. It touches the reader too; you cannot be unmoved by the work. As Marechera is a writer, an artist, this violence is in his work indeed metaphorical. However, there is evidence that he was violent at times in his actual life (see Veit-Wild [1992] 2004: 175–176) and his early demise can be interpreted as being violent towards himself, abusing his body so systematically.

The poem below deals therefore with the familiar colonial prohibition "don't touch" and "don't speak". It is from Marechera's unpublished work *Choreodrama*. The section *Portrait of a Black Artist in London* was written in the Africa Centre in London in the early 1980s and published first in 1992. Marechera's "metaphorisation" here is indeed perhaps close to abject – the expulsion of the unbearable – angry here at the notion of a "distinct culture", which is somehow ethnic and therefore researchable outside the simple human norms. We know (Veit-Wild [1992] 2004) that British author David Caute found the manuscript after the author's death in Harare in 1987 and submitted it to Heinemann who turned it down repeatedly for publication. It was eventually published for the first time in a collection of interviews and contributions gathered, collated and edited by German scholar Flora Veit-Wild in 1992, who also was instrumental in having the work performed in Harare in 1992 as a performance of poetry, prose and music.[11]

The encounter with the Other that Marechera refers to here is heavily sexualised. He accuses the colonisers of over sexualising the touching but then he himself uses sexual metaphors to describe his anger: for example, of nearly ejaculating as a way of describing the sense of never quite succeeding in the post-colonial world. He can never feel at home – anywhere. He is always "fucked out of house and country". But, despite the despair, or because of it, he writes. He metaphorises: for us to read, analyse, remember, understand, to be touched by. The words full of rage have a potential healing power because they are also the holder of the truth enunciated, as Spivak would say, by the subaltern. Marechera demands to be heard as he ridicules the white colonial 'don't touch me' which he cites once more:

> Sure I'm bollocking off like I'm
> always being fucked out of house
> and country
> Christ, *don't touch me.*
> What the shit, I'm beating a hasty

retreat like I've always done in
your fucking history
I'm always going off somewhere but
you pigs always make sure I never
arrive
I'm always on the point of
ejaculation but you fucking bitch
of a country just fall dead asleep
snoring
You talk of culture that I come
from you know I got a distinct
culture and know too
But I don't want to know
You say I've got it this authentic
ethnic balls
But you don't give much room you
define it so small I can't get
in. ...

It is beyond the scope of this chapter to offer a close reading of the text above. The poem's extraordinary power lies in the attempt at naming both the very fear of the Other (a white coloniser's offensive assumption regarding the black people) and the rage of the poet who tries and fails to get through the polite consciousness of the white European culture. The poem's phraseology and imagined iconography is deeply offensive – he calls Britain 'you fucking bitch of a country' for example which can be seen as a desperate gesture and an attempt to reclaim some kind of control over the way the sublatern never "arrives" anywhere – another sexualised image. Marechera's work in its entirety is characterised by its violent and evocative imagery and expression of rage, which bursts out in the language of the coloniser, to touch the readers and change them.

Flora Veit-Wild and concluding remarks

I have tried in this chapter to present some ideas regarding touching and the voice in the colonial and post-colonial encounter, looking in particular at the relationship between Mary and Moses in Lessing's *The Grass Is Singing* and Dambudzo Marechera's poetry. I have suggested that the work's fictional nature can perhaps teach us more than any factual accounts of the pain and despair surrounding the near prohibition of any human communications between the colonisers and the colonised.

There is perhaps something else worth adding here: Prof. Flora Veit-Wild was a friend of Marechera in the early 1980s in Harare and went on to become his major academic advocate throughout the 1990s, editing his work and organising inter-national conventions to promote it in her capacity as the full professor of African Literature at the Humboldt University in Berlin. Only a couple of years ago she revealed the fact that she and Marechera were more than friends: they were lovers for a time in early 1980s in Harare and friends forever (Veit-Wild 2012). She was the only person by his bedside when he was dying in 1987. Veit-Wild then went on to do her doctorate and proceeded to publish work on Marechara's novels and poetry, including the *Sourcebook* ([1992] 2004), which has become the invaluable resource for any scholar researching the poet.

In her personal essay of 2012 she states:

> While I have generally come to be known as "The Marechera Authority", there have always been two narrative strands behind this persona: the public and the private. While the public one has stood out as strong and clear, my private life has been interlaced with love and passion, loss and pain, with illness and the threat of death. Yet, what I have gained is so much more than what I have endured that I am filled with gratitude and, I might add, with laughter. My personal involvement with Dambudzo Marechera has affected my professional life in a way I would never have expected. The many ironic twists, the tricks that Dambudzo played on me even posthumously, make our story an immensely rich and funny one, one that I now, more than twenty-five years after I came to know him, want to tell. (1)

Why did she reveal the intimate nature of their relationship, which after all she had kept secret for more than 25 years? When I asked her in person and by email in 2014 and in person in 2015, she said simply "it was the right thing to do".

To my mind, there is something quietly beautiful and bold in her gesture of reclaiming the secret passion that she had for this iconic Zimbabwean writer, one of the first clear voices of the post-Independence period. The relationship was very complex, according to Veit-Wild's writings, and the challenges of dealing with the (post) colonial legacy ever present in their very intimate relationship. There was an illicit element to her romance as she was married at the time. Her revelations aroused incredulity on the one hand amongst the academic community and a sense of disapproval on the other amongst the Zimbabwean community, whom I interviewed in early 2014 and 2015. And yet it was very clear to me why Flora Veit-Wild was disclosing the romance, perhaps to her own detriment as a scholar, as academics are meant to be objective, detached, fair handed, rather than passionate and emotionally and physically involved with the subjects of their research.

In some ways, for me Veit-Wild's announcement at last redeems the tragedy of Mary Turner and Moses, which in Lessing's book had to remain partially secret and unexplained to the public: a forbidden mystery, as the truth would have been impossible to accept by the general public, and too subversive. It is here that the notions of trans-generational loss and trauma, which translate themselves into challenges in everyday private relationships, could be considered again. Emma Wilson in her book, *Love, Mortality and the Moving Image* (2012), which I referred to above, draws from the seminal work of Barthes (1980 and 2002) but takes it elsewhere, towards the notion of touching and the notion of the language of mourning. She writes about artists, photographers and filmmakers who have created works involving words and images, still and moving, of their loved ones as a kind of "amorous relation to the dead. Art is imagined here as a form of pain management, offering the living a mode of absorption and distraction" (2012: 3). Wilson sees the process of creating as an attempt at *an embodied* encounter with the dead: a form of touching, if you like. More, she calls the endeavour "palliative care", which she proceeds to define as follows: "there is a wish to create a living relation to the dead one in memory work and commemorative acts" (ibid.: 11). For a writer, the process of writing is not dissimilar to that. The embodied encounter – the touching of the lost ones through the writing and through images, through a metaphorisation of the pain, through a profound re-narrating of the loss – is perhaps what both Lessing and Marechera were doing: in their different ways reclaiming the unrepresentable pain of the absence in the colonial encounter. It is also perhaps what Veit-Wild is doing, and perhaps in the de-colonial context, which is not just about systems but about personal pain, her bold statement is particularly important.

Wilson in her interrogation invites us to embrace an occasional need to make grief public and, through doing it, she invites us to be touched by the work. Wilson herself embraces the challenge: "I am opened up to what I cannot ever touch or hold. I am anxious about the act of looking, its violence, and its desire. I am led to imagine a longing for connection, a wish *to touch*, and to be held in return" (ibid.:141, my emphasis). It is that loss of an ordinary human interaction with which perhaps inter-race relationships are still coming to terms in Zimbabwe and elsewhere; it is that sadness and that longing, to my mind, that are being expressed in both Doris Lessing's and Dambudzo Marechera's work.

In addition, I wonder whether Flora Veit-Wild has agreed to my making a fiction film of her relationship with Marechera in order to try and hold onto his presence and their passion a little longer. As previously mentioned, Lacan says truth has always a structure of fiction, in the clinic and elsewhere; the pain is never representable in language but telling and writing stories and making films might help us get closer to metaphorising that pain and eventually to working through the loss.

Notes

1 Derrida focuses on Blanchot's story "The Instant of My Death" in which he recounts in a fictionalised way a moment when he was almost shot by a firing squad. Derrida said he had been talking about it for decades before writing the short story.
2 The details of his complex childhood can be found, for example, in Benoit Peeters's biography of the philosopher entitled *Derrida* (2012).
3 Here "*la pédagogie*" could be perhaps more elegantly translated as "education" or "scholarship" rather than "pedagogy".
4 I have used her concept extensively in my article (Piotrowska 2014a).
5 See Muzondidya (2005: 202) and the section on interracial marriages in Wang (2009: 206).

6 For cases of touching and healing see, for example, Zinter (2007).
7 See a discussion of the touch also in Stibbe (2011).
8 Azzedine Haddour, for example, in a talk given at UCL on 19th September 2015 during a seminar on Frantz Fanon took vociferous issue with Khanna's linking post-colonial violence to the issue of trying to find a voice. The talk has not yet been published.
9 For further discussion of whiteness as a signifier of dominance it is worth consulting Richard Dyer's classic *White*.
10 I have offered a thorough discussion of the Lacanian notion of "not giving up on one's desire" in my article (2014b) on *Zero Dark Thirty* (2012). That desire of course has nothing whatever to do with conscious wanting of material or other things; it is rather an unconscious element of our structure that makes us who we are and the denial of which constitutes a betrayal of a fundamental sense of the self.
11 This detail was confirmed by Veit-Wild in private correspondence on 20th December 2015.

References

Abraham, N. and Torok. M. (1994 [1972]) *The Shell and the Kernel: Renewals of Psychoanalysis*. Trans. T. Rand. Chicago: University of Chicago Press.

Barthes, R. (1980) *Camera Lucida*. Trans. R. Howard. New York: Hill and Wang.

Barthes, R. (2002) *A Lover's Discourse: Fragments*. Trans. R. Howard. London: Vintage.

Blanchot, M. and Derrida, J. (2000) *The Instant of My Death. Demeure: Fiction and Testimony*. Trans. E. Rottenberg. Paolo Alto: Stanford UP.

Butler, J. (2004) *Precarious Life: The Powers of Mourning and Violence*. London: Verso.

Butler, J. (2005) *Giving an Account of Oneself*. New York: Fordham UP.

Deleuze, G. and Guattari, F. (1986) *Kafka: Toward a Minor Literature*. Trans. D. Polan. Minneapolis: University of Minnesota Press.

Derrida, J. (1988 [1985]) *The Ear of the Other: Otobiography, Transference, Translation*. Trans. P. Kamuf and A. Ronell. Lincoln: University of Nebraska Press.

Derrida, J. (2001) *Writing and Difference*. Trans. A. Bass. London & New York: Routledge.

Derrida, J. (2002 [1967]). *De la grammatologie*. Paris: Minuit.

Derrida, J. (2005 [2000]) *On Touching. Jean-Luc Nancy*. Trans. C. Irizarry. Stanford: Stanford UP.

Derrida, J. and Stiegler, B. (2002) *Echographies of Television: Filmed Interviews*. Trans. J. Bajre. London: Wiley.

Fanon, F. (1975 [1952]) *Black Skins, White Masks*. London: Pluto Press.

Furlong, P. (1983) *The Mixed Marriages Act: An Historical and Theological Study*. Cape Town: Centre for African Studies.

Ibrahim, H. (1990) The Violated Universe: Neo-Colonial Sexual and Political Consciousness in Dambudzo Marechera. *Research in African Literatures* 21(2): 79–90.

Khanna, R. (2003) *Dark Continents: Psychoanalysis and Colonialism*. Durham: Duke UP.

Kristeva, J. (1982) *Powers of Horror: An Essay on Abjection*. New York: Columbia UP.

Lacan, J. (2006) *Écrits*. Trans. B. Fink. New York: Norton.

Lessing, D. (2013 [1950]) *The Grass Is Singing*. London: HarperCollins.

Marechera, D. (2004 [1992]) The African Writer's Experience of European Literature. In F. Veit-Wild (ed.) *Dambuzo Marechera: A Source Book on His Life and Work*. London: Africa World Press.

McClintock, A. (1995) *Imperial Leather*. London: Routledge.

Muzondidya, J. (2005) *Walking a Tightrope: Towards a Social History of the Coloured Community of Zimbabwe*. New York: Africa World Press.

Nancy, J. L. (2008) *Corpus*. New York: Fordham UP.

Peeters, B. (2012) *Derrida*. London and New York: Polity.

Piotrowska, A. (2014a) Mourning and Melancholia at the Harare International Festival of the Arts. *The Journal of African Media Studies* 6(1): 111–30.

Piotrowska, A. (2014b) Zero Dark Thirty – 'War Autism' or a Lacanian Ethical Act? *New Review of Film and Television Studies* 12(2): 143–55.

Roberts, S. (1993) Sites of Paranoia and Taboo: Lessing's *The Grass Is Singing* and Lessing's *July's People*. *Research in African Literatures* 24(3): 73–85.

Said, E. W. (2006 [1978]) *Orientalism*. New York: Vintage Books.

Scully, P. (1995) Rape, Race, and the Colonial Culture: The Sexual Politics of Identity in the Nineteenth-Century Cape Colony, South Africa. *The American Historical Review* 100(2): 335–59.

Self, W. (2015) A Point of View: Does Technology Make People Touch Each Other Less? Available from: http://www.bbc.co.uk/news/magazine-31026410. [Accessed 15 September 2015].

Spivak, G. (1988) Can the Subaltern Speak? In C. Nelson and L. Grossberg (eds.) *Marxism and the Interpretation of Culture*. Macmillan: Basingstoke.

Stibbe, M. (2011) *One Touch from the King Changes Everything*. Milton Keynes: Authentic Media.

Stoler, A. (2000) *Carnal Knowledge and Imperial Power*. Berkeley: U of California P.

Straker, G. (2013) Unsettling Whiteness. In G. Sevens, N. Duncan and D. Hook (eds.) *Race, Memory and the Apartheid Archive*. London: Palgrave.

Veit-Wild, F. (ed.) (2004 [1992]) *Dambuzo Marechera: A Source Book on His Life and Work*. London: Africa World Press.

Veit-Wild, F. (2012) Me and Dambudzo. *Wasafiri* 27(1): 1–7.

Wang, J. (2009) White Postcolonial Guilt in Doris Lessing's "The Grass Is Singing." *Research in African Literatures* 40(3): 37–47.

Zinter, P. (2007) *A Time to Heal: The Biblical Ministry of Divine Healing*. Maitland: Xulon Press.

Filmography

The Grass Is Singing (1982) Directed by Michael Raeburn. Zambia/Sweden: Chibote/SFI.

6
POINTING AT THE OTHER

Goran Vranešević

If we are content with simple beginnings, this chapter could be summarized with the question: why are people inclined to point with their finger? It seems a marginal topic where we could easily be content with a simple description of external features (movement of hand, outstretched finger) and/or inner motivations. However, the gesture of pointing is also pervaded by a certain discrepancy, where it seems that the above question doesn't sufficiently articulate the problem. The intended meaning of pointing is framed by the overlapping of language and body. It could be interpreted as neither one nor the other, but something that emerges in the junction of both, in the movement from one to the other. The focus will therefore lie in establishing an overview of this peculiar habit and in unravelling its basic characteristics, but let's begin with a detour: a commentary on a classical work of art.

Commissioned as a fresco sequence on the public part of the Vatican apartments, Raphael's *Scuola di Atene* is considered, together with Michelangelo's fresco *La creazione dell'uomo* in the Sistine Chapel, as the pinnacle of the Renaissance era. And perhaps it isn't a coincidence that both are designed around a certain gesture of habit. The center of the first fresco (its vanishing point) is conveniently occupied by two prominent central figures of ancient philosophy, Plato and Aristotle, who are commonly associated with two opposing modes of knowledge. Both are embodied in their gestures: one pointing at the sky's limitlessness and the other pointing at the physicality of presentness. We are thus confronted with a split in knowledge: a fissure between ideas (ἰδέα) where our heads can quickly get entangled in clouds of error and thus miss the truth of heaven and potentialities (*entelécheia*) of logic that are ultimately structured as dirty empirical jokes to be repeated by whoever coincidentally stumbles upon them.

This is the standard approach to interpreting the painting, but there is also a more interesting perspective, a slight speculative refocus of the theme. While the emphasis is usually on the meaning that permeates the gestures, a more formal look at the image reveals that Aristotle is pointing towards the ground, while Plato is pointing at the pointing gesture itself. But why is there a need for such an elaborate explanation? Wouldn't a simpler approach produce the same, or at least similar, results? Lacan articulated one part of the answer with his *bon mots* through which he formulated his fundamental theoretical insights. In one such moment, he deliberated on the question of what does one think with and adamantly maintained that "thinking is above all a thing of the feet" (Roudinesco 1999: 489), as they are the only point to touch the ground. Contrary to common sense, it is not an easy feat or a natural endeavor, if one is ready to conceive it as the "locus of both thought and touch" (Dolar 2008: 79). The idea behind Aristotle's downwardly directed hand is thus based on the difference created by touching: a topic that has been scrupulously interpreted by Mladen Dolar.[1] Meanwhile, the act of pointing itself, utilized specifically by Plato, remains mostly obscured.

There are ways of showing or elaborating on things: by description, thinking, using sense, or in some cases, by pointing. While the goal is to make the object of interest tangible, the natural inclination is to view these approaches as interchangeable. Although the act of pointing is present in every society, it is nevertheless the least conventionalized means of communication. It is incidentally also treated as a simple task with immediate implications: namely, highlighting the desired subject matter. However, its inherent aporias tell another story. Even though it requires a minimum of understanding, it is a highly complex operation. It is "dialogic, since it is *used* for someone else's interest; it serves to single out an entity which the recipient understands to be the referent; and it defines the direction of the referent as being away from the pointing hand, along an axis defined by it" (Tallis 2010: 17). Furthermore, it is inseparable from its social function. If we follow certain universal manners, then we shouldn't directly point at the matter at hand or even translate it into discursive signs. Simply put, it is not polite to point, as the pointed finger accuses the person of being guilty of something, if nothing else of being the right person. In this sense, there appears to be a clear transition from intention or motivation to the object of interest. The conclusion would therefore be that, unlike in speech, nothing is lost while pointing. And so, the simplest approach would then be to identify (with) the scope of Cratylian theory of communication and reject the idea that words are always in flux and thus unable to sufficiently render their intended meaning. We will proceed differently.

Our analysis will remain attached to the initially illustrated disjunction embedded into philosophy. If there is an inner junction between thought and touch, what does the pointing finger represent? And more significantly, what does one have in common with the other? A distance is present in both, so they are clearly related. If touching is something clearly tangible as a sensible experience that is even too near to us, pointing is immanently ostensible, unable clearly to grasp its object of interest. It is something infinitely distant and evades any palpable sense, even though it functions as one. It seems that a touch cannot miss, while the pointing gesture has to take a chance. But on the other hand, touching is a very delicate procedure, which can hardly be said about pointing. You can point at a general direction, and its meaning will nevertheless be clear by the context. Undoubtedly, there is an unexpected coincidence between touching and pointing, as if one triggers a reaction in the other and vice versa. However, it is not clear how this is possible.

Even if we are touching a surface with our finger, let's say our forehead, we are still performing a pointing gesture. It is in this sense that they are coupled, but also furthest apart. While touching makes an incision into the symbolic and then takes the same tools and stitches it together, pointing does the exact opposite. The movement highlights the subject's self-referentially—a recognition of oneself—whilst simultaneously exposing its nothingness. In this sense it is no surprise that touch was used as a magic proxy in analytical practice by Freud.[2] In the moments when words fail, touch produces a supplementary cure in analysis. With pointing, things are turned upside down. The subject foresees the impossibility of solely articulating a situation and uses the finger to separate itself from its closeness. But thereby it also produces an attachment that is symbolically registered as an empty space. This is why the pointing gesture (as a silent act) is always accompanied by words. It is a sort of double fixation: first on the lack of essence and then to the singularity of the situation that is pointed out. And contrary to what it seems, our pointed finger at the Other points to something in us. The connection between the two will be dealt with in greater detail later on, but the general idea is that pointing is an imaginary function that leaves a trace of the link between language and body. The cut-off finger in von Kleist's *Die Familie Schroffenstein* testifies to this. Tossed into the midst of two families gathered around the murdered bodies, it functioned as a clue to hidden entanglements. Our task will hence be quite straightforward: to show the inner tension that permeates the gesture of pointing, analyze the limits of language and body, and expound its relation to the Other.

A remark

So far, the argumentation is in line with one of Hegel's rarely mentioned insights, which is incidentally his basic discursive strategy: to begin in an inappropriate manner, not with the "thing itself" or methodological background but a remark. As such, it is not an aimless act as it leaves a mark behind, a trace indicating signification and with it the question: what kind of signification? All respective attempts to capture the truth behind such endeavors change the latter, as it is not separated from knowledge. We could linger on the implications of this prescription, but it is paradoxically also a prerequisite for establishing a systematic insight into the thematic field of pointing. And isn't the pointed finger in the last instance just that, a remark?

A few centuries ago, the Pope issued a Papal Bull announcing that the Jews had to convert or be expelled from Rome. Because of a huge outcry from the Jewish community, the Pope called in the chosen representative of the Jews, Rabbi Moshe, but was beforehand warned that he didn't speak Latin, while the Pope didn't speak Yiddish. As a solution, the Pope decided to communicate with the Rabbi by gestures. When the latter came into his chamber, the Pope showed three fingers. The Rabbi responded by pointing up to the ceiling with his middle finger. The Pope looked back and made a circle in the air. Rabbi Moshe pointed to the ground where he sat. The Pope then brought out communion water and a chalice of wine. So Rabbi Moshe pulled out an apple. As a result of this interchange, the Pope tore up the Papal Bull and permitted the Jews to stay. Later that day, the Cardinals met with the Pope asking what had happened. The Pope said, "First I held up three fingers to represent the Trinity. He responded by holding up one finger to remind me that there is still only one God common to both our beliefs. Then, I waved my finger to show him that God was all around us. He responded by pointing to the ground to show that God was also right here with us. I pulled out the wine and water to show that God absolves us of all our sins. He pulled out an apple to remind me of the original sin. As a result of this, I tore up the bull." Meanwhile the Jewish community was gathered around Rabbi Moshe. "How did you convince the Pope to let us be?" they asked. Moshe explained: "First he said to me that we had three days to get out of Rome, so I said to him, "up yours!" Then he tells me that the whole country would be cleared of Jews and I said to him, "we're staying right here." "And then what," asked a woman. "And then" said Moshe, "He took out his lunch so I took out mine." There are numerous variations to this joke, but what they all have in common is a general misunderstanding, and a joke is clearly a fitting solution to this unsolvable problem as it renders visible that there is something inherently uncertain in the act of pointing. Even if the interaction in the joke seems straightforward, the outcome couldn't be resolved by means of rational debate, but rather with the joke's "surplus-sense that was produced from that very failure or nonsense" (Zupančič 2008: 119). So, it was saved by a slightly different approach: by an insight that even a carefully gestured point points the wrong way, although producing an excess of content.

A joke is thus a perfect transitional point for expounding the cunningness of the gesture of pointing.[3] It does its work without effort, as a sort of automated generation of speech that is perturbed by a surprise pleasure when a symbolic signifier (spirit, thought, idea) suddenly emerges and retroactively rearranges the meaning of the situation at hand. When we point at an accused person in an argument, we immediately feel the impact of the act. Not by validating some arbitrary presuppositions but in the uneasiness, joy, or anxiety of the person who is pointed at.[4] It's as if the finger is directing our attention elsewhere, away from the (accompanying) rational narrative of the situation. The question is, where are we supposed to look for its meaning?

The pointing act functions by materializing an image out of nothing; this is why it is interwoven with a kind of spectrality. There is nothing to see but the gaze itself. There is nothing to hear but the words uttered with the pointing. But it nevertheless produces a satisfactory outcome. Still, it is not clear why this extra layer of symbolization persists in everyday relations? Pointing could be easily reduced to a medium with which it is unambiguously possible to present the object of knowledge or desire, but we will try to outline a certain impasse in its realization. In the same manner as a joke short-circuiting two mutually excluding realities, pointing discloses the distortion between the trauma of being and the nothingness of signification, an expression of the relationship between body and language.

While Freud does not elaborate a theory on pointing, there are certain clues present in his work that could give us an idea how to think this form of declaration. In *Aus der Geschichte einer Infantilen Neurose* (1918), he mentions two events, one fleetingly and the other more precisely.

The first example is the Wolfman's hallucination of the cut finger (see Freud 1966), which was accompanied not by pain, but with a sense of castration anxiety. The finger, a sort of enabler of touch, was mutilated, castrated, disabled, and unable to execute its function of inserting a cut into the social fabric. Because "the touch as cut is what defines the social, and hence the properly human dimension" (Dolar 2008: 90), such an act doesn't just present an inscription of the modern impasse, the impossibility of touch into the flesh (don't touch), but also a facet of pointing (don't point). It is a curious case, where even Lacan remains reluctant while interpreting it. In short, the whole scenario is predicated on a rejection of access to castration and therefore the access to the symbolic order: an act which is based not on a radical foreclosure but rather on the excess of signifiers that were not incorporated into the meaning of speech. Even though the surplus is usually interpreted as that which "is refused in the symbolic order [and] re-emerges in the real" (Lacan 1993: 13) or through a psychotic frame, this was not the case here as the "hallucination was the perception of the traumatic representation of castration as real" (Vergote 2003: 71). In this sense we could say that certain degraded symbolic leftovers become the primary fixating points that cannot be uttered, and this is also the reason the Wolfman was unable to recount this episode in speech. The aim was thus to establish some certainty. The proposition "what can be shown, cannot be said" (Wittgenstein 2001: 31) should therefore be slightly reformulated: that which cannot be said, can be shown. In this manner, we are operating with immediacy where we are caught in the here and now, where the positive moment of nowness (or hereness) is always-already negated with its disappearance. A (pristine) certainty is therefore irreversibly lost, but as such it produces the condition of possibility of speech. Such a detour through a seemingly psychotic landscape was needed to highlight how the inhibition of the finger, a failure to touch but also to point, unveils its embeddedness into the symbolic field.

Then there is also a more explicit example of pointing present in the aforementioned text. In the course of therapy, the Wolfman recalled a forgotten dream:

> He saw himself riding on a horse and pursued by a gigantic caterpillar. He recognized in this dream an allusion to an earlier one (...) In this earlier dream he saw the Devil dressed in black and in the upright posture with which the wolf and the lion had terrified him so much in their day. He was pointing with his out-stretched finger at a gigantic snail. The patient had soon guessed that this Devil was the Demon out of a well-known poem, and that the dream itself was a version of a very popular picture representing the Demon in a love-scene with a girl.
>
> *(Freud 1966: 101)*

Freud's own interpretation of the dream is exactly what one can expect from him. While the snail is presented as a symbol of female genitals, the demon's finger points to the last missing piece of the puzzle, which is sexuality. It is an intriguing approach, but the analysis will follow a different lead. I will inquire into the vagueness of the patient's explanation of his dreams that is left behind by Freud. He doesn't bother to explain the role of the central figure, the demon, who is in literature usually appropriated as a foreign body inherent to self-awareness. In pointing at the snail, the demonic finger not only expounds an inner kernel of the symbolic sphere, but also produces a disruptive effect in the symbolic, or rather bends it. The demon is also an intermediary between dreams and reality, the middleman that holds together the universality of the dreamland and the materiality of the picture. And following Freud's phrase that interpretation of dreams (or a deviation) is the royal road to knowledge about the unconscious (1961),[5] which is by Lacan's account structured like language, the out-stretched finger is thus clearly pointing to an impasse in the discursive universe (between being and nothingness).

Why must we talk while pointing?

There are no predefined situations that would encapsulate a meaningful codex of pointing. This is, in one form or another, evident in Hollywood films. They contain a curious imperative of self-censorship in regard to the suitability of issues such as sexual content, violence, substance abuse, and naturally, language (profanity, impudence, or other types of mature content). However, there is a gesture that is noticeably absent or just habitually overlooked from such lists, namely, the act of pointing. There is a long-lasting silent pact, which is a reflection of social preconditioning, to remove such acts from the film medium, not through unconditional suppression but by delimiting its role to certain genres and situations.[6] For this reason, it is only in the context of peril, danger, comedy, and exceptional situations, such as moments of demonstrating love or when a witness is obliged to point to the defendant in courtroom that the gesture appears. One could even argue that it is the camera itself that assumes the function of pointing. Such considerations lead us to the impression that there is a correct use of the pointing motion, usually permissible in strictly defined situations or uncanny scenarios.

It might seem that this is merely a dilemma of costumes. For example, Filipino tradition explicitly uses another medium: instead of pointing the forefinger to an object, one will shift his or her eyes towards the intended object, or "purse the lips and point with the mouth" (Morrison and Conaway 2006: 388). But the problem itself appears to lie elsewhere. In the fact that these acts cannot be articulated or reproduced by means of language, yet are nonetheless symbolically (linguistically) structured.[7] At the same time, it seems clear that the circumstances become complicated at the moment when we arbitrarily point at someone or thing, as a direct engagement with the sensual world clearly misses the point because there is a need to further articulate the intended purpose. Pointing is inadequate. That is why it appears one is always inclined to speak when pointing at something.

So, even if the medium of pointing is non-lingual, it is structured like language, as it always misses a pure desired outcome. The topic of pointing is thus inherently linked to language.[8] Or, to go a step further, as Lacan liked to put it, "the very foundation of interhuman discourse is misunderstanding" (1993: 163). Even a casual talk is never just a straight conversation, there is also the presence of the Other. That is to say, just like in dreams, we produce something that wasn't intended.

When using language we are not aware of the impact of our own words, and pointing similarly raises the question: what does it actually produce? In the vein of Heinrich von Kleist's reformulation of the French saying, "appetite comes while one eats (*l'appétit vient en mangeant*)", which he parodies and says, that "an idea emerges as one speaks (*l'idee vient en parlant*)" (see 1986), we could similarly say that speech is produced when one points. Being structured like language, this bodily movement also involves linguistic operations such as metaphor, which interrupts, suspends, or even cuts the consistency of the world, and metonymy where the meaning is endlessly postponed in the next signifier.[9] In both cases, we create an irreparable split between the imaginary experience and the field of inter-subjective symbolic network. Consequently, we have to ask ourselves what is then the specific function of pointing, if it is not capturing the reality itself? Where does it inscribe itself?

The pointed other

A long-lasting series of studies by the Max Planck Institute for Evolutionary Anthropology has proven that the act of pointing is (un)surprisingly an inherent human characteristic while its meaning remains vague. Infants use such a gesture to refer to various space-time categories and practices (future, past, present, absent, etc.). They are able to grasp the relevance of complex gestural meanings and in such manner constitute a shared experience of the world with other subjects. In contrast, primates are fixated solely on the gaze, tracking where another individual is looking; they are incapable of performing pointing gestures, although they have the ability or physical flexibility to perform the gesture (Tomasello 2006: 506–524). Whereas a primate can "discern simple signalization of the location of objects, thus, partaking in an imaginary construction of the image" (Lacan 2005: 19–20), human communication is subjected to the symbolic dimension. While the role of language is unique to homo sapiens' construction of the world, the need for it to be complemented by pointing is puzzling. Even if we envision pointing in its simplified mode that precedes the practice of formed language constructions, its existence is possible only through language. It has to be thought of as immersed in this symbolic edifice. Children are born into a preformed linguistic universe, which is in psychoanalysis commonly referred to as the big Other. The essence of the latter can be deduced from the very end of Lacan's *Seminar on "The Purloined Letter"*, where he famously declared that "a letter always arrives at its destination" (2005: 30). It is necessary to bear in mind that true addressees are never flesh-and-blood others, but the Other, the symbolic order itself. "The moment the sender 'externalizes' his message, delivers it to the Other, is the moment the Other takes cognizance of the letter and thus disburdens the sender of responsibility for it" (Žižek 2007: 10). One could argue that the act of pointing is no exception, as it is embedded into the same logic.

We can elaborate the Other's willingness to be pointed at more precisely if we delineate its dual nature. First, the functioning of the Other is paramount to the subject but cannot be directly interacted with. Strictly speaking, the Other is not another name for the symbolic order as it is upholding this very realm, functioning as the guarantor of signification: a necessary supposition without which the subject would fade away. As such, it produces effects even if we don't judge ourselves against it and ignore it. It inconspicuously lingers in the background and constantly addresses our inner kernel of being, never leaving us be. Consequently, the subject seems to be lost to the necessity of predetermined and all-encompassing network of rules, costumes, and habits, which permanently presuppose a meaning. In this way, it affects or even dictates our every movement and speech, operating as a Godly ventriloquist, simultaneously compelling us to disavow it.

Yet the Other is nothing more than a presupposition, a fiction working only insofar as individuals believe in it and therefore functions according to pre-established practices. Irrespective of its ubiquity, we as speaking beings are bound to the appearance of its non-existence. Hence Lacan's guide to understanding its anti-nomical role: *L'Autre manque* or the Other does not exist, though it still functions. Even though its omnipotence is real, it is a broken one. But, and this is essential, this flaw is in the last instance the structural principle of the Other. In failing, it reveals a gap, a dwelling of the unconsciousness, which is where the structure slips. It is also the place where desire is born (see Lacan 2005: 287). There is a convenient example concerning the oblique nature of these concepts.

In one of the most famous propaganda posters from the early twentieth century, the image of Uncle Sam addressed the passers-by and demands they must unconditionally respond to the call: "Your country needs YOU". This message is intensified with his extended pointed finger. Observers being addressed by the poster, regardless of their will and/or intention, are enchained by its signification, while the pointing gesture misses them. If everything is already present in the slogan, why is it then necessary to add the image of pointing? Even though the attempt to capture the positive patriotism of the masses fails, it does not lead into its opposite state of treachery, but into the sublation of the immediate "here and now" through negation and thus returns to the starting position that no longer has the same character as in the beginning. What initially expresses the spirit of the time ("Your country needs YOU") exposes in the next moment its perverse side ("I Want YOU"). "We can see that the demand is actually based on a desire, while its truth articulates itself in the very distortions of the 'factual accuracy' of my speech" (Žižek 1997: 148).

It may seem that such a maneuver is meant to signal an idea that the subject is merely an afterthought of a symbolic process: a view mostly associated with Althusser's concept of interpellation introduced in his essay "Ideology and Ideological State Apparatuses" (2001). Simplified to the utmost, the theory presupposes an interaction between an individual and a subject who embodies the social injunctions of the Other. The sole purpose of the latter is to address the individual with a simple "Hey you". By answering or turning around, the individual acknowledges this call. Knowing its meaning, he or she recognizes him/herself as a subject ("It is I"). This is only possible because the subjectivity was always-already present in the symbolic. The subject's emergence is thus preceded by a structural necessity that substantiates it, a process of which the subject is not aware.

There is also another reading, closer to the topic of pointing. In his eleventh seminar, Lacan introduces the well-known parable of the dream of a butterfly (1977: 76). In it, the ancient Chinese skeptic Choang-tsu poses the question of how, after waking from a dream of being a butterfly, he can't tell whether he is Choang-tsu who has woken from the dream of being a butterfly or the butterfly now dreaming he is Choang-tsu. Althusser's model solves this riddle by essentially assuming that there must be a material background in which we believe. This is paradoxically achieved by repetitive praxis and not true inner belief: "Kneel down and you will believe!" (cf. Pascal 1958: 250).

The solution to the aforementioned quandary of self-recognition is therefore supposed to be entailed in a gesture of subjectivization. Yet, there is something amiss here. As already elaborated, the subject presupposes that it has to respond and recognize itself with the calling. What is missing is that the subject must first assume the Other's existence. In doing so, the formal gesture of belief is not merely directed at a pre-established medium but is a gesture that enables the emergence of the Other. It is such a supposition to which the subject addresses his discourse. While the subject gains a certain independence from recognition, he or she posits an existence anterior to him/herself, which is lost but also never existed. Consequently, self-identity is never fulfilled, always lacking its being. Something can fail in the mechanism of interpellation and in this way incapacitates the subject's ability to be whole.

The failure of the subject to accept unquestioningly the Other's call by surrendering his/her own being points to a blind spot in signification or meaning. While such a conceptualization irreversibly leads to the loss of self-sufficiency, psychoanalysis inversely embraces the tradition of the cogito but not without due consideration. In psychoanalysis, the issue of subjectivity is not tied to the question of (mis)recognition (or the philosophical consciousness) that is inherently a product of the Imaginary dimension. Undeniably such an approach to subjective genesis has its merit, but it is rather Lacan's insistence on the symptomatic point of non-recognition—the declaration "this is not me", as an integral part of subjectivity—which is relevant for understanding the act of pointing. The moment we recognize ourselves as the addressees of the call of the ideological Other (state, religion, nation, money, and so forth), when this call "arrives at its destination" in our inner being, we spontaneously misrecognize the fact that it is only in the act of recognition that we become that as which we have recognized ourselves. It is essential to keep in mind that one doesn't recognize oneself in the call because one is its addressee, one becomes its addressee the moment one recognizes oneself in it. This is also the reason a letter always reaches its destination: "because one becomes its addressee when one is reached" (Žižek 2007: 12). It is in this context that we have to read the pointing gesture. By pointing we do not just address the Other, because the Other also addresses us. It is the one pointing and thereby binding the sender to follow. The letter was not alone; it was accompanied by a slip, a slip of the finger.

A slip of the finger

So far, I have formulated different aspects of the pointing maneuver. However, it is only now that I come to the crux of the matter. The nearest proxy for expounding the inner mechanism of the relationship between the pointed finger and the Other is Freud's case of the *Fortsein* game in *Jenseits des Lustprinzip* (1968). In the standard reading of the game, the thrown object (spool)—which is retrieved by a thread—is supposed to simplify the trauma of the mother's absence and reappearance. The anxiety of the disappearance is thereby corrected or sublated. Such a reading contains seeds of truth, but the real problem revolves around the cause of desire,[10] the thing that the mother desires in him: as such it is a piece of externality in the subject that ties him to the m(Other), more commonly labeled as object. The structure of the game is subverted; it is a method by which the subject escapes the suffocating confines of the mother's *jouissance*. In a way, the child stages his own disappearing act. By throwing the object, the child constructs a pathway to his own desire. "The thrown spool belongs neither to the mother nor to the child (...) it is an intersection of the two sets" (Žižek 2003: 59) but something more as the sum of both. In short, the demand to circumvent the mother's desire is not realized as a successful separation but as a surplus in the form of a speech act (*Fort! Da!*).

Reading this great cultural achievement in terms of pointing, the logic appears to coincide. Isn't the outstretched finger just a re-enactment of this game of subjectivity? In throwing the spool, the child is working out the impasse of his being. He resolves it only through a bypass: with an externalization and a return to himself (identification) effectuated as "its own straying away from itself" (Dolar 2013: 230). The spool represents, or rather functions, as a sort of a prerequisite of the child's symbolic world, by evoking the difference of his being. In a similar sense, the finger pointing maneuver reiterates this act of alienation in the realm of the Other.

By reaching out into the world, one doesn't just encapsulate a piece of reality but rather brings to light a lapse in causality (in one's own being). The extended finger fails to grasp directly the intended object, as it impossible to make an explicit correlation between the intention, the pointing move, and the desired object itself located in the certainty of the tactile and visual field. Something slips in the process, but it nevertheless evokes the Other. This slight touch—which is archived in the form of condensation and displacement and is incidentally the ground whereon dreams operate—incurves the Other and touches upon a basic insight.

One could easily argue that the pointed finger just coincidentally slips and touches upon an impasse. Rather, the gesture itself is the slip. We view the pointed finger as a mechanism for a simplified interpretation of circumstances, while in fact the procedure is plagued by a self-induced imbroglio. As such, it is of the same fabric as the demon from the Wolfman's dream, unhinging the symbolic edifice and thus bending the realm of reality. In a way it could also be said that there is a speculative dimension present: the pointing finger is a slip that enables the subject to peek behind the curtain of its own subjectivity, where it can behold its own lack and the Other's desire, foreign to its user. Hence, one has to compensate and repeat the intention with speech, respond and recognize oneself and thereby construct a fantasy: the truth of the Other.

This is something that demonstrates very well the ambiguity of the Other. It is simultaneously the bearer of existence and its reaper. However, the problem is not the existence of the Other but our own existence. And pointing is practically a repetition of this impasse which produces *jouissance*.[11] In pointing, the finger slips and misses the intended target and simultaneously produces a repetition in the guise of speech. The interaction could be summed up in the following manner: the subject shamelessly asks the Other, "What do you want from me?" Although the answer is returned, it is not an expected one. It replies with a question "What do *you* want?" and thereby pushes the subject towards its own desire. The interaction does not end there, as the subject stubbornly continuous: "What do you want from me?" Given that the subject's desire is the desire of the Other, the question posed is directed/pointed at the object of desire or a lack in his being.

In a certain sense, the act of pointing can be understood as a backwards movement. While the desired object—at which one can point—seems like a neutral entity, there is of course a twist present. We cannot point at something without its pointing back at us. At first, the gesture necessarily fails, touching upon a lack inherent in the Other. Subsequently, the failure itself demands a repetition in the guise of speech, which points back at our own desire. The pointed finger enables a brief traversal of the fantasy, a slight bend, which is enough to produce a speech effect, a verbalized repetition that retroactively establishes a certain meaning. The subject aims at a preconceived image and misses it but hits the inner core of its own subjectivity. Strictly speaking, it becomes apparent that pointing is an effect that retroactively posits its own cause. It doesn't matter what is intended with pointing, as this "will have been determined"; what comes afterwards gives meaning to what happened beforehand. Between one and the other, there is a cut, a reshaping of previous events, and an emergence of meaning. The latter is therefore not grounded in some material or idea, but on a practice of retroactive denotation. This also confirms the argument that the pointing gesture is an integral part of subjectivity: the reason being that the pointed finger itself is already inscribed into the pointed object, functioning as a slip. As such, it is an effect of the Other but not an unnecessary one. Quite the opposite: it is an indicator of the minimal difference on which the symbolic structure of reality is premised.

Let us summarize: what is the point of pointing? Ultimately there shouldn't be any doubt left that pointing cannot be explained with regard to intentions or natural inclinations. It is a curious function. Taking into consideration the concretization of the concept of pointing, we saw that the truth of pointing (at a certain phenomenon) resides in the intersection of two interpretations: on the one hand, pointing as a retroactive activity of self-differentiation and, on the other, as a curvature of the symbolic edifice. The point is to think of their manifestations together, a cut and a swerve. When pointing at a thing, we do not try to touch its pre-established meaning, because meaning is not prefabricated. Meaning is in this case only grasped through a misunderstanding and *post facto* formation based on the gesture of pointing. To point is, therefore, not to point at a meaning grounded on some substantial image (*Urbild*) that fills the entire canvas of reality, but on a practice of retroactive denotation.[12] It is as if the repetition of this gesture requires subsequent confirmation of intentions. This sets in motion a continuous affirmation of a failed encounter. Although every signifier is destined to signify nothing, this consequently doesn't presuppose a state where nothing is signified. On the contrary, the more pointing (or words) miss and signify something unintended, the more the subject's own being is solidified.

Pointing can therefore be understood through a literal reading of the pirate motto "Take what you can, give nothing back", made famous by the *Pirates of the Caribbean: The Curse of the Black Pearl* (Verbinski, 2003), which can be best summed up in psychoanalytic terms: interpret, look for clues, little slips of tongue, metaphors, and symptoms, but do not touch the nothing that is my being. It is the lack, or bend, in the Other (*jouissance*) that institutes the relation to one's own body. And isn't the whole point of pointing already evident in the title of Freud's classical work *Traumdeutung*, where Dreams (*Traum*) are coupled with pointing (*Deuten*), with dreams structured around a navel or a gateway to the unknown (*Unerkannt*)[13] and the finger bending the fantasy, which gives consistency to what is usually referred to as reality?

Notes

1 Thought can be only touched through a mediation of an object, and inversely thought is possible with a touch of an object. For a detailed interpretation of touching, see Dolar (2008) and Nancy (2008).
2 See Freud (1961: 97). He thereby enabled the analytic community to think about its practical role: as a material act of performing thoughts and desires for the observers; as a stage in the libidinal development, acting as an all-pervasive power of thought; or as a mediatory in the form of "touch, called in at the point where the word fails" (Dolar 2008: 97).
3 See Hegel on "cunning" (1986: 190).
4 It is clear that pointing is not an innocent function, as explicitly depicted in the *Invasion of the Body Snatchers* (Philip Kaufman, 1978), where the extraterrestrial beings alert others that a human is among them by pointing at her or him and emitting a shrill scream.
5 Dreams are not merely a neutral process of translating thoughts, because something is constantly added: a desire that dislocates, deforms, and transforms the content without having an original appearance. The role of interpretation is therefore not to grasp some real meaning behind dreams and words but to read the analysand's discourse in the same manner as if reading a text.
6 For instance, the pointing finger is often used by children as a sign for a gun. The most famous example is Travis Bickle in Martin Scorsese's *Taxi Driver* (1976). After the climatic shootout, his last act is to motion with his forefinger to his bloody forehead and trigger it. The symbolic field he occupied broke down, so there was nothing else to point at but himself.
7 Belonging to a society imposes on us certain norms and practices, such as love for our parents, but also aims to uphold the appearance of free choice. In reality, there is none. We must blindly oblige.
8 The related German words *Deuten* (to explain, interpret, but also to point) *Deutbarkeit* (interpretability) and *Bedeutung* (meaning, importance) clearly attest to this.
9 Pointing doesn't have to be understood in the context of immediate physical consideration, as it has an extent as wide as the metaphorical use of the phrase "to illustrate this point".
10 As mentioned, desire is not to desire a certain thing but the impossibility for a word to work as a word. Cf. Lacan on desire in "The Direction of the Treatment and the Principles of its Power" (2005).
11 The child establishes an object that represents a signifier that is always-already missing. His response is to try again; maybe the second time he will be successful. The spool is thrown again and again, the child always finding some enjoyment in failing, but thereby also playing with his own constitution.
12 In this context, it becomes clear why the psychoanalytic trauma is not conceptualized as a reflection of a shocking and unexpected event that shakes the stable everyday picture of the world, but as an inconsistency of meaning, which is usually constructed several years after the actual experience.

13 More precisely, the navel to the dream is an intertwined cobweb of the symbolic realm, where the hard kernel of the Real (the object cause of desire hidden in the Other) and the surplus signifier touch.

References

Althusser, L. (2001) *Lenin and Philosophy and Other Essays*. New York: Monthly Review.

Dolar, M. (2008) Touching Ground. *Filozofski vestnik* XXIX: 79–100.

Dolar, M. (2013) Tyche, clinamen, den. *Continental Philosophy Review* 46(2): 223–39.

Freud, S. (1961) *Gesammelte Werke IX. Totem und Tabu*. Frankfurt am Main: S. Fischer Verlag.

Freud, S. (1966) *Gesammelte Werke XII. Werke aus den Jahren 1917–1920*. Frankfurt am Main: S. Fischer Verlag.

Freud, S. (1968) *Gesammelte Werke XIII. Jenseits des Lustprinzips / Massenpsychologie und Ich-Analyse / Das Ich und das Es*. Frankfurt am Main: S. Fischer Verlag.

Hegel, G. W. F. (1986) *Jenaer Schriften 1801–1807*. Frankfurt am Main: Suhrkamp.

von Kleist, H. (1986) Über die allmähliche Verfertigung der Gedanken beim Reden. In *Werke und Briefe in vier Banden*. Frankfurt am Main: Insel Verlag.

Lacan, J. (1977) *The Seminar, Book XI. Four Fundamental Concepts of Psychoanalysis*. New York: W. W. Norton & Co.

Lacan, J. (1993) *The Seminar, Book III. The Psychoses*. New York: W. W. Norton & Co.

Lacan, J. (2005) *Écrits*. New York: W. W. Norton & Co.

Morrison, T. and Conaway, W. A. (2006) *Kiss, Bow or Shake Hands*. Avon: Adams Media.

Nancy, J. L. (2008) *Noli me tangere*. New York: Fordham UP.

Pascal, B. (1958) *Pensées*. New York: E. P. Dutton & Co.

Roudinesco, E. (1999) *Jacques Lacan: An Outline of Life and History of Thought*. New York: Polity Press.

Tallis, R. (2010) *Michelangelo's Finger: An Exploration of Everyday Transcendence*. London: Atlantic Books.

Tomasello, M. (2006) Why Don't Apes Point? In N. J. Enfield and S. C. Levinson (eds.) *Roots of Human Sociality. Culture, Cognition and Interaction*. Oxford & New York: Berg.

Vergote, A. (2003) Freud and Lacan on Neurosis and Psychosis. In J. Corveleyn and P. Moyaert (eds.) *Psychosis: Phenomenological and Psychoanalytical Approaches*. Leuven: Leuven University Press.

Wittgenstein, L. (2001) *Tractatus Logico-Philosophicus*. London: Routledge.

Žižek, S. (1997) Desire: Drive = Truth: Knowledge. *Umbr(a)* 1: 147–52.

Žižek, S. (2003) *The Puppet and the Dwarf: The Perverse Core of Christianity*. Cambridge: MIT Press.

Žižek, S. (2007) *Enjoy Your Symptom! Jacques Lacan in Hollywood and Out*. London: Routledge.

Zupančič, A. (2008) *The Odd One in: On Comedy*. Cambridge: MIT Press.

Filmography

Invasion of the Body Snatchers (1978) Directed by Philip Kaufman. USA: Solofilm.

Pirates of the Caribbean: The Curse of the Black Pearl (2003) Directed by Gore Verbinski. USA: Walt Disney Pictures.

Taxi Driver (1976) Directed by Martin Scorsese. USA: Columbia Pictures.

PART III

Impossible poetics

7

IS POETICS A FICTION ABOUT TRUTH – IN A POEM? SOME REMARKS ABOUT PAUL CELAN

René Rasmussen

This text is an attempt to examine the relationship between poetics and poems regarding four poems by Paul Celan and some ideas about truth.

What is truth?

First a few words about how we may understand truth. We must not understand truth in the way positivism does, namely, as a positive, present and available fact connected to a given thing or phenomena. We can of course talk about a certain objective truth connected to given things or phenomena: for example, gravity, the existence of trees, or of black and white people. However, the problem, as we know it with regards to gravity, is that the referent included in such an objective truth is never unequivocal. The law of gravity only exists under certain circumstances, and as a law it makes no sense if we do not include at least a globe and a body. But where is gravity: in the globe, in the body or in their relationship? And do body and globe know the law of gravity? There is no simple answer to these questions. It becomes even more confusing when talking about blacks and whites, in so far as the words black and white belong to a code of colours, not to mention all the possible racist or biological discourses connected to various colours of skin.

Hence, the referent is never unequivocal, and the objective truth can hardly be distinguished or separated from a given discourse. Such a discourse can be physical, biological or racist, but in any case a given discourse excludes some statements and opens towards others. Talking about gravity, we do not talk about a god in the apple, which Newton saw falling from a tree, or about a god on earth, on to which the apple falls. When some Danes proclaim "Danishness", because they are born and raised in a country named Denmark, they do not talk about the somewhat fictive correlation between a nationality and a birthplace. The power connected to their nationalistic discourse excludes a further look at the fictive aspect associated with it. Such a fictive aspect is both a created as well as a creative element, which is not guaranteed by any positivistic idea about a so-called objectivity. Every kind of discourse contains a certain power, a certain inclusion and exclusion of possible statements; and its possible consistency is built on at least one element that is not included in such statements. Such an element is considered unnecessary to debate in the discourse. So a given discourse may perhaps be consistent, at a certain level, but is also incoherent at another level.

Furthermore, if a subject meets a so-called given truth, it often becomes confused. Being a passenger in a car accident, where the car falls off a bridge, or being black and surrounded by members of a violent nationalistic group of white men gives rise to such confusion or even anxiety or anger. At the moment the car falls or when a violent attack occurs, any discourse collapses. The situation has no words, or the subject meets the Real, as Jacques Lacan calls it.

Connected to the Real we also have fiction. Whatever we may say about the Real, it is never the truth, but just an (impossible) representation of the Real. We can only represent or imagine the Real, because it never can be grasped or understood in any discourse. Such a representation – imagination – is also fiction about or of the Real, but a rather different kind of fiction compared to the inherent incoherency connected to a given discourse. Language can never describe the Real. The trauma connected to meeting the Real will forever shake language, although it may shake less, the more distant the trauma is.

On the other hand fiction in a discourse is something preventing the discourse from shaking too much or something that gives the discourse a certain stability. Fiction in the discourse is linked to the idea of a word saying something true about something different from itself. This is a specific fiction, which makes us believe in the words we hear, although we may know that the person uttering them is lying. Fiction makes the semblance of word, a semblance connecting for example a name to that which is named, while fiction about the Real is an impossible attempt to represent: what cannot be represented and what is unbearable in the life of the subject. Fiction in a discourse prevents language from shaking too much. Fiction about the Real is fiction about what shakes any discourse.

Hence there exist two kinds of fiction: the first is the (impossible) attempt to grasp the Real and the second is connected to the incoherency of a given discourse. Fiction connected to poetics is different from fiction connected to poems: in so far as poems (also) are "representations" of the Real, while poetics is a discourse, although such a discourse may contain some poetical aspect. Hence, the answer to the question "Is poetics a fiction about truth – in a poem?" is that of course poetics is fiction (linked to a discourse) about truth in poems, which are about the Real. But we can never say everything about the Real, the truth about it. We can never express the truth, because there are not enough words, as Lacan says in

Télévision (1973: 9). This is why we are forced to read or write poems or to see a psychoanalyst, so we can elaborate or change our fiction about the Real and thereby hopefully reduce the weight or the trauma of the Real in our life.

Paul Celan

Celan was born in 1920. His parents were German-speaking Jews in Czernowitz in the Romanian region Bukovina. In the 1930s, this region of Romania was strongly anti-Semitic, and in 1941 Germany invaded. Celan was in a working-camp in Romania in 1942–43. His parents died in another working-camp, Michailowka (Ukraine), in 1942; his father died of typhus, and his mother was shot. The death of his mother (with whom he often spoke German) marked him very much, and Celan saw himself as "the child of a dead mother" (see Maulpoix 2009: 33). In 1945 he wrote the very famous poem: "*Todesfuge*" ("Fugue of Death").

In 1948, Celan emigrated to Paris and later became a French citizen but wrote most of his poems in German. He married a French painter, Gisèle de Lestrange, in Paris. Even though they stayed together until the very end of Celan's life, it was not an easy marriage. From 1965 Celan was struck by many crises of delirium, and he attempted suicide in 1967 (ibid.: 34). On the night between the 23rd and 24th of November 1965, he tried to stab and kill his wife. Shortly after, he was committed to a psychiatric hospital in Paris for about six months. For the rest of his life, he was in and out of psychiatric wards. Not only did he have problems with his wife, but he was also accused of plagiarism by the widow of his friend Ivan Goll, who was a poet as well. These accusations, which were not true, were repeated twice by the widow, in 1953 and in 1960, and Celan felt he was being persecuted. He committed suicide, around the 20th of April, 1970, by drowning in the Seine, Paris, where he was found days later. The intention of these few biographical remarks is not to say whether his stays at psychiatric wards and his suicide were determined by his psychotic structure or by the Holocaust (although they were probably shaped by both) but to underline that there is no doubt that the Real plays an important role in his life and in his poems.

The Meridian and four poems

Let us first take a look at his poetics in *The Meridian* and then at four poems. The poetics of Celan, as he develops it in his famous speech *The Meridian*, can be seen as an essay on anti-metaphoric resistance. Here Celan talks about art as being child-less, although he insisted on writing his poems in German. Is a childless child also a homeless child? I am not sure what the answer may be to this question, but at least there is not much home in poetry as such. Rather his poems seem to be a home for the homeless, for that which stays homeless.

Furthermore, Celan underlines, that art is also a problem, an "eternal" problem (2003: 38). This problem is connected to a retreat from the canny (*das Heimliche*) and a journey towards *das Unheimliche*, the uncanny, which turns away from human beings. "The *Unheimliche*, the estrangement, is the estrangement of the human given the meaning. It hence affects existence. It derealizes it" (Lacoue-Labarthe 2004: 71). Art is connected to a strangeness, and thereby it seems to exclude the I or to create an alienated I (Celan 2003: 46). The subject is fundamentally alienated in poetry.

However, the poem talks: it talks on behalf of itself and only on behalf of itself. But doing this, it is not so much a question about talking about strangeness, but that the poem talks about something different, something other than itself. Poetry talks on behalf of something totally different. A poem hence creates a different world, not only a strange world, but an irreducible otherness (which also constitutes an alternative to the homogeneity in Nazism, where there was no place for a heterogeneity including the Jews). Celan uses the word *Das Andere* in the original text to stress this otherness, which can be translated both as the other (the other subject) and as the opposite of the same, namely otherness (I am using both possible translations or connotations).

The poem screams and stretches out to move from an *already-no-more* to its *still-here*. The poem exists between an *already-no-more* and a becoming *still*. For example, a poem – this is an obvious example in Celan's poems – may talk about the dead of the Holocaust, but, of course, without mentioning it, and these dead are *already-no-more*, and still (*still-here*); they are there, in so far as the poem attempts to give life to them (ibid.: 49).

This movement between an *already-no-more* and a *still-here* is also an attempt to meet the radical otherness, which explains why Celan talks about the loneliness of the poem (ibid.). The poet, the writer, follows the poem to the meeting – the unsayable or secret meeting – with the totally different, with the other. Everything and every human in a poem is a shaping or an elaboration of this Other. A poem, including such a meeting with the otherness, constitutes a conversation with the otherness, but often a despairing conversation.

Here the I meets a "you", if we understand the "you" as the absolute other. This meeting between the I and you, in the absolute otherness, may explain the emerging of the often rather strange "we" in many of Celan's poems.[1] Or the I, this strange I, which is neither an imaginary I or a shifter, meets or is presumed to meet the Real incarnated in a you (although Celan does not use the words "the Real"). The meeting between the I and the Real – for example, the dead – constitute the "we" in many of his poems. For example in "*Blume*" from *Sprachgitter* (1959), the I speaks to an unnamed person evoked by the eye. Together they create darkness, but they also find the word "flower", while their eyes give for or "take care / of water" (quoted in Szondi 2003: 110). The word "flower" seems to be created out of the meeting between the seeing eye (I) and the blind eye. The I meets the Real (represented by the blind eye or the stone), and out of this meeting we get "flower", which also can be seen as a metaphor for the poem. Hence, the poem is also created out of this meeting. Celan's poems search, according to his poetics, the strange place, or this absolute other, where the I meets the Real. This is not possible, according to Celan's ideas, if the poems use figures and tropes.

Although a poem that really may create a meeting with the Real does not exist, a poem avoiding figure and trope seems to be close to the idea of giving existence to a non-existing place for absolute otherness. This explains the resistance to tropes and figures in *The Meridian* (cf. Räsänen 2007). But what about his famous "*Todesfuge*" from *Mohn und Gedächtnis* (1952), where there seem to be many tropes or figures? Here "a grave in the air" is literally the ashes from the dead in the gas chamber (quoted in Felstiner 1995: 31). On the other hand, Celan's idea also insists that, for example, "black milk" is not a metaphor (ibid.), which however leaves us with the question about this black milk: Was the milk in concentration camps black? And furthermore: Did the man in the camp have a snake? And is death really a master from Germany? These words cannot escape a metaphorical interpretation, although Celan's idea in *The Meridian* is that, in a poem, "the words *mean to be* untransferable, untransportable, unmetaphorizable" (Räsänen 2007: 174).

Furthermore, it is also possible to understand them as living metaphors: to use a metaphorical distinction between living and dead metaphors, where living meta-phors are new, un-expected metaphors, and dead metaphors are metaphors we meet all the time. However, nearly all words, at least all nouns, are metaphors or semblances: they are substitutes for something outside themselves. The word "snake" in this poem is a semblance; the word is a linguistic reference to something outside itself, either an undefined snake or the snake with which the man in the camps actually plays. When Celan stresses the necessity of avoiding metaphors, it must be understood as an attempt to avoid (too) living, transferable and transportable metaphors. This resistance against tropes and figures also assures that poetry exists or comes forth to a non-existing place. Celan can thus talk about a utopia connected to the poem: a u-topia connected to a non-existing place. Here the I meets itself in a meeting with the Real. This is the only moment where such a meeting can be localised. It is a kind of homecoming to non-existing places: "None of these places can be found. They do not exist. But I know where they ought to exist, especially now, and … I find something else" (Celan 2003: 54).

It is easy to understand this resistance to metaphors (and other figures and tropes) as an attempt to give existence to someone dead – for example a mother who died in a working-camp – who you at the same time never will be able to meet. It could be understood as a meeting with the absolute otherness to such a dead mother, who does not exist any longer but still has to exist in the poem. In this sense poems contain what does not exist any longer and what *still* has to exist. Confronted with the Real, Celan's poems, according to this poetics, have to recreate what is forever lost or out of reach. The only way to name the nameless (the Real is only a para-dox name for that which is without a name) is to avoid living and transportable metaphors: in so far as metaphors, which give birth to linguistic associations, bring the reader away from the Real. However, we can only imagine the Real or only represent it in a language that is different from the semblance normally connected to words. Such a "representation" can be without metaphors, but it can also be with metaphors, as is the case with poets other than Celan.

Nevertheless, Celan's poetics underlines that the Real cannot be named (although he never use the words "the Real"), but only evoked in a language that cannot grasp the Real. That is the main paradox of literature and its "truth": not only are there not enough words, but words fail to grasp and maintain the Real. Even so, every poet tries in his/her own language to grasp and maintain that which cannot be understood. A poet develops his/her own style by reducing common and public language to his/her own language, to his/her mother tongue or *lalangue*, as Lacan calls it in *Encore*. Celan's mother tongue or *lalangue* is German, which he spoke with his mother and in which he wrote his poems, but it is also a language in which he develops a style avoiding (too) living metaphors, so the I – the subject in the poem – can meet the other.

However poetics is fiction – linked to a discourse – about truth in poems, which is about the Real. Hence, Celan's poetics is not the truth about the Real, which his poems also fail to represent; neither is it the truth about his poems. Nevertheless, this shall not exclude us from using his poetics to open towards some of his poems. So let us briefly look a two of his shorter poems, the first one from *Zeitgehöft* (1976). In "All Those Sleep Shapes", it is possible to see "you" as the Other or the radical otherness, which the I attempts to meet, but only in so far as the I leads its own blood to "the language shadow" (quoted in Carson 2002: 70), which may mean that the I has to give up his/her present life. Hence the I has to become a stranger to itself, has to be alienated, and the blood is "the place where a poet's understanding takes place (*Erkenntnis*)" (ibid.). Furthermore he/she loses his/her grief in meeting the Other or the "language shadow", or the I gives its grief to the Other. Such a "language shadow" does not exist outside the poems but may be understood as an attempt to grasp that which is without a name. The "language shadow" should not – according to Celan's poetics – be understood as a metaphor, but as speech reduced to language's material form of which the poem consists.

A last poem from *Atemwende* (1967) can underline this material form. In "No More Sand Art", we see even more clearly the material form of language with the triple reduction of (the unwritten but presumed) "deep in snow": "Deepinsnow, / eepinnow, / e-i-o" (quoted in Felstiner 1995: 220), where spaces between the word and consonants disappear, whereby the material reduction of the letters themselves also disappears deep in nothing or in "e-i-o". But what does the song know deep in the snow? Is there knowledge in the snow? Or is this a metaphor for knowledge of non-knowledge? "No more sand" can be seen as no more urns of sand, no more Holocaust, no more Nazism (cf. Carson 2002: 114). Sand is metonymically connected to urns of sand. It is also possible to understand "no masters" – no more masters – as a reference to the masters of the Holocaust evoked by "*Todesfuge*": no more death in camps. On the other hand, it can be read as a criticism of the metaphors in "*Todesfuge*": no more metaphors or "Death is a master from Deutschland". "Dice" may be a reference to Stephanie Mallarmé's famous poems about dice, "A Throw of the Dice" ("Un coup de des"), while such a throw can be seen as a naming or a metaphor and thus a too-obvious approach to what has no name.

No more throw of dice, of metaphors. Snow seems to be connected to death, mostly the death of his mother, in other poems (cf. ibid.). "Seventeen" could be seen as a reference to the Jewish eighteenth prayer, which is thanks to God and the miracle of life. However, we never come to this thanks: language becomes mute. Or *das Andere*, the non-existing place, evoked by the poems exists only deep in the snow or in the (reduced) material of words or of letters. But this reading, which attempts to follow Celan's poetics, cannot avoid the existence of metaphors (knowledge in snow) or the metonymy ("no more sand" instead of "no more urns of sand").

Summary about Celan

Celan's poetics is a discourse, although containing lyric elements, and as such is different from his poems, which break with any discourse. This is especially clear regarding his resistance to figures and tropes, which his poetics wants to avoid, whilst the poems do not. It is also clear that something else or more is going on in his poems than is explained in *The Meridian*, which the material reduction of "Deep in the snow" to "e-i-o" in the poem "No More Sand Art" manifests. The radical otherness is not only a meeting with a strange unnamed Other, or it is only such a meeting if this other includes a space where language stops. Or the reduced letters ("e-i-o") are only an indication (or an epitaph) of that which no longer has a space in the poems. But although his poetics does not tell the (full) truth about his poems, it opens for an examination of the truth searched by the poems: a truth about the Real, which escapes any true representation.

Note

1 The idea about such a meeting is inspired by Martin Buber's considerations about I and you in a religious context, but as James K. Lyon underlines (1971), Celan is not occupied with God.

References

Carson, A. (2002) *Economy of the Unlost*. Princeton: Princeton UP.
Celan, P. (2003) The Meridian (1960). In *Collected Prose*. Trans. R. Waldrop. New York: Routledge.
Felstiner, J. (1995) *Paul Celan. Poet. Survivor. Jew*. New Haven: Yale UP.
Lacan, J. (1973) *Télévision*. Paris: Seuil.
Lacan, J. (1975) *Encore*. Paris: Seuil.
Lacoue-Labarthe, P. (2004) *La poésie comme expérience*. Paris: Christian Bourgois Editeur.
Lyon, J. K. (1971) Paul Celan and Martin Buber: Poetry as Dialogue, *PMLA* 86(1): 110–20.
Maulpoix, J-M. (2009) *Commente Choix de poèmes de Paul Celan*. Saint-Amand: Folio/ Gallimard.
Räsänen, P. (2007) *Counter-Figures. An Essay on Antimetaphoric Resistance: Paul Celan's Poetry and Poetics at the Limits of Figurality*. Available: https://helda.helsinki.fi/bitstream/ handle/10138/19366/counterf.pdf?sequence=2. [Accessed 20 August 2015].
Szondi, P. (2003) *Celan Studies*. Stanford: Stanford UP.

8
PRESENTING THE UNREPRESENTABLE IN PRESENTABLE WAYS

Pia Hylén

Donne

Interanimating Souls

I am not done with John
and Donne is not done with me
for his Ecstasy
runs around with me
'til the mixture of things make one

PART I

Desire in the poetry of John Donne

In the beginning of *Séminaire* VI, *Le désir et son interprétation*, Lacan says that the use, transmission and function of the word "desire" are particularly well illustrated in poetry, although not in all kinds of poetry (2013: 14).

My chapter is an observation of John Donne's structural approach to desire. "John Donne is Shakespeare's heir, muscular, theatrical, and metaphor-ridden. Donne fills even devout religious poems with flamboyant sexual personae and eccentric transposition of gender" (Paglia 1991: 228).

History

John Donne is considered one of the greatest poets of the English language. He was born late in the reign of Elizabeth I, a time when Britain turned Protestant. It was also the time of the great transformation of ideas. The world vision evolved from a concrete and self-centered state, to the expansive and enriched outlook with broader and more eloquent views so characteristic of the Renaissance. The phenomenal discovery that the Earth was not the center of the universe but revolved around the sun was established.

Times were tumultuous and violent. Elizabeth I was the daughter of Henry VIII and Anne Boleyn, his second wife. For Henry VIII to marry Anne, he had to free himself from the Catholic Church because the Pope would not grant the annulment of his first marriage to Catherine of Aragon. Henry VIII therefore turned to Protestantism. Three years after marrying, in 1536, Queen Anne was accused of adultery, incest and witchcraft. These accusations appear to be false, but gave enough coverage to Henry VIII to order her execution and then marry Jane Seymour. Elizabeth was at the time two and a half years old.

Before the reign of Elizabeth I, Henry VIII attempted to annul his marriage to her mother, Queen Anne, which was temporarily canceled, and Elizabeth was for a while declared illegitimate. Once Elizabeth became Queen, she properly severed the ties with the Catholic Church and became famous for establishing the Protestant Church of England. She was known as the "Virgin Queen" and the "Queen Warrior".

It was during these hectic times that John Donne lived. So why is this important? John Donne lived in an era very different from ours. Major political and scientific events were structuring Renaissance England. Radical changes took place regularly, with effects upon daily life—both concerning stability of life and congruency of thought—affecting the symbolic and the imaginary. The real was very close.

The symbolic is a construction of our understanding of the outside world. As long as our understanding rests in itself, life can go on undisturbed. When our world perception is stirred, such as when the Earth goes from being the center of the universe to being an element in motion, or when the king has his queen executed, we are shaken by the real. These events change the subject's perception of the outside world: the symbolic is shaken by the real and then reconstructed.

The Petrarchan conceit

The most characteristic style in Elizabethan poetry, a particularly prolific period, is the Petrarchan conceit, forming clichéd comparisons between closely related objects, such as rose and love. The writing style in the second half of the sixteenth century is furthermore characterized by an extensive allusion to classical myths. There is a revival of Greek and Roman theater, and poetry is guided by ideals and platonic romance. The regularity of prosodies and trochees is applied to build very precise traditional pentameters. Melodic and conventional beauty reigns, and this period, characterized by literature of exceptional quality, is generally referred to as The Nest of Singing Birds (see Norbrook 2002).

During the reign of Elizabeth I, both contents and form were confined to a smaller place than Donne considered suitable to express his desires in poetic form. They had so been constrained that metaphors became very extraordinarily banal and hardly evoked any true feelings. Limitations were imposed by religion and confined by rhymes which diminished the content: in short reduced by what grew to become the Petrarchan conceit. This rigid structure, which during the second half of the sixteenth century had helped so many poets and writers to write, was unacceptable to Donne. He broke the rules when possible. It was a revolution in poetry. Donne broke out; he broke free. Even if keeping certain clichés, he challenged rhymes to be able to speak of his devotion, his desires and his sexuality. Donne was a poet who began his writing in the Elizabethan era; his creative inspiration was, however, of a different cantor than most of his contemporaneous poets. He is more blunt; in highly religious times he names a poem "Ecstacy" and he goes on:

> This ecstasy doth unperplex,
>   We said, and tell us what we love;
> We see by this it was not sex, (1974: 54)

Donne speaks rather freely about sex when other poets prudently mention roses as a metaphor for love, and Donne ventures into the more physical aspects of love and sex saying it straight out, which was considered highly inappropriate at the time.

Shifting basic values in society is part of the evolution of times. Thomas Kuhn speaks about shifting paradigms: theories endure a certain time until they can hold no longer. When there is political pressure, scientific discovery or social movement it branches out into the arts, strong reactions are formed and, as in Kuhn's theorem (1975), the rules that govern the system break up and new rules are laid down, which begin to structure according to new theorems. A different theoretical system is created with new structures and new references. When the real breaks through, a new symbolic structure has to be erected.

One could argue that the rigidity of Elizabethan poetry was too much for Donne. Something had to give. Donne broke out; he defied all and started to talk openly about his desires and openly about sex. What Donne did was to break down the norm of an epoch; he changed the norms of a society; he changed the paradigms. He did this by demolishing the walls of the literary system and making room for his individualized access to desire through new metaphors and metonymies.

The metaphysical conceit

Donne is the most prominent of the metaphysical poets; they are characterized by their use of metaphor, which is fundamentally different from that of their contemporaries. The poetic style is called metaphysical because the metaphors do not have much in common with the romantic metaphors that the other poets used. The metaphysical poets use vivid images and a strong visual power, which easily stir the mind. Their use of metaphors is furthermore particular in that they combine images and ideas that are hardly related in either form or content and that under normal circumstances would never be thought of as being even remotely related.

Donne often used intellectual metaphors, which can be either complex or subtle and in some cases offensive; in this construct a link is established between a feeling or a desire and a seemingly inappropriate physical object and brings the symbolic and the imaginary together by a daring and often metaphysical image. This creates an unusual context because associating two things that do not appear to have any connection with each other, this unexpected circumstance, stirs the reader.

An example can be observed in Donne's poem "The Flea": the word "flea"—far from the things of love—allows the lovers to unite: rather unorthodox and quite paradoxical. The noble transcendence, created by Donne, induced via the flea, consists of the fact that as they both have been bitten by the same flea their blood is already mixed, therefore the sexual act is only a confirmation of something that has already taken place: the two souls are already united. The originality of the metaphor gives love strength. The desire escapes, escapes metonymically, from confinement to a particular object via the smooth gliding transformation to another object. Metonymically sliding from one object to the next, as when you kiss the hand and then the cheek, you kiss the cheek and then the mouth, you kiss the mouth and then....

Ecstasy in Donne's philosophy of love

Donne is known mainly for his erotic poetry, but paradoxically also for his religious devotion. What may have joined these two elements—sex and heavenly matters—which both appear harmonious and natural to the poet, elements that ordinarily are not associated? One way to answer this question is to say that it was neither sex nor deity that created Donne, but his symptoms, his (poetic) know-how concerning ecstasy.

What is ecstasy? The poem of that title by Donne concerns not only a natural, sexual impulse, but the outcome of a struggle of the union of organs, souls and minds. Donne's philosophy of love does not differ much from the ideal described by Aristophanes in Plato's *Symposium*, where elements that appear to be linked by nature are associated only in an illusory way (1955: 44). Both take the sublime starting point, the unification of subject and object. The difference lies in their use of style; their desire is what makes it possible to transcend the bleak loneliness of the subject.

Desire

In "Ecstasy" Donne clearly states that desire is not just sexual. There is no doubt that the man desires the woman, but in the poem the woman is above all an occasion for Donne to launch his long and arduous riddles of love and passion. However, as his desire is not only to focus on the carnal, his desire also hits the spiritual. At the end of the battle, he feels that something escapes both the winner and the loser.

Let us therefore assume that sexuality for Donne is not merely physical; it is also an entrance to an elevated mental residence where lovers for a while share a space.

But as neither the physical nor the mental lasts—we are dealing with momentary visits—another step follows. It is like the waves of the sea: when one comes in, another is moving out. Here again we are dealing with the metonymic sliding. How does Donne do this? Brodsky explains that "while reading Donne you measure not the number of syllables but time" and compares this to Mandelstam "drawing out the caesura", which entails:

> holding back an instant, stopping … for something which seems wonderful to the poet for one or another reason. Or the other way around, like in his "Voronezh Notebooks", there you have unevenness, jumps, and truncated feet, truncated meter, feverish haste – so as to hasten or eliminate the instant which seems terrible. (2013)

On the other hand we have Chater who says that Donne is too close to that which moves, and that he is unsuccessful in gaining control. In a kind of psychoanalytical analysis she states that Donne:

> depicts the agony of a man who has lost the once-cherished physical contact of his lover and instead of humbling himself, is using manipulative passive-aggressive behavior. We sense that the poet knows the feel of the lover's touch and craves to feel it again. And not gently. He's so desperate to regain the sensation that he longs for the touch to be violent and masculine and even painful. He wants the touch to convince him beyond a doubt that he is in contact with his beloved: that he's under the power and coercion of God to the point of being sadistically victimized, maltreated, even persecuted to the extent of physical abuse. He's begging for the return of something he once had. But how did he lose the one thing he loved the most in the first place? (2004)

Here we maintain the idea that Donne's ideal—his perfection of love, which in "Ecstasy" is a woman—is combined with a loss, which is not only on-going but structural. Donne desires the woman, he worships her, but he never manages to get her: she is lost forever. It is his own desire that drives him, and therefore she can continue to exist as the unattainable.

Lacan

Lacan introduces the word "desire" into psychoanalysis. It does not exist in post-Freudian theories; nor does Freud talk very much about desire. Before Freud spoke about "*Wunsch*" in *The Interpretation of Dreams*, the concept of desire was evoked better by philosophers and poets. In philosophy, Lacan highlights Spinoza and Hegel. And in poetry, he talks about the metaphysical poets, whose highest exponent is John Donne. Lacan sets the metaphysical poetry of Donne up against the figurative poetry.

When describing desire, the latter calls immediately upon the senses, while the metaphysical poets create a new poetic language and introduce a new poetic form.

Metaphysical poetry does not eliminate the body but returns to the body through language, soul and intelligence. What is new about it is not the concept of love—which is still stuck in the Platonic sphere, in the primeval androgyny—but the way that it is said. In other words, the descriptive poets place themselves in a duality with the object. For instance, love becomes a rose: beginning with one object, love, which, via a simple metaphor, is named a rose, whereby the second object is introduced. The metaphysical poets, on the other hand, invest themselves in the underlying relationship the subject has with the symbolic, more precisely with the signifiers.

An illustration is in the second line of "Ecstasy" where Donne talks about "A pregnant bank swell'd up" (1974: 53), referring to the meaning and the consequence of his desire, that she falls pregnant. "Ecstasy" is one of Donne's later poems. He has a classical structure of verse (stanza, rhythms and rhymes, abab/cdcd). It is in this literary space that Donne introduces the conflict among body, soul and intelligence, and he solves the conflict in perfecting this new poetic form. Instead of saying that he desires the woman, or that her body evokes feelings in him, he instead refers to the effect his desire has, as if it were already a *fait accompli*.

Donne speaks of a "pregnant bank": we not only get a visual image of the bulging riverbank, but also understand that Donne desires the woman and wants her to become bulging, to fall pregnant. The signifier "pregnant" requires a whole series of actions, the first of which is sex; but he will not stop here—he takes it further—he desires the woman, but he does not stops with the physical action, he continues in a metonymic way S1, S2, S3… and ends up with a family. As Lacan says in *Séminaire* VI, desire is the fruit of the passage of all, which is considered natural in an individual (instinct, needs, tendencies, etc.), via the structure of language. But not all desire is language; something escapes, the alienation of the signifier, what Freud calls "the lost object", a loss that Lacan assigns a metonymic character. A desired object continually escapes the individual, who therefore can continue to desire.

Donne tries to catch the flight of what escapes with a network of signifiers that are his poems. The ideal object, not real, should then be women. The hope of love is the re-unification with the lost woman. The metaphorical process of substituting one signifier for another seems apt to give access to this idealized object, but the terrible metonymy imposes itself by sliding away from what the metaphor sought to achieve. The metonymic movement is an active process. It is above all that which allows Donne to continue writing throughout his lifetime in a different way than the usual, using the most prolific forms. This inspiration sustains not only the desire, but also the fantasy of a greater proximity to the object that causes it, that Lacan calls *petit a*. As no one ever reaches his or her object of desire, as it is lost in the structure, Donne continues his quest on the road of metaphysical poetry. From the clearance of this path, we now know, we are all left enriched.

PART II

The role of poetry in the disturbance of the symbolic order in the twenty-first century

Le Poème

La forme en elle même déjà dérange comme elle peut être sans forme –
sans forme conforme à la forme d'un langage.
Le fond également ne fait pas comme les fonds forcement font –
alors avec ce fond et cette forme non conforme le sujet peut inscrire et s'inscrire dans un
discours hors comme-une –

The Poem

The form already disturbs
since it can be without form
conform with the form of language.
Neither does the content do
what contents usually do –
so with this form and this content non-conform
the subject can inscribe and be inscribed in a discourse out of the norm –

Lacan mentions in *Séminaire* VI that desire is hard to access but that Donne paves us a very fruitful way (Lacan 2013: 12, 14) and illustrates that poetry can break paths and pave roads. Daniel Tutt, following Judith Balso, confirms that poetry creates a new space for thought and imagination and that it lends its frame for a new onto-logical capacity of thinking (2011). In this sense, poems are so much more than mere artistic events of aesthetic contemplation; they are a forum for thought, for new kinds of thinking. Poetry is a discourse in which the subject establishes itself and has the power to establish new capacities and new avenues of thinking (2011).

The other side is that poetry becomes more dangerous than thought because it exists in concrete terms and can therefore be disclosed; it is not just imaginary, but it is part of a token, a portion of the structure to which we are subjected, part of the symbolic order. Poetry can be viewed as dangerous because it cannot be limited; it is not subject to the same structural standards as prose. It flows into and is flooded and penetrated by the real and consequently cannot be contained, cannot be controlled and you cannot trust it. It produces a singularity; it can even create a new ontology. A poem produces something unique; it is a unique place, where things can happen that cannot happen elsewhere.

Poetry is a structure, a collection of words chosen by the poet and composed in exactly the way she/he wishes. There are no limits, and there are no restrictions, there are only consequences. Poetry creates order where none was—an order that might be a disorder—an order that inscribes itself in a discourse out of the ordi-nary, an order out of something that comes from the real. Poetry structures and de-structures because the situations for desire are riveted to a specific function in the language, exactly where subject's relation to the signifier is concerned.

A more recent example of poetry breaking the norms is the American poet Allen Ginsberg, who felt restricted and oppressed by society's limiting moral standards. In 1957 legal action was taken against him: one of his poems, "Howl", was accused of being obscene because it explicitly described hetero- and homosexual sex. Ginsberg won his lawsuit; the judge proclaimed that it was not for the law to enforce bland and innocuous euphemisms (see Morgan and Peters 2006).

In a recent film *Kill Your Darlings* (John Krokidas, 2013), Daniel Radcliffe plays Ginsberg. It is a portrait of Ginsberg who tears down the walls of conventional literary norms in society, just as Donne did 250 years earlier, and both do so in order to make room for their personal desires, expressed through new metaphors and metonymies. This has immediate reverberations in the social world. Ginsberg broke the sexual taboos prevalent in America in the 1950s (see Morgan and Peters 2006). He felt the hypocrisy of society offensive, and for him there was nothing more natural than talking about what was so important to him: namely his desires, his sexual desires and specifically his homosexual desires. Many felt offended and outraged and could not accept that such "vulgarity" should be available in print. When the symbolic order becomes too narrow, the real breaks through and breaks down part of the existing symbolic system. Donne and Ginsberg are examples of poets at the forefront of the symbolic: where the symbolic meets the real.

The use of metaphors and metonymies can change the ontology, as what is said lies beyond the immediate meaning of the words' nominal sense. When metaphors and metonymies are used, there is a parallel impact at another level. Something can be said, without its actually being written. The symbolic importance may go beyond the norm and make something understandable without its actually appearing. The poetic context allows for such expression because of its freedom of form. This freedom makes it possible to touch issues that cannot be addressed directly. The content of a sentence is limited to what the words mean, and the specific use of the words in a grammatical context defines it. Once the structure is no longer restricted, the content is not either. Because poetry has a much looser structure than prose, poetry can get around where prose does not reach.

Donne and Ginsberg are two examples in the history of poetry where poets break not only with the linguistic structure, but also with the normative structure, that is, with the symbolic as such. Because desire desires desire, and it is not the object that is the driving force, the symbolic must be restructured to be accommodative anew.

To represent the unrepresentable

After the Holocaust it was said that about this matter poetry could not be written (Adorno 1997: 34). A description of the Holocaust is doomed to fail because it will be a violation not only of moral character, but also of epistemological character: an offense that moves away from what Wittgenstein states can be talked about in this world. To nominate the real is not possible. This was disproved because poetry also represents a truth outside that which can be said. Paul Celan was able to do it and in German, which was not his native language but the language of the enemy. He was able to go further and to symbolize that which is considered unsymbolizable and unrepresentable: namely horror. With Celan we learn that one can represent the unrepresentable. It can be presented in a poem. Experiences too cruel for words can be said, but in a poem. That which is not accessible to language can be accessed in a poem. Where language ceases to be sufficient, the poem becomes viable, because the poem, as a form, goes beyond the symbolic.

Poetic structure

Poetry is difficult to understand because of its structure, which is a lack of structure, that is to say its lack of conformity to the standards of grammatical rules. Poetry is written in words, but written in a style that does not conform to common writing style. A poet can use language in the way she or he wishes. Poetry may appear as *lalangue,* a personalized colloquialism, a language full of idiosyncrasies, a space of pleasure defying normality. Poetry can be personalized words understood only by the individual who writes them, and it can be confused with *lalangue*, as common language structure can be overridden, words can be created and shaped as the poet wishes. Therefore, poetry can appear as private inaccessible thoughts, but the difference between *lalangue* and poetry is precisely that poetry is understood by others: poetry transcends *lalangue*.

The freedom that makes it possible for poetry to break with the structure, to break our limitation by the symbolic, this freedom is present because poetry has access to the real. Ginsberg is an example of how a poet's work can start restructuring an era, breaking down and building back up the symbolic. Ginsberg writes about desire and touches signifiers that are taboo. He creates a scandal—far from the first one—but one that starts a re-structuring of the symbolic of the time. This poem, "Howl", challenges society's norms and begins to celebrate the individual. The father is now sitting on the edge of the chair and is sliding downwards.

Ten years later *Naked Lunch* is published. I will not describe *Naked Lunch* as an epic poem, but more like an odyssey: a journey through a trip that lasted 15 years. William S. Burroughs portrays a world beyond the symbolic, a world where drugs, violence, suffering, death, addiction, hallucinations, killings, sarcasm, fear, torture and manipulation, all of which are real, track him down. And when this happens, well-being in the symbolic world ceases to exist. Ginsberg uses his poems to reach out: to reach outside. He destabilizes the symbolic world, and just after him comes Burroughs, doing more of the same. But Burroughs goes further, he undermines the symbolic. Many poets before him had represented the unrepresentable without its having had drastic structural consequences. But Burroughs, after Ginsberg, opens up for the abject—breaks down the boundaries between subject and object, creates havoc—and the symbolic world is in full slippage.

Kristeva coins the term "abject", which epistemologically refers to a place in language where opinions cease to exist: it is outside the realm of the symbolic:

> There looms, within abjection, one of those violent, dark revolts of being, directed against a threat that seems to emanate from an exorbitant outside or inside, ejected beyond the scope of the possible, the tolerable, the thinkable. (1980: 9)

The outbreaks of the real, which are usually only seen on the fringe of our lives in phenomena such as death, break down the boundary between subject and object and consequently degrade meaning. Poetry can touch this because poetry is a place where the language can be reconciled with that which is more than miserable, with the abject. Burroughs lived on the edge of society and took the law into his own hands; he always carried a gun and he did—accidentally—kill his wife. His world was not nicely ordered within a respectful frame, within a recognized symbolic order as most of us know it. His taste, his desire for that which lays above and beyond characterizes his writings: where you encounter the abject, clashing encounters with violence and death, with the real, which according to Kristeva (1980: 13) shows the recognition of a basic lack of any solid foundation, the lack of sense in our lives.

On our way – but where to?

By treating the abject as a privileged signifier, by dealing with that which intentionally destroys us, drugs, violence, decay and death, by elevating it as if it were something sublime, something worth striving for as the worthwhile value in life, the crisis in the twenty-first century is well engaged. The symbolic consists of a structure through which the values of our society are maintained. The real, however, is without structure and is located in a parallel universe, to which we have access now and again. Poetry is closer to the real than prose, and through its access to the real it can break down the symbolic. Because of outbreaks from the real the borders of the symbolic are damaged. When the metonymies are driven so far out that the signifiers become real, the symbolic falls apart. While Ginsberg is talking about different kinds of sex, Burroughs addresses violence, abuse and murder: he romanticizes decadence, and he smashes the symbolic, as he reaches through to the real.

The order of our society governed by a legal system and functioning in a democratic spirit based upon certain moral and ethical aspects is what carries our society, is what makes it possible to maintain our culture. When respect for this structure ceases to exist, there can be a breaking of the structure, which can begin in the arts. And if what begins in art, which is a transgression of norms, becomes so strong that it takes to the streets—if breaking down the structure no longer is limited to the arts but turns into a provocation that everyone wants to take a go at—then the established order will no longer be upheld, the structure holding up our society breaks down.

Oedipus has mythically laid a basic structure for our society, but centuries have passed and borne witness to his passage; not even he cries any longer from his gouged-out eyes. The paradoxical pleasure of our *plus-de-jouir* is getting closer and closer to the abject, and in that sense desire is getting closer to perversion. If we desire the abject, then we lose the connection to the object, to the Other, to a structure defined by the symbolic, and we fall out somewhere, where meaning ends. The symbolic structure is normative for the values the subject has. Where we have major changes (consisting of many smaller parts that amongst themselves are unrelated)—when, for instance, homosexuality is no longer illegal—then fundamental values have shifted; and, in addition, where substance abuse is becoming commonplace and violence is on the menu every day, we can talk about slippage of the symbolic. *Naked Lunch* is not only an odyssey through Burroughs' excesses; it is our odyssey out of the symbolic. Ginsberg fucks the father, and Burroughs kills him, and today we are without.

In the seventeenth century Donne broke with the contemporary values of Elizabethan standards; he broke with the prevailing symbolic structure, where love was defined as sweet as a rose and a sense of religious awe was dominating so that desire had to be cultivated within these frames. Donne distinguishes himself twofold: *le fond et la forme*. First he spoke quite openly about sex, and second he used language that did not appeal directly to the senses, but to the fundamental relationship that exists between a subject and its signifiers.

Donne's strength was that he took the step all the way out; he broke with tradition by rejecting limiting symbolism—rose-love—and going straight to the signifiers, which he related openly in his poetry. He broke with the prevailing symbolic order; he named the signifiers and thus initiated a paradigm shift; he helped to change the way poetry is written, the way desire is expressed. There is a shift, in which one symbolic order collapses and another one is built. I wanted to show how Donne through his poetry was creating a new order. Poetry is an entrepreneur, the instigator, because it is closer to the real than prose; because poetry has more access to the real it instigates a passage between the real and the symbolic. Poetry is at a permeable point in the symbolic.

References

Adorno, T. (1997) *Cultural Criticism and Society*. Cambridge: MIT Press.

Bailey, J. (1920) The Sermons of a Poet. *Quarterly Review* 463: 317–28.

Brodsky, J. (2013) *On Donne, The Poet Is Engaged in the Translation of One Thing into Another*. Available: http://www.rferl.org/content/Brodsky_on_Donne_The_Poet_Is_Engaged_In_The_Translation_Of_One_Thing_Into_Another/2051105.html. [Accessed 6 November 2015].

Burroughs, W. (2008) *Naked Lunch*. London: Harper Perennial.

Chater, V. (2004) John Donne: Bulimic Bore? *Absinthe Literary Review*, Winter. Available: http://www.absintheliteraryreview.com/archives/chater.htm. [Accessed 6 November 2015].

Donne, J. (1974) The Complete English Poems. Ed. A. J. Smith. London: Penguin.

Eliot, T. S. (1921) The Metaphysical Poets. *Times Literary Supplement* October: 669–70.

Flinker, N. (1999) John Donne and the 'Anthropomorphic Map' Tradition. *Applied Semiotics* 3(8): 207–15.

Ginsberg, A. (1986) *Howl*. New York: HarperCollins.

Haven, C. (2013) Brodsky and Donne in the Arctic: "the image of a body in space." Available: http://bookhaven.stanford.edu/2013/01/john-donne-in-the-arctic-the-image-of-a-body-in-space/. [Accessed 6 November 2015].

Kristeva, J. (1980) *Pouvoirs de l'horreur*. Paris: Éditions du Seuil.

Kristeva, J. (1987) *Soleil noir*. Paris: Éditions Gallimard.

Kuhn, T. S. (1970) *The Structure of Scientific Revolutions*. Chicago: University of Chicago Press.

Lacan, J. (1966) *Écrits*. Paris: Seuil.

Lacan, J. (2013) *Seminaire VI, Le désir et son interprétation*. Paris: Éditions de la Martinière.

Miller, J. A. (2013a) L'Autre sans Autre. Congrès de la NLS. Available: http://www.amp-nls. org. [Accessed 6 November 2015].

Miller, J. A. (2013b) Une réflexion sur l'Oedipe et son au-delà. Congrès de la NLS. Pipol News 64. Available: http://www.amp-nls.org/page/fr/171/le-congrs-de-gand-2014/0/1187. [Accessed 6 November 2015].

Morgan, B. and Peters J. N. (2006) *Howl on Trial: The Battle for Free Expression*. San Francisco: City Light Books.

Norbrook, D. (2002) *Poetry and Politics in the English Renaissance*. Oxford: Oxford University Press.

Paglia, C. (2005) *Break, Blow, Burn*. New York: Pantheon Books.

Paglia, C. (1991) *Sexual Personae*. New York: Vintage.

Plato (1955) *Symposium*. København: Gyldendahl.

Rahimi, S. (2012) Subjectivity at the Intersection of Metaphor and Metonymic Functions. Available: http://somatosphere.net/2012/12/subjectivity-at-the-intersection-of-metaphoric-and-metonymic-functions.html. [Accessed 6 November 2015].

Tutt, D. (2011) Metaphysicians in the Dark: Poetry, Thinking and Nostalgia for the Idea. Available: http://www.thethepoetry.com/2011/09/metaphysicians-in-the-dark-poetry-thinking-and-nostalgia-for-the-idea/. [Accessed 6 November 2015].

Filmography

Kill Your Darlings (2013) Directed by John Krokidas. USA: Killer Films.

9

DURAS AND THE ART OF THE IMPOSSIBLE

Carin Franzén

Marguerite Duras' writing is constituted by a paradox. Throughout her work, which to a large extent is autobiographical, a prerequisite seems to be the impossibility of telling her story, the story of her life. In our own time, when the subject's intimacy is exposed and made public by new media practices, it is rather astonishing to return to Duras' literary work and its undermining of the confessional imperative that has been dominating Western subjectivities for centuries.[1] In the following I will try to relate the negative affirmation, the "story of my life doesn't exist", to a fundamental necessity of writing that is also articulated throughout Duras' work. One of the main points is that her writing demonstrates that the borderlines of subjectivity are delineated by an impossibility of representation that tends to be foreclosed in aesthetics in recent years.[2] In other words, I will argue that the relation between the impossibility to tell the story of her life and the necessity to keep on writing is a very good illustration of a more general impossibility.

Actually, Duras' writing, which has often been described in terms of a feminine desire or as an expression of a specific feminine melancholia (Kristeva 1989: 234), can more thoroughly be assessed as a specific form of arrangement of the unrepresentable within a symbolic practice. The point of departure for the assessment of this more general impossibility in Duras' art of writing is taken from Lacan: "the path of the subject passes between the two walls of the impossible" (1977:167). In his 1964 seminar on *The Four Fundamental Concepts of Psychoanalysis*, Lacan explains that the Real constitutes one wall and that the other designates the impossible fulfillment of drives and desire. When Duras writes that there is "no path, no line" in the story of her life, the statement could be understood as an approach to these two impossibilities that Lacan identifies as constituent for the subject: the fundamental lack at the core of subjectivity and its relation to the real.

To be sure, the real is an evasive term in Lacan's theory. It stands out as a limit of the human being's symbolic and imaginary relation to reality, which for the sake of self-awareness and autobiographical writing implies that subjectivity is anchored in something unknown, or more correctly put, in something that cannot be known. By emphasizing the category of the impossible and by forging the concept of the Real, Lacan takes Freud's discovery of the unconscious as the fundament of the human being a step further. Today however, we seem to live in a world dominated by a reality-based aesthetic or an imaginary belief that the Real can be totally grasped and mastered, in particular through writings that claim to be 'the true story' of a person's life, or by the exposition of personal intimacy by other media technologies such as reality TV shows or the expanding sphere of networking platforms. If this trend is revealing of the relation between the late capitalist order and subjectivity in our society, psychoanalytic experience could be used as "a hindrance, a stumbling block, a point of resistance and a starting point for an opposing strategy" (Foucault 1998: 101), based on the insight that the impossible is an essential part of the human condition.[3]

This impossibility has to do with the fact that language defines human life in a specific way, or as Lacan describes the consequence of the infant's entrance into a symbolic order: "The ready-to-speak that was to be there (…) disappears, no longer being anything but a signifier" (2006: 713). The speaking subject is someone that forever has lost something of its primary being. Thus, the subject is decentered and split between a symbolic order where it has to find its place and the Real "that was to be there". Civilization has always tried to arrange itself according to or rather against this human condition, not least with ideas that aim at reconstituting the centrality and wholeness of the self, as for example Cartesian rationalism or romantic ideas of love. However, in art and literature as well as in science and philosophy we also find articulations of the limits of the subject and an acceptance of the forces that supersede it. Furthermore, in present-day artistic practices the divide between the nostalgia for wholeness and 'the real thing' on the one side and the acceptance of loss on the other, is negotiated against the backdrop of a social order dominated by a neoliberal ideology preaching the supremacy of the individual and the maximization of self-interest. A reminder of some central aspects of the modernist aesthetics of which Duras' writing is part can be an illuminating contribution at least to some of the impasses in that negotiation.

Against a short backdrop of the general historical context of Duras' writing, I argue that her art of the impossible reveals the imaginary illusions in contemporary trends reflective of late capitalist and neoliberal subjectivity that share a belief in individual freedom supported by the slogan that everything is possible.

A crisis of representation

The major experiences from the 20th century have all been connected to catastrophes and crises, such as the two World Wars and the new weapons of destructions that came with technological evolution. Progress and a radical questioning of the values of modern civilization seemed to go hand in hand. It has been argued that "Europeans especially felt anguish in regard to their existence, since some perceived that they were entering times of meaninglessness" (Salecl 2004: 2). The post-World War period has moreover been seen as affected by a "crisis of representation" (Kristeva 1989: 221). This description is relevant also for Duras' minimalist aesthetics, which nevertheless bear clear subjective and autobiographical traits. Through Duras' work one can actually follow a history of the subject from the depiction of the traditional bourgeois family in her first novel *Les impudents* from 1943 to its bankruptcy in the 1960s and the 1970s. During this time, Duras' writing changes from a realistic narration to her famous elliptic style. However, the need to elaborate her "*Familienroman*" seems to follow her through her writing, which at the same time becomes more openly political and critical of contemporary society and its capitalist order. This critique goes hand in hand with a reflection on her own writing, and she has on various occasions underlined that literature must be set free from moral constraints, not in the name of individual freedom but in response to a demand that seems to come from the symbolic practice itself. However, I think that this modernist *credo* of the autonomy of art in Duras' case is based on an experience of the limits of subjectivity that I will try to highlight in the following.

In the short text "Solitude" from the 1980s published in the French film magazine *Cahiers du Cinéma* and reprinted in *Green Eyes*, Duras describes the writing of a book as a kind of submission in the sense that it has a life of its own and furthermore a life that is unknown. The writer can only subject her self to its force: "You have to go through this journey with the book you are giving birth to, this hard labor, the whole time of its writing. One acquires a taste for this wonderful misery" (1990: 69). A "misery" that she in the same context also describes as a kind of fundamental unawareness – "You don't know. You know nothing about what you're doing" (ibid.: 7) – which can also be seen as a certain relation to the Real or a will to represent the unrepresentable without reducing it to some presumed translatable essence or hidden truth.

In addition, when Duras talks about her writing she often underlines the integrity of the creative process itself. Even if the product, the finished book, is inevitably part of the logic of the market, the editorial or commercial business, it's writing is not. The becoming of a literary book for Duras is not negotiable by the fact that writing is tied to the unknown. Could it be predicted, the act of writing would not be necessary, or as she puts it in a reflection on her writing from 1993: "it's impossible to speak to someone about a book one has written, and especially about a book one is writing" (2011: 17).

Thus, the integrity of the book is linked to the impossibility of speaking of its becoming. This may sound as a romantic and even mystic view of literature, but it can also be based on the acceptance of the impossibility of filling up the lack at the heart of the subject's being. A revealing example of this acceptance is formulated in Duras' novel *The Ravishing of Lol Stein* from 1964, when the narrator tries to understand the protagonist Lol V. Stein's enigmatic character. The narrator talks about her silence and believes that it is due to a specific lack, namely the absence of a unique word – a word that could precisely tell the story of her life. This word does not exist, but if it did it would be an absence-word, a kind of black hole in which all other words would have been buried (1966: 38) Like Lol's silence, Duras' writing is driven by something unrepresentable that risks burying her words, but unlike Lol, the writer concedes to continue writing in a vain attempt to put the absence-word into words. This paradox is at any rate characteristic of how Duras describes her writing: "Writing is the unknown. Before writing one knows nothing of what one is about to write" (2011: 44). This, in fact, makes her art transgressive in the sense that it goes beyond any mimetic representation of the already-known.

Even though Duras' work seems to be part of a more general crisis of representation in the post-World War period, her expressed trust in the force of writing indicates a specific adherence to the symbolic order in contrast to the imaginary search for the real thing or the real story in today's aesthetics.[4] Duras' acknowledgement of the unknown – "writing is the unknown" – could be seen as a parallel to a psychoanalytic experience, to quote Lacan again: "since the opposite of the possible is certainly the real, we would be led to define the real as the impossible" (1977: 167). Transposed into literary writing, and in particular into Duras' writing, this idea of the Real as a limit for what can be articulated by the symbolic is nevertheless expressed through a poetical sensibility based on an absence-word, a hole-word, whose center is the subject's constitutive lack. This poetical arrangement of the real impossibility of the symbolic does not mean that silence or resignation is at the basis of Duras' aesthetics.

In her reading Kristeva suggests that Duras' writing gives expression to a specific feminine melancholia through a refusal of linguistic proficiency that "absorbs political horror into the subject's microcosm" (Kristeva 1989: 234). But it could also be argued that Duras' art of the impossible gives literary writing a specific implication that transgresses both a singular feminine desire and a given historical crisis of representation in a re-configuration of its elements into a critical operation of the traditional representation of subjectivity and politics (see Rancière 2010: 211).

Subject to truth

Kristeva describes Duras' style as deriving from an aesthetic that imitates and reproduces an experience that can be tied to a feminine melancholia but also to the major events from the 20th century. Her main point is that the aesthetic refusal or minimization of literary devices that characterized art and literature in the post-World War period was directed by a desire to stay true in the face of exterior as well as interior traumas as if pain were the only faithful expression of these crises. However, the force of this pain and the breakdown of ideologies that followed the

Second World War did not imply that Duras gave up her belief in the necessity to write or political change, even though her style becomes more and more naked and her adherence to a political party no longer seems to be an option, as she says looking back to the 1960s:

> We are sick with hope, those of us from '68. The hope is the one we placed in the role of the proletariat. And as for us, no law, nothing, no one and no thing, will ever cure us of that hope. I'd like to join the Communist Party again. But at the same time I know I shouldn't. (2011: 26)

In one perspective the crisis of representation and the theme of melancholia that Kristeva wants to discern in Duras' writing could seem to reflect a political failure as well as a personal experience. Motifs, such as the crazy mother, the colonial experience, the Second World War, are recurrent through her work and could easily be related to her biography.[5] However, the autobiographical narrative in Duras' work is at the same time undermined by negative affirmations such as the one quoted at the beginning of this essay.

If the story of Duras' life does not exist, then what does exist is writing and through this symbolic practice an articulation of experiences that cannot be fully represented.[6] Furthermore, Duras' underlining of the unrepresentable is tied to a specific exigency of her aesthetics. In a revealing passage in her novel *The Lover*, she talks about writing as something that has lost its meaning. For writing to regain importance, she says, it needs to confront to things: on the one side, an inexpressible essence, and on the other a basic offensiveness (Duras 1997: 8). Thus, for the author of *The Lover*, writing on the late capitalist market has turned into nothing at all, which could be read as a description of the consequences of a reification of literature.

When writing *The Lover*, this great public success in 1984, Duras was 70 years old. To be sure, the autobiographical themes – childhood and the drama of growing up, the drama of sexual desire – have captivated the public and made the book into material for perhaps an even more successful film. At the same time these captivating themes are articulated as something beyond reach. Duras' description of contemporary literary writing as nothing at all could also be read as an indication of a literary institution conditioned by the liberty to say everything and to say it in the way one wants. Nevertheless, Duras insists here that this nothing, or absence of literary moral constraints, must be directed by something that it is not possible to express in public. If this quality is lacking, *writing is nothing but advertisement* (1997: 8), a sentence to which I will return. Thus, even though writing is no longer a moral occupation, Duras points to the necessity of some sort of protection against the actual exposure of literature, not least in regard to the autofictive and autobiographical trend that dominates it today.

Differently put, if writing shall be something other than a more or less automatic response to the demands of the market, then it must obey something essentially unrepresentable. This exigency of Duras' aesthetics is also apparent in the configuration of a kind of primal scene of writing at the beginning of *The Lover*. Duras talks here about her childhood as an area where silence begins. As a literary author she can only watch it from a distance, but that is also why she continues writing, as if writing actually could bridge this distance of time and death that separates the writer from her past. In the novel Duras also talks about her writing as a continuous waiting outside the closed door of childhood (1997: 25). This impossibility at the core of autobiographical writing also distinguishes Duras' project from the proliferation of the autofictive and autobiographical genre today, which can be seen as part of a new regime where storytelling has become a central part of a neoliberal "narrative order" (see Salmon 2010). Duras' art of the impossible can therefore also be assessed as a counter-discourse to that order. Furthermore, the subjective and singular experience articulated in her writing is made general by a juxtaposition of passion and politics, and it is often done in ways that are unseemly in a politically correct sense. In *The Lover,* for instance, she compares the French collaborator during the Second World War with her own political engagement in a way that points to a kind of solution that tries to escape the impossibility at the core of every personal identity. Collaboration and resistance or political engagement is, says Duras here, based on a lack of judgment that consists of believing in political solutions to personal problems (1997: 68). It could be this somewhat cynical declaration that leads Kristeva to her conclusion that Duras "scrutinize[s] only the spectrum of suffering" (1989: 236). Nevertheless, in Duras' work the "personal problem" is also transformed into a radical stance going against the compromises of social life and the resignations following the failures of ideologies, which I will demonstrate by considering her configurations of love and the political consequences that one can draw from them.

Subject to love

When Duras writes about passion – drives and desire – she often seems to criticize a conception of romantic love as a dream about an everlasting relation where two become one. Against this traditional representation of love that is still rather dominant in our culture, her art reveals a dissymmetrical configuration of the sexual relation with a bearing even for a radical conception of a social community, and it comes as no surprise that it should reverberate in thinkers on subjectivity such as Lacan and Blanchot. Lacan tried to assess main traits of her art of love in his famous "Homage to Marguerite Duras, on 'Le ravissement de Lol V.Stein'" from 1965 (Lacan 1987: 122–129), and it still echoes in his famous declaration regarding the impossibility of the sexual relationship to which I will return. Blanchot also made appreciative comments on Duras' short fiction *The Malady of Death* one year after its publication in 1982 in his work *The Unavowable Community* (1988).

In Duras' condensed novella about a man, a woman and their sexual relation, the man is constantly referred to as "you" and the woman as "she". By its specific narrative form it illustrates love not only as a force – in the story love is also represented as a specific power structure, underlined by the fact that the man pays the woman to spend her time with him, and is therefore something absolutely dissymmetrical. Blanchot sums up the main theme with the following question:

> What then is the difference between these two destinies, one of which pursues a love refused to him while the other, through grace, is made for love, knows everything about love, judges and condemns those who fail in their attempts to love, but herself only offers herself to be loved (under contract) without ever giving any sign of her ability to go from passivity to limitless passion? (1988: 40)

Blanchot admits that he cannot answer his question and concludes that the dissymmetry between the man and the woman remains "an inscrutable mystery" (1988: 40). I will not go further into Blanchot's comment here, but I want to underline the link that exists between his own conception of an unrepresentable and impossible core in every community – that he calls "the unavowable community" (1988: 53) – and Duras' configuration of love.

For Duras, love is aligned with a passion that cannot be mastered by will as Descartes once thought.[7] In her writings she often points to a profound incompatibility between passion and will, an impossibility at the heart of every community and *a fortiori*, the one that lovers dream of, as for example in these lines from the already quoted text "Solitude" in *Green Eyes*:

> Most people marry to get out of solitude. (…) Solitude is blurred but not defeated. (…) A lover's couple is shortlived. It never survives marriage. (…) One cannot do anything from within the couple but wait for that wonder, the days of love, to run out. (1990: 66–67)

Thus, in love we seek to transgress solitude, but this blessing is not a secure basis for a community of two, but rather a consecration of "*the always uncertain* end inscribed in the destiny of the community" to quote Blanchot (1988: 56).

In Duras' representation of love as incompatible with the couple we can find an obvious parallel to the psychoanalytic theory of sexual difference and love that Lacan developed in *Encore*, the twentieth Seminar, from 1972–1973. Furthermore, even though Lacan here states the impossibility of a union of the two sexes (1998: 9), he also points to the fact that there have always been different ways of compensating for this failure, with for example the imaginary dream of completion as a union with one's "other half", as we find it in Aristophanes' discourse in *Symposium*, or the creation of an object of desire that is inaccessible, as in the code of courtly love for instance.[8] A more truthful approach to this absence of sexual relation or impossible union of two into one is to be found in the experience that goes beyond the imaginary solutions and which Lacan designates in terms of a *jouissance*. In *Encore* Lacan illustrates this thinking by a reference to female mystics such as Saint Teresa and the Beguine Hadewijch d'Anvers who, as he claims, experience a *jouissance* that transgresses the symbolic order (1998: 76). This experience has also been related to Duras' writing (see David 1996), which can be qualified as supported by a *jouissance* that operates as a corrosive force that undermines every romantic idea of love as a unification of two into one. Nevertheless, this experience is articulated through the symbolic – through her literary work – which is why Duras can also be said to write the unrepresentable without relating it to an imaginary idea such as God in the mystical wordless experience. By letting the experience of *jouissance* be transformed into writing, Duras not only destabilizes the Symbolic, leading "to an aesthetics of *awkwardness*" according to Kristeva (1989: 225), she also puts an hegemonic imaginary of love into a process, thereby making the impossible Real a ground for its representation.

A short passage in *The Lover* highlights this process in a tangible way. The scene is zooming in on the narrator as a young girl just after her meeting with the Chinese man, the lover. She expresses her desire for him, but he wants her to wait and criticizes her for loving love more than him (1997: 42). The idea of being in love with love can be traced back to Augustine's *amans amare*,[9] as well as to the tradition of courtly love where idealization makes of the beloved woman an abstract entity for the male subject's narcissistic desire.[10] When Duras lets the lover in this story inscribe the young girl in these traditional discourses on love she nevertheless also turns them around and deconstructs their idealization of passion. Beyond a psychological reading of the passage, where the lover's anticipated jealousy points to the sexual dissymmetry as a recurrent theme in Duras' work, I would like to underline that Duras' account of the girl's desire in this passage indicates the author's fidelity to the unrepresentable Real. Through the symbolic and the imaginary dreams of union Duras reveals the impossible ground as a condition for every community, be it a couple or a social group, and by doing so she also shows the political potentiality of aesthetics in terms of *dissensus,* to use Rancière's term.

Even though Rancière seems to criticize a notion such as the Lacanian Real for being a "strange contemporary figure of apophatic dogmatism", his description of the function of *dissensus* as the political core of the community is as far as I can see also applicable to Duras' art of the impossible and its undermining of any "policing of domains and formulas" (Rancière 2010: 216–218). Duras' writing moves between an always-deceiving symbolic order and the Real that can only be sensed as "an absence-word", but her art transforms this narrow path into a dissensual practice that therefore becomes a necessity that transgresses private life.

Coda

Duras' description of love and writing is in many aspects inscribed in an actual literary institution conditioned by the liberty to say everything and to say it in the way one wants. Nevertheless, Duras insists that the modern absence of literary moral constraints must be directed by something that is not possible to express in public. If this quality is lacking, as is said in *The Lover*, then *writing is nothing but advertisement*. Differently put, if writing is to be something other than a more or less automatic response to – or mimicry of – the demands of the neoliberal market, then it must obey a counterforce that disrupts the coherence of narratives and precludes any attempt at totalizing a story of one's self. One such counterforce is constituted by Duras' specific arrangement of representing the unrepresentable, which corresponds to the analytical observation regarding the impossibility of fulfilling desire and grasping the Real. In other words, in Duras' writing the path between the two walls of the impossible that Lacan pointed out for the subject is transformed into an art preventing the aesthetic practice, as well as love, from being reduced to the consensus dictated by the ruses of power, which resonates in the late capitalist imperative of storytelling.

Notes

1 For a genealogy of confession and its relation to subjectivity, see Foucault (2014: 102–103, et passim).
2 Anselm Kiefer gives a clear-cut description of this trend in an interview: "The formerly subversive expression '*l'art c'est la vie*' is being perverted into a pure mimicry. The war in the head – the long way from the first idea, from the concept until the result – is reduced to one point. Everything is possible while art actually resides in the fact that almost nothing is possible", "*Pour survivre, je crée un sens, et c'est mon art*", *Le Monde* August 3rd, 2005.
3 Even though Foucault in his work on the history of sexuality from 1976 sees psychoanalysis as part of a more general bio-power, this essay is inspired by the thought that his analysis of the techniques of the self opens up for a radical view of the subversive function of psychoanalysis in actual societies.
4 I have especially in mind the current trends toward autofiction that can be analyzed in the light of the imperative of storytelling in the neoliberal "narrative order" (see Salmon 2010).
5 See for example Adler (2000). When Adler's biography was published in France in 1998 it became a bestseller, which once again indicates the actual interest in the "true story".
6 With Rancière it could be argued that it is only possible to conceive of the unrepresentable within an aesthetic regime where "everything is representable" (2010: 208), which of course is characteristic for Duras' defense of the autonomy of art.
7 In his treatise *The Passions of the Soul* from 1649, Descartes states that "even those who have the weakest souls could acquire a quite absolute dominion over all their passions if one employed enough skill in training and guiding them" (1988: 49).
8 From a psychoanalytic point of view love can be understood as a specific solution to the constitutive lack in every subject formation, which the other is supposed to fulfill, and this imaginary wish for plenitude is manifest in dreams as well as in literary configurations. In his seventh seminar, on *The Ethics of Psychoanalysis* (1959–1960), Lacan first illustrates this idea by referring to the structure of courtly love where the impediments to sexual union can been seen as a way of making up for its absence. Lacan returns to this topic in the twentieth seminar *Encore* (1972–1973).
9 See the third book in the *Confessions* written in Latin between 397 and 400 AD where this experience is depicted as a state before the conversion into a true Christian who only loves God: "I came to Carthage, where a caldron of unholy loves was seething and

bubbling all around me. I was not in love as yet, but I was in love with love; and, from a hidden hunger, I hated myself for not feeling more intensely a sense of hunger. I was looking for something to love, for I was in love with loving" (2002: 31).

10 Drawing on Lacan, Slavoj Žižek argues that the courtly love code's "elevation of woman to the sublime object of love equals her debasement into the passive stuff or screen for the narcissistic projection of the male ego-ideal" (1994: 108).

References

Adler, L. (2000) *Marguerite Duras: A Life*. Trans. A-M. Glasheen. Chicago: University of Chicago Press.

Augustine, A. (2002) *The Confessions of St. Augustine*. Trans. A. C. Outler. New York: Dover.

Blanchot, M. (1988) *The Unavowable Community*. Trans. Pierre Joris. New York: Station Hill Press.

David, M. (1996) *Marguerite Duras: une écriture de la Jouissance*. Paris: Desclée de Brouwer.

Descartes, R. (1988) *The Passions of the Soul*. Trans. S. Voss. Indianapolis: Hackett Publishing.

Duras, M. (1966) *The Ravishing of Lol Stein*. Trans. R. Seaver. New York: Pantheon Books.

Duras, M. (1990) *Green Eyes*. Trans. C. Barko. New York: Columbia UP.

Duras, M. (1994) *The Malady of Death*. Trans. B. Bray. New York: Grove Press.

Duras, M. (1997) *The Lover*. Trans. B. Bray. New York: Pantheon Books.

Duras, M. (2011) *Writing*. Trans. M. Polizzotti. Minneapolis: University of Minnesota Press.

Foucault, M. (1998) *The Will to Knowledge. The History of Sexuality: 1*. Trans. R. Hurely. London: Penguin Books.

Foucault, M. (2014) *On the Government of the Living. Lectures at the Collège de France, 1979– 1980*. Trans. G. Burchell. New York: Palgrave Macmillan.

Kristeva, J. (1989) *Black Sun: Depression and Melancholia*. Trans. L. S. Roudiez. New York: Columbia UP.

Lacan, J. (1977) *The Seminar of Jacques Lacan, Book XI. The Four Fundamental Concepts of Psychoanalysis*. Trans. A. Sheridan. New York: W. W. Norton & Company.

Lacan, J. (1987) Homage to Marguerite Duras, on "Le ravissement de Lol V. Stein." In *Marguerite Duras*. Trans. P. Connor. San Francisco: City Light Books.

Lacan, J. (1992) *The Seminar of Jacques Lacan, Book VII. The Ethics of Psychoanalysis*. Trans. D. Porter. London: Routledge.

Lacan, J. (1998) *The Seminar of Jacques Lacan, Book XX. Encore*. Trans. B. Fink. New York: Norton.

Lacan, J. (2006) *Écrits. The First Complete Edition in English*. Trans. B. Fink. New York: W. W. Norton & Company.

Rancière, J. (2010) *Dissensus. On Politics and Aesthetics*. Trans. S. Corcoran. London: Continuum.

Salecl, R. (2004) *On Anxiety*. New York: Routledge.

Salmon, C. (2010) *Storytelling: Bewitching the Modern Mind*. Trans. D. Macey. London: Verso.

Žižek, S. (1994) *The Metastases of Enjoyment: Six Essays on Woman and Causality*. London: Verso.

PART IV
Without words

10
REPRESENTATION WITHOUT LANGUAGE

Freud and the problem of the image

Annie Hardy

Psychoanalysis, as both a theory and a practice, is intertwined with language. At a bare minimum, the pragmatics of conducting analysis require the presence of two people who are able to exchange ideas through speech. Theoretically, Freud took language beyond a practical necessity: his creation of a metapsychology to accompany his psychoanalytic practice saw him developing intricate and sophisticated views of the role of language in psychic functioning, presenting it as the archetypal vehicle of representation for the conscious, reality-oriented thinking (see Freud 1961: 20).

Freudian metapsychological models are dynamic, rather than static, systems in which thoughts that are represented in different modes are able to influence and communicate with one another (see Freud 1957: 190). In what follows, I will consider the relationship between linguistic and imagistic thought in Freud, with particular emphasis on philosophical issues this can raise for psychoanalysis.

Mental imagery, interestingly, is one of two exceptions that Freud gives to his rule that human consciousness is linguistic (see Freud 1961: 20). As the other is *affect* (Freud 1957: 177), visual thought is the only exception to this rule with an inherently *representational* character. Unlike language, which Freud affords a definite structural position as the representational vehicle of conscious thought, mental images are presented as part of neither the conscious nor unconscious mind. In contrast to other forms of non-verbal representation, such as a conversion hysteria, an act of visual thought does not achieve the status of psychopathology, yet Freud nevertheless states that it is incapable of reaching the level of "full consciousness", which in turn involves the ability to make connections between ideas (Freud 1961: 20).

The fact that Freud makes an exception of the image, I hope to show, potentially betrays some of the key philosophical influences on Freudian metapsychology. Jean Paul Sartre, in his early work *The Imagination*, argues that the relationship between the image and thought in both Western philosophy and early empirical psychology is highly important because it is indicative of the philosophical assumptions (for instance, assumptions about how the mind relates to the body) that each theory adopts (see Sartre 1936: 20). In Freud's case, I will argue, the fact that his presentation of visual thought is shifting and indeterminate throughout his work indicates an underlying metaphysical ambiguity at the heart of psychoanalytic theory.

Before continuing, it is worth clearing up the use of certain terms. Freud falls victim to a natural ambiguity in his use of the term "thought", at times using it to denote the totality of psychological processes and at other times reserving for a certain type of psychological process: namely one that is conscious, minimally rational and reality oriented (see Holt 2009: 3). As Robert Holt has noted, "Freud's theory posits two antithetical forms of cognition, a more primitive form sometimes called 'ideation' and a more sophisticated form worthy to be known as 'thinking'" (ibid.). This confusion in terminology should be acknowledged upfront: whether certain forms of mental activity warrant the label "thought" whereas others (such as imagistic experience) do not is precisely what is at stake in this argument. For clarity, where the term "thought" or "thinking" is used to denote a *specific kind* of mental activity it will be presented in quotation marks.

I will also occasionally use the term "imagination" in the place of "mental images" or "visual thought". This is because several of the philosophers discussed – including Descartes, Sartre and Kant – opt for it as a preferred term for "visual thinking". It is vital to note, however, that they do not intend to imply a sense of creation or fantasy that can accompany the term "imagination" and so these qualities should not be assumed for the sake of the current argument.

Language and the mental image

It could be argued that a "psychoanalytic" way of thinking was born when Freud realised that linguistic mental representations had the potential to become divorced from other forms of mental activity. Although psychoanalysis has been said to have truly begun with the publication of *The Interpretation of Dreams* in 1901, many important features of Freud's uniquely psychoanalytic approach to the mind were present in his creative insights into the language disorder aphasia, which he published as a monograph in 1891. Writing strictly as a neurologist, Freud aimed to challenge contemporary accounts of aphasia, which tried to explain the loss of linguistic ability in aphasic patients by uncovering localised lesions in specific areas of the brain designed for generating and comprehending language (see Freud 1891: 1). He argued instead that aphasia was a disease of *function*, a whole-person phenomena that could not be reduced to the presence or absence of neurological lesions but instead reflected the fact that linguistic mental representations can be divorced from other forms of mental representation, creating problems in expression and understanding (see Freud 1891: 78). The dichotomy forged in "On Aphasia" between language and other forms of mental activity continued to define Freud's division between conscious and unconscious psychic representations throughout his career, with the ability to reclaim lost ideas by articulating them in speech forming the backbone of psychoanalytic therapy and the representation of an idea in "word-presentations" a defining feature of consciousness (see Freud 1957: 200).

The idea that conscious thought and language are interdependent, despite enjoying popularity in philosophy and psychology throughout the twentieth century, has been drawn under increasing scrutiny in recent years. In many psychological sciences it has been common practice since "the cognitive revolution" to consider some species of animals and non-human infants as "thinkers" despite the fact that they are not language users (see Bermudez 2003: 3). This paradigm shift is slowly making its presence felt in philosophy of mind, with Jose Luis Bermudez arguing in his recent work *Thinking without Words* that a sufficient amount of empirical evidence has now been accrued demonstrating that non-linguistic thought is possible, and the task ahead is to fine tune our understanding of the nature of non-linguistic thought, rather than questioning its existence:

> Relatively little work has been done on elucidating the types of thinking that are being attributed to different types of non-language using creatures. The consequences of this basic assumption have been far more deeply explored than its theoretical background. This, of course, is how science proceeds. Niceties of conceptual framework are not at the fore when there is a major paradigm shift. But the new paradigms in ethology, development psychology, and the study of hominid prehistory are sufficiently well established for the more theoretical questions now to demand attention. (2003: 5)

As non-linguistic thought is often taken to be visual in nature (see Gauker 2011), the shift of emphasis towards non-verbal thinking that Bermudez describes has brought with it a wealth of new work on the subject of mental imagery. Contemporary philosophers such as Christopher Gauker and Colin McGinn have argued that the image has mistakenly been cast by philosophers as a form of sensory, bodily activity, when in reality it would be more appropriately seen as a different kind of *thinking* with a greater span of cognitive abilities than previously assumed (see Gauker 2011: 158–159; McGinn 2004: 5). In June 2015, 124 years after Freud's publication of "On Aphasia", a new form of psychological disorder was proposed by Adam Zeman et al. called "Aphantasia", which could be considered the visual counterpart to aphasia. Sufferers of "Aphantasia" undergo a form of visual agnosia that manifests as blindness in "the mind's eye", preventing them from either conjuring or experiencing mental imagery (see Zeman et al. 2015). The phenomena that this diagnostic category targets (imageless mental experience) is not a recent discovery; psychiatric textbooks have described such patients for decades, with Anderson and Trethowan's 1973 publication of *Psychiatry*, for instance, describing a patient who reports:

> I cannot even imagine what my husband or children look like. When I look at something I know what it is, but as soon as I put it away it is completely gone. It is as if you asked me to imagine what air looks like. (1973: 17)

The creation of a new diagnostic category *at this point in time* could therefore be significant, potentially reflecting the growing interest in mental imagery as a topic worth further investigation.

Recent years have also seen an increased effort to unite classical Freudian theory with empirical neuroscience (see Hopkins 2012). I would like to suggest that the two go hand in hand: the developments in perceptual neuroscience that form the back bone of emerging disciplines such as neuropsychoanalysis are the same as those that re-evaluate the idea that linguistic thought is different in kind to mental imagery. Following Sartre's claim that the relationship between thought and the image sets the tone for an overall philosophical worldview, it makes sense that a shifting view of the mental image comes alongside a shifting view of psychoanalysis.

In order to explore this further, I will divide the relationship between mental imagery and language into two broad camps. The first derives from a philosophical tradition that understands linguistic, conceptual thought as fundamentally different in kind from visual thinking, which in turn is cast in the role of a sensory experience. According to this view, rational, conceptual thought is the hallmark of the "mental" (as opposed to the physical) and the bearer of free will in an otherwise causally determined universe. Freudian psychoanalysis has been considered open to similarities with this philosophical worldview, as its concept of personhood includes both a biological, psychically determined unconscious and a rational ego that can freely bring about change in the mind.

The second considers linguistic thought and mental imagery as the exercise of conceptual capacities: the automatic organisation of neural stimuli according to the concepts that an individual possesses. According to this view there is no difference in kind between words and images; both are constituted from the same representational building blocks. As mentioned above, this account owes great debt to the growing field of perceptual neuroscience, where advances in our understanding of the mechanisms that underlie perception have shown that even bare sensory experiences are "cognitively penetrated" (subject to influence and distortion by higher-order brain mechanisms) (see Raftopolous 2009).

The image in metaphysics and metapsychology

Freud's notion of a linguistic consciousness was developed in the context of his "topographical model", which centres on three distinct mental systems: the system unconscious, the system preconscious and the system conscious (1957: 173). According to this model, an idea is dynamically unconscious (or repressed) if it resides within the system unconscious, which represents mental activity in "primary process" thought structures. The "primary process" is a mental event that predates conceptual thought and continues to exist unconsciously in the adult mind throughout life. It only rises to the level of awareness in dreams, psychosis and to a smaller extent in jokes and slips of the tongue. In "The Unconscious" Freud sums up the features of the primary process as follows:

> These instinctual impulses co-ordinate with one another, exist side by side without being influenced by one another, and are exempt from mutual contradiction ... there are in this system no negation, no doubt, no degrees of certainty. ... To sum-up: exemption from mutual contradiction, primary process (motility of cathexis) timelessness and replacement of external by psychical reality. (1957: 185)

The "primary process" is a different Freudian construct from visual thought. Despite a natural resonance between the irrational unconscious and mental imagery, which comes out in particular through hallucinations and dreams, Freud's theory of unconscious thought could not be summed up simply as "visual"; as not only does this fail to incorporate the descriptively unconscious aspect, but Marcia Cavell has shown that a close reading of Freud's writings on unconscious "primary processes" reveals that they presuppose a capacity for rationality and language almost as often as they disavow it (see Cavell 1996). The secondary process represents according to language (the word presentation), tolerates causal and temporal relationships, does not tolerate contradiction and can contain negations (see Freud 1957). The fact that the secondary process is a linguistic thought process underpins Freud's assertion that human consciousness is linguistic; the conversion of an idea from dynamically unconscious to preconscious involves the addition of a linguistic element:

> We now seem to know all at once what the difference is between a conscious and an unconscious presentation. The two are not, as we supposed, different registrations of the same content in different psychical localities, nor yet different functional states of cathexis in the same locality; but the conscious presentation comprises the presentation of the thing plus the presentation of the word belonging to it, while the unconscious presentation is the presentation of the thing alone. (ibid.: 200)

Even if we allow for the fact that the primary and secondary processes may represent two ends of a spectrum rather than a binary distinction (see ibid.: 190), it is hard to give mental imagery a place within them. Freud acknowledges this in his 1923 paper "The Ego and the Id" where he states:

> We must not be led, in the interests of simplification, perhaps, to forget the importance of optical mnemic residues, when they are of things, or deny that it is possible for thought-processes to become conscious through a reversion to optical mnemic residues, and that in many people this seems to be the favoured method. (1961: 20)

Freud's treatment of the mental image as "outside" the standard metapsychological framework has conceptual similarities with Sartre's "problem of the image": the failure of Western metaphysical systems properly to assimilate visual thought into their models of the mind. In terms resonant with Freud's contrast between "word" and "thing" presentations, Sartre argues that philosophers of the early modern period cast the mental image as a "thing": inert and deterministic, comparable to a passively received piece sensation.

> In these three solutions, the image remains an identical structure. It remains a thing. Only its relations to thought change according to the point of view that one has taken on the relations of man to the world, of the universal to the particular, of existence-as-object to existence-as-representation, of the soul to the body.
>
> *(Sartre 1936: 20)*

Sartre argues here that the manner in which a philosophical model characterises the interaction between imagery and "thought" is indicative of the fundamental metaphysical commitments it embodies. His analysis is particularly striking because he shows that philosophers who otherwise adhere to radically different worldviews, such as empiricists and rationalists, nevertheless use the same strategy in regards to the mental image. Throughout the rest of the work, Sartre proceeds to show how the treatment of the mental image in early modern philosophy came to impact the treatment of the imagery in early empirical psychology (ibid.: 21–76): an intellectual climate in which Freud would have been immersed when he was forging the beginnings of psychoanalytic theory. Although it is beyond the scope of this chapter to investigate this period of intellectual history, the relationship between early modern philosophy and early empirical psychology is worth noting for two reasons. For one, it justifies the focus on this particular period of philosophy when drawing conceptual parallels with Freudian metapsychology, as there is some evidence that there are direct currents of influence and not just wide thematic similarities. On a more fundamental level, it demonstrates how empirical studies are susceptible to inheriting implicit philosophical assumptions, allowing these assumptions to shape their general form. Arguably, Freud takes two distinct but interrelated lessons from philosophical theories of the mental image: that imagination is not part of the "thinking" mind (but is closer to a bodily act) and that it cannot be a representational vehicle for acts of reflection. He comments on both of these qualities in the same passage from "The Ego and the Id":

> We learn that what becomes conscious in it is as a rule is only the concrete subject-matter of the thought, and that the relations between the various aspects of this subject matter, which is what specially characterises thoughts, cannot be given visual expression. Thinking in pictures is, therefore, a very

incomplete form of becoming conscious. In some way, too, it stands nearer to unconscious processes than does thinking in words, and it is unquestionably older than the latter both ontogenetically and phylogenetically. (1961: 20)

The idea that the image is closer to the body because it cannot be the vehicle of rational reflection can be found in the rationalist metaphysics of René Descartes. For Descartes the radical dichotomy between thought and sensation parallels several other philosophical dualisms: that between body and soul, rationality and animal instincts, freedom and determinism. His approach gives rise to the classic version of the mind-body problem: asserting that "thought" and the mind are radically different from physical phenomena makes it difficult to account for the ability of thought to integrate or interact with the body or other physical phenomena. In creating this dichotomy of thought and sensation, mind and body, Descartes places the imagination closer to the material body than the rational mind: rather than being a mental activity in the strict sense, the imagination is a mechanism of the body that mysteriously traverses the abyss between the mind and the brain and excites "innate" ideas so that they are experienced as conscious intellectual activity (see Sepper 1996). Descartes justifies this by appealing to the second quality of the image that Freud identifies: its inability to form rational links or reflect back upon itself. Descartes argues that visual thought "differs from pure intellection only in this respect, that the mind in conceiving turns in some way upon itself, and considers some one of the ideas it possesses within itself; but in imagining it turns toward the body, and contemplates in it some object conformed to the idea which it either of itself conceived or apprehended by sense" (1637: 113) A Cartesian mental image, as Sartre describes it, is "an object by the same right as external objects. It is exactly the limit of exteriority" (1936: 9).

Although Cartesian Dualism has lost popularity over the years, the idea that imagistic thought differs from its linguistic counterpart because it cannot act as a representational vehicle for reflection persists to this day. Bermudez argues in *Thinking without Words* that linguistic, conceptual thoughts can be differentiated from non-linguistic thoughts according to their ability to have "intentional ascent" (2003: 151), a psychological function that implies reflective capacity. Reflective thought requires not only thinking about the content of the thought but also its "vehicle" or representational structure. It could be possible to explain Bermudez' reasoning as follows: a linguistic thought can take an imagistic thought or another linguistic thought as its object, but an imagistic thought cannot take a linguistic thought as its object. This is presumably because it is not possible for a mental picture to have a linguistic statement as its representational content without transforming into a linguistic representation itself; words describe images in a way that images cannot describe words. Linguistic thoughts have the built-in potential to be metarepresentations (thoughts about thoughts) whereas imagistic thoughts do not.

Freud's comments on the differing natures of verbal and visual thought can therefore be placed within an established and continuing tradition. This does not necessarily *commit* him to a metaphysical or functional dualism but it does, arguably, reinforce his own claim that acts of visual thought cannot act as vehicles for rational thinking in virtue of their pictorial nature. This insight can then be helpfully woven into the seemingly paradoxical statement that the conscious experience of a visual thought is not "fully" conscious (1961: 20). In asserting this, Freud is not denying that we have phenomenally conscious experiences of mental images but is drawing attention to the fact that the image's lack of linguistic structure necessarily limits the mental operations it can perform. In this regard, Freud's theories of the conscious and unconscious minds are concerned as much with the functional ability of thoughts and ideas as with the awareness that accompanies them.

Freud, arguably, differed from the philosophers Sartre discusses by positing that the mind has *two* distinct ways of relating to the body and the outside world: the unconscious primary process and the conscious secondary process. As Alfred Tauber has argued in *Freud, the Reluctant Philosopher*:

> Basically, Freud divided the mind between the unconscious grounded in the biological and thus subject to some natural causation, and a rational faculty, which lodges itself in consciousness and exists independent of natural cause. (2010: 117)

If Freud's conception of linguistic consciousness shares similarities with the Cartesian model of rational thinking, his portrayal of both imagistic thought and the primary process (in other words, all psychic activity that is not linguistic consciousness) may be better compared with Hume's empiricism. Hume operated at the opposite end of the philosophical spectrum from Descartes: a staunch empiricist, he denied the possibility of a difference in kind between psychological processes, allowing only for differences in degree, claiming that mental images, which in turn are the building blocks of thought, are simply a dimmer version of sensory perceptions (Hume 1739: 56).

It is important to note that while Hume does re-establish an equality between imagery and "thought", he achieves this by showing that both are ultimately a variation on sensory activity. Rather than the image being recognised as a form of mental activity that disrupts the traditional dualism of "thought" and sensation, "thought" itself is revealed as an illusion. What the Cartesians perceive as "rational" or "reflective" connections between ideas are in fact associations formed by habit after repeated exposure in experience:

> Whenever any object is presented to the memory or senses, it immediately, by the force of custom, carries the imagination to conceive that object which is usually conjoined to it.
>
> *(Hume 1777: 31)*

Freud's theory of "primary process" thinking adopts a similar style of associationism. In the system unconscious, chains of ideas form associatively through the mechanisms of "condensation" and "displacement", which connect ideas that have an affective resonance with one another. Consider, for instance, his famous example of Little Hans, whose phobia of horses was formed through the unconscious association between horses and Hans' father (see Freud 1955). Psychic symptoms are formed through primary process mechanisms, and "cured" through the transformation of associative ideas into secondary process thoughts. Freud, in this sense, can be seen as creating a model that pulls elements from empiricism and rationalism. As neither creates a satisfactory account of the mental image, it may be no surprise that it is also an underdeveloped area in Freud's work.

Freud and Kant: dynamic mental systems

The problem with seeing Freudian theory as a hybrid between empiricism and rationalism is that it forces a more drastic split between the conscious and unconscious minds than Freud intended. In other words, it denies that dynamic aspect of the mental functioning: the fact that different forms of representations are capable of influencing and interacting with each other, albeit imperfectly. One answer to the rationalist-empiricist debate in the late eighteenth century was the philosophy of Immanuel Kant, who proposed a "transcendental" solution to the question of how our minds are able to know anything about the world. Kant and Freud, it can be argued, share a certain kinship: both are responsible for generating massive upheavals in our view of our own minds by showing, in distinct ways, how the mind is capable of affecting its own contents. It is therefore through a comparison with Kantian metaphysics that it is best seen how the "problem of the image" manifests for Freud.

Kant's relationship to Freud is explicitly picked up by Tauber, who argues that Freud's later concept of the ego takes on the role of a Kantian rational regulator, one that is able to act freely in the face of a deterministic biological unconscious and steer the path of the individual:

> The critical distinction resides in Freud's acceptance, as a psychologist, of a functional mind-body dualism, and in the higher functions of the mind, he places the repository of interpretative reason. This is essentially a Kantian construction, whereby reason assumes an independent character that allows for a detached scrutiny of the natural world.
>
> *(Tauber 2010: 117)*

The functionalist dualism that Tauber attributes to Freud has ramifications for the possibility that psychoanalytic theory could be consistent with empirical findings in neuroscience, because (like the Cartesian) it introduces an element of mental life that cannot be characterised by physical description alone. Strangely, empirically oriented readings of Freud such as those presented in neuropsychoanalysis can also be traced back to Kantian insights, although the interpretations of his metaphysics in each case differ widely. George Makari, noting the vast range of readings to which Kant is open, has quipped, "Reading the history of post-Kantian philosophy tempts one to conclude that the history of philosophy is a history of misreadings" (Makari 1994: 553). This accusation could just as well have been levelled at Freud: the fact that Tauber's reading of Freud lies at odds with that of neuropsychoanalysis represents just one tension amongst a vast tradition of Freudian scholarship, which tugs him in various ideological directions. In what follows there will be no attempt to canvass the range of interpretation, theory and thought that Freud and Kant have inspired. Rather, to return more directly to the problem of the mental image, I will match two divergent approaches to Kantian philosophy with two divergent approaches to reading Freud. In both cases, the emphasis will be on drawing out the shared philosophical approaches and how this naturally brings with it a conception of the image as a kind of sensory experience or a kind of "thought" respectively.

Although it is far beyond the scope of this argument to give a satisfactory account of Kant's transcendental philosophy, and as a result many subtleties will be missed, it is worth noting how Kant's treatment of the image evolved from the philosophers discussed so far. If one had to nail down a starting point to Kantian metaphysics, it would be the question of how mental representation is possible at all: what capacities must be present in our minds in order to allow us to represent the external environment in the way that we do? To explain the features of human consciousness, most notably its unity, Kant creates a set of transcendental arguments that demonstrate the necessary features of cognitive experience. He operates from the starting point that we cannot know things as they are in themselves but only as they appear to us. As such, he was overtly opposed to Cartesian metaphysics, arguing that Descartes mistook his subjective experience for objective reality. Descartes, Kant argued, was in the grip of a "transcendental illusion", an act of mistaking the experience of oneself (or the world) for its "reality", as though a truly external vantage point were possible. Kant equally rejected "naïve" empiricism: Patricia Kitcher, in her work *Kant's Transcendental Psychology*, has argued that he is best understood as implicitly replying to deep problems in Hume's philosophy of mind by showing that association alone could not possibly account for how we have the stable, unified experience of objects (see Kitcher 1990). As discussed above, Hume attempted to explain how we have the consistent experience of objects in our environment using the "Law of Association" (see 1777: 31), but Kant shows that this is problematic: if habit alone were responsible for the combination of certain sets of sensations into objects, then our constant exposure to a match being struck and catching fire should, in theory, cause us to see the match and the flame as the same object, but this does not happen. We do, however, consistently see different parts of the same telephone as the same object (see Kitcher 1990). Teasing out the difference in kind between these two cases requires us to look at the ways in which our minds use certain principles to synthesise sense data.

Kant begins by acknowledging the rudimentary fact that to represent an object a set of cognitive states must be consistent and coherent. I cannot have the (accurate) representation of a book in front of me as both red and blue at the same time; the sensory stream must be united into an overarching representation that remains consistent. Although unity is necessary for representing objects, we cannot derive it from objects because the unity itself is not given in perception. The unity of conscious experience is achieved by the synthesis of the manifold of sensory data in the "productive imagination". A key aspect of Kant's metaphysical project is his assertion that there are two forms of imagination: the reproductive imagination and the productive imagination. The former, in a comparable manner to the philosophical theories of the image outlined so far, consists of the rebirth of inert sensory experiences that occur in the mind but are nevertheless "thoughtless". The productive imagination, in contrast, consists of the same representational building blocks as thought.

The productive imagination, importantly, is a "transcendental" faculty of the mind. The term "transcendental" should not be confused with "transcendent": Kantian metaphysics is not concerned with what goes beyond experience but what is constitutive of experience itself. When Kant argues in the "Transcendental Aesthetic" that whatever we perceive in the world we necessarily perceive as occurring within space, he is not trying to establish a relationship between the individual and the world where one asserts something about the other in a primarily one-directional manner. Rather, his idea is that a certain kind of being is open to reality in a way that is shaped by the kind of being it is. Due to its status as a transcendental faculty of the mind, the exact notion of the productive imagination is incredibly complex. It is also of paramount importance to the current discussion, as whether one views Kantian philosophy as compatible with empirical data depends, in part, upon the interpretation of the productive imagination that one adopts. On the one hand, the productive imagination may be considered as a metaphysical construct that allows for the possibility of organised knowledge that is nonetheless grounded in experience. On the other, it can be read as a *naturalistic* theory: a description of the mechanisms that the human brain puts to work when creating experience.

Kitcher argues that current empirical evidence demonstrates that the constitution of our minds may influence knowledge in very basic ways, in a manner that can be directly derived from Kant. More specifically, she sees him as responsible for drawing attention to effects of contemporary assumptions about synthesis, which have re-emerged in experimental psychology as "the binding problem": an area of research that attempts to explain how shape, colour, luminance and other properties of objects can be brought under one consistent representation. The fact that this kind of "binding" must occur has been established by studies that demonstrate that we erroneously engage in binding in certain experimental conditions. For example, participants will often combine features of shape and colour in separate pictures that are shown quickly one after the other, despite the fact that the various features belong to different objects (see Kitcher 1990).

The existence of an active combining mechanism was acknowledged in neuroscience from the time that Freud was developing the roots of psychoanalysis. Most notably, Hermann van Helmholtz and Theodore Meynert, both of whom worked closely with Freud, argued that Kant had hit upon fundamental truths about brain operations in his attempt to create a transcendental metaphysics (see Makari 2008). This, Makari has argued, could have been derived in turn from Schopenhauer's interpretation of Kant in which he argued that Kant "showed everything that makes real perception possible, namely space, time and causality, to be brain function. He refrained however, from using this physiological expression, to which our present method of consideration necessarily leads" (Makari 2008: 554; Schopenhauer 1844: 285). This reading of Kant flattens out the transcendental aspect of his metaphysics, seeing him less as philosopher in the strict sense and more as a thinker who intuitively pre-empted later scientific findings.

Once again, the same could be said of Freud as a pioneer of psychoanalysis. Much of the recent work in neuropsychoanalysis has argued that Freudian theories of mind should be seen as providing a subjective account of objective neurophysiological brain processes. In some cases, Freud is seen as actively pre-empting later empirical conclusions (see Hopkins 2012). The theoretical claims of neuropsychoanalysis are grounded in the same model of perception that Freud would have been exposed to via Helmholtz and Meynert, which it has been shown was inspired by Kant. As Jim Hopkins explains in his recent paper "Psychoanalysis, Representation and Neuroscience: the Freudian Unconscious and the Bayesian Brain":

> Helmholtz wrote in a tradition founded by Immanuel Kant (1781). His neuroscientific work partly embodies Kant's idea that we can see our basic concepts (Laurence and Margolis, 2011)—that is, our basic but everyday ways of thinking of space, time, substance, objects, events, and the relation of cause and effect—as performing an unconscious synthesis of the "manifold" of sensory intuition (…) This philosophical perspective, at once straightforward and profound, has been carried forward via Helmholtz, Hinton, Friston, and others, into the conception of the Bayesian brain.
>
> *(Hopkins 2012: 7)*

While Helmholtz's models have been expanded on over the course of the last century, the basic Kantian assumptions have remained the same. These may be necessary for establishing the fact that we play an active role in "warping" our own experience, a premise to which all psychoanalytic models of the mind adhere in one form or another. Within neuropsychoanalysis in particular, the "face-house experiment" is often used to provide an example of how the Bayesian brain can act as an empirical cradle for Freudian theory. In this experiment, a picture of a house is projected onto a participant's right eye and a picture of a face is projected onto his or her left eye, with the result of the phenomenological impression of a face gradually turning into a house, and then gradually back into a face again. This occurs because the brain "knows", from experience, that there is no such thing as a "face-house", so it uses the visual data available in the right eye to conclude that it is looking at a face and suppresses the contradictory data coming in from the left eye. This succeeds momentarily, but there is so much contradictory data (it makes up half of the visual field) that the brain is forced to change its hypothesis, and concludes that it is seeing a house. The cycle repeats, creating the undulating image for the participant. This experiment may explain why individuals appear to act with unified intentions despite the fact that they experience mental conflict, because it demonstrates how conflicting information can be suppressed outside of awareness, compelling us to conclude that the mind engages in the repression of its own contents (see Hopkins 2012).

This experiment, alongside other interpretations that link Kantian philosophy with cognitive psychology or neuroscience, relies heavily on a *naturalised* account of the productive imagination. It solves "the problem of the image" by appealing to empirically realised mechanisms that define all mental activity, from perception to rational thought, as an exercise of "top-down" conceptual capacities. Philosophically, what is lost in such theories is a place for the unmediated sensory "given", a direct access to the world that is not shaped by conceptual capacities (see McDowell 1996). This dissolves the difference in kind between image and thought by transforming the image, along with all visual experiences, into a rudimentary form of thinking.

Although there are theorists who argue that non-conceptual sensory experience is compatible with the findings of contemporary neuroscience, these claims tend to be based upon admittedly speculative experimental interpretation (e.g. Gauker 2011) or have such a limited scope (for example, by applying only to a minute portion of the most primitive perceptual mechanisms) that they have no impact on the wider philosophical issues (e.g. Raftopolous 2009). In other words, it seems less than hopeful that contemporary neuroscience is compatible with a metaphysical worldview in which the image is a form of sensory mental activity that is different in kind from conceptual thought. This represents a drastic reversal of dualist metaphysics, which appeal to the difference in kind between the thought and the image in order to preserve the possibility of freedom of reflection. If both visual and verbal thought are considered an exercise of conceptual capacities, in a manner consistent with scientific interpretations of the Kantian "productive imagination", many of the salient differences between the two collapse.

Conclusion: the image as a psychic symptom

The two diverse readings of mental imagery in Freud, traced through two divergent understandings of Kant, therefore deliver up two very different psychoanalytic models. To characterise this division in the form of a question could be to ask: is a "thinker" simply a range of connected mental states, produced by in-built neurological organising mechanisms, or an agent that connects those states in virtue of reflecting on itself as a thinking being?

Although the former option may serve up a viable and empirically testable solution to Sartre's "problem of the image", this comes at a price: where "thought" is seen as different in kind from other mental processes, it allows space for thought to turn back on itself and for rational reflection to play an active role in shaping mental contents. Although this is by no means impossible in a naturalised reading of psychoanalysis, the need for it is greatly diminished. The "organising" force becomes the brain, rather than the mind, as it constantly creates new perceptual experiences of the world. This, nothing more, can act as a guiding principle for a discipline that is potentially entering a time of great change.

If this work has had one aim above others, it has not been to support or discourage attempts to marry Freudian theory with the neurosciences but, like Sartre, to emphasise that it is impossible to have a descriptive model of mental functioning that is free from underlying philosophical assumptions of the nature of thought and its relationship with the external world, the body and the senses. The fact that Freud and Kant can be interpreted so diversely by scholars from different intellectual backgrounds only serves as testament to this. To finish with an analogy, the mental image in Freud could be compared with a psychic symptom: not because it is inherently pathological, but because it is in fact a *solution in the guise of a problem*. The fact that the image is not integrated into "thought" can be seen as a side-effect of the need to preserve the *sui generis* nature of linguistic and rational thinking, a free sphere of the mind that is defined in contrast to all other kinds of deterministic mental activity and that can meaningfully act as a free agent.

References

Anderson, E. W., and Trethowan, W. H. (1973) *Psychiatry*. London: Bailliere.

Bermudez, J. L. (2003) *Thinking without Words*. Oxford and New York: Oxford UP.

Brook, A. (2003) Freud and Kant. In M. Cheung and C. Feltman (eds.) *Psychoanalytic Knowledge*. New York: Palgrave Publishers Ltd.

Cavell, M. (1996) *The Psychoanalytic Mind: From Freud to Philosophy*. Cambridge: Harvard UP.

Descartes, R. (1641 [1924]) *Discourse on Method and The Meditations*. Trans. J. Veitch. New York: Cosimo Publications.

Freud S. (1955) Analysis of a Phobia in a Five Year Old Boy (1909). *The Standard Edition of the Complete Psychological Works of Sigmund Freud, Volume X (1909): Two Case Histories (Little Hans and The Rat Man)*. Ed. and trans. James Strachey. London: Hogarth.

Freud, S. (1957) The Unconscious (1915). *SE XIV (1914–1916): On the History of the Psychoanalytic Movement, Papers on Metapsychology and Other Works*.

Freud, S. (1958) The Interpretation of Dreams (Second Part). *SE V (1900–1901): The Interpretation of Dreams (Second Part) and On Dreams*.

Freud, S. (1961) The Ego and the Id (1923). *SE XIX (1923–1925): The Ego and the Id and Other Works*.

Freud, S. & Stengel, E (1891). *On Aphasia: A Critical Study*. USA: Literary Licensing.

Gauker, C. (2011) *Words and Images: An Essay on the Origin of Ideas*. Oxford: Oxford University Press.

Herman, A. (2014) *The Cave and the Light: Plato versus Aristotle, and the Struggle for the Soul in Western Civilization*. New York: Random House.

Holt, R. (2009) *Primary Process Thinking: Theory, Measurement and Research*. Lanham: Rowman & Littlefield Publishers Inc.

Hopkins, J. (2012) Psychoanalysis Representation and Neuroscience: the Freudian Unconscious and the Bayesian Brain. In A. Fotopolou, S. Pfaff, and M. A. Conway (eds.) *From the Couch to the Lab: Psychoanalysis, Neuroscience and Cognitive Psychology in Dialogue*. Oxford: Oxford UP.

Hume, D. (1777 [1977]) *An Enquiry Concerning Human Understanding*. 2nd edn. Indianapolis: Hackett Publishing Company.

Hume, D. (1739 [1985]) *A Treatise of Human Nature*. London: Penguin Classics.

Kant, I. (1781 [1900] [2007]) *The Critique of Pure Reason*. Trans. J. M. D. Meiklejohn. New York: Dover Publications Inc.

Kitcher, P. (1990) *Kant's Transcendental Psychology*. New York: OUP.

Livingstone Smith, D. (1999) *Freud's Philosophy of the Unconscious*. Dordrecht: Kulwer Academic Publishers.

Makari, G. J. (1994) In the Eye of the Beholder: Helmholtzian Perception and the Origins of Freud's 1900 Theory of Transference. *Journal of the American Psychoanalytic Association* 42: 549–80.

Makari, G. (2008) *Revolution in Mind: The Creation of Psychoanalysis*. New York: HarperCollins.

McDowell, J. (1996) *Mind and World*. Cambridge: Harvard University Press.

McGinn, C. (2004) *Mindsight: Image, Dream, Meaning*. Cambridge: Harvard UP.

Morgan, L. (1894) *An Introduction to Comparative Psychology*. London: Walter Scott.

Raftopoulos, A. (2009) *Cognition and Perception: How Do Psychology and Neural Science Inform Philosophy?* Cambridge: MIT Press.

Sartre, J. P. (1936 [2012]) *The Imagination*. Trans. K. Williford and D. Rudrauf. London and New York: Routledge.

Schopenhauer, A. (1844) *The World as Will and Representation*, Vol. 2. New York: Dover, 1969.

Sepper, D. L. (1996) *Descartes Imagination: Proportion, Images, and the Activity of Thinking*. Berkeley, Los Angeles and Oxford: University of California Press.

Tauber, A. (2010) *Freud, the Reluctant Philosopher*. Oxford: Princeton UP.

Zeman, A., Dewar, M., and Della Sala, S. (2015). Lives without Imagery – Congenital Aphantasia. *Cortex*. doi:10.1016/j.cortex.2015.05.019. Available from http://www.sciencedirect.com/science/article/pii/S0010945215001781. [Accessed 10 October 2015].

11
UNDERSTANDING WITHOUT WORDS

John Miller

Some 20 years ago, I was conducting a psychoanalytic session when it suddenly felt to me as if I were experiencing a heart attack. Violent shooting pains occurred in my arms and my chest. I felt uncontrollable spasms and could hardly breathe. By using yoga breathing techniques I was somehow able to manage my symptoms until they abated, and the patient on the couch was not aware of what I was going through. After the session medical checks revealed no signs of anything the matter with my heart and circulation. I then realised that the session had been the last one before a holiday break with an emotionally, extremely disconnected patient whose father had suddenly died of a heart attack during a holiday when she was a child. The patient was massively insulated, against taking anything in or expressing any genuine emotion, by a chronic state of manic defence. She also had an eating disorder, which had resulted in her being morbidly obese, so that she was physically insulated from the world around her. I have since come to believe that my "heart attack" was a spectacular countertransference phenomenon where the patient projected into me the inexpressible feelings about a father who died of a heart attack during a holiday break by somehow making me feel that I *was* the father dying at the beginning of the holiday break.

Although she was an intelligent and educated woman with a university degree, which enabled her to get a responsible job in industry, she had been completely unable to process the disastrous experiences in her childhood, which had left her so unable to cope with the emotional pain of life. Being unrepresentable, it could not be communicated symbolically and so was only available to me because the psychoanalytic relationship enabled her to communicate to me in the same non-verbal ways in which the baby makes the mother understand its distress.

A woman colleague of mine had a similar experience with a young male patient who had come for an initial consultation. A few minutes into the consultation my colleague suddenly found that she had a desperate urge to empty her bladder so extreme that she was really worried she might wet herself. She excused herself from the session with some embarrassment and when she returned, the young man was in tears. It transpired that a core issue in the difficulties for which he had come for analysis was the abrupt way in which his mother had abandoned him when he was very small, as a result of which his childhood had been plagued by a history of enuresis. The un-representable – perhaps unspeakable and unthinkable – experience could not be put into words, but it could nevertheless be communicated to someone who was receptive or "tuned-in" enough to pick it up.

These may seem to be mysterious and unusual examples, which might even border on the paranormal, but in fact they are simply rather dramatic demonstrations of countertransference. This is a fundamental aspect of psychoanalytical practice and refers to the emotional experience the analyst has of the patient. This is generally recognised as taking two forms: neurotic countertransference, where the analyst projects his or her own unconscious material onto the patient, and syntonic countertransference, where the analyst picks up unconscious communications from the patient. The only way in which these examples are unusual is the extent to which the repressed mental pain had been compressed, so to speak, into such a tangle of pain and confusion that all its components had to be emotionally projected into the analyst *en bloc*. Consequently, I had to feel that I *was* the father dying of a heart attack, and my colleague had to be made to experience herself as *being* the enuretic child while simultaneously being forced to behave like the abandoning mother. We only sit up and take notice when examples are as dramatic as this – and even then the tendency is to dismiss meaning on the grounds of coincidence or fanciful thinking – but the truth of the matter is that all human beings (as well as animals) send and receive vital complicated communications all the time in ways that are seldom dependent on words.

Let us start with the communication between mother and baby. In the crucial, formative, early weeks and months of life, the baby is incapable of expressing or understanding articulate language. Nevertheless, within a few days of life, the mother starts to be able to interpret the baby's cry as well as its expression, and the baby similarly begins to interpret both the expression in mother's voice and on her face. When it comes to auditory communication (notice I am carefully avoiding anything as specific as the notion of "verbal"), it is the music of mother's voice – what is known technically as the prosody – to which the baby responds. A simple demonstration of this is the way in which, if the mother of a small baby starts to have a quarrel or an argument with someone in the baby's hearing, the baby is very likely to become immediately distressed and start crying. This response to the prosody is a fundamental factor in verbal communication throughout adult life. At the crudest level this is demonstrated by the importance of emphasis, as illustrated by the very different meanings of the following three statements:

I don't believe you!
I don't *believe* you!
I don't believe *you*!

In subtler ways, the music of a person's speech is something upon which we unconsciously rely continually in order to know what he or she is "really" saying and generally to get a feel for his or her attitude and point of view.

There seems to be no doubt that the development of music in the course of civilisation antedates language just as poetry antedates prose. This is because music and poetry involve a living emotional experience whereas the prose of both spoken and written language is, strictly speaking, a code that can convey messages that can be completely devoid of personal or emotional content or even meaningless.

In the 500 years since the invention of printing, written and spoken prose has gradually come to dominate human activities, reaching its apogee in the second half of the nineteenth century with the advent of universal education. During this process, the emotional and relational experiences that used to be mediated by music and poetry have gradually become buried, disguised and in some cases distorted. The general consequence has been a gradual increase in focus on the objectivity and logos of the masculine principle with the gradual loss of contact with the feminine principle of subjectivity and relatedness. As a consequence, humankind has become progressively more advanced technically at the same time as it became more and more disconnected emotionally. The net result is that there has been more and more of the human condition that has become un-representable, which at earlier times in history would have had a voice, a medium or a means of expression.

Consequently, it is no accident that the Unconscious was discovered, and psychoanalysis originally developed, as a result of research into hypnosis and the treatment of hysteria (Freud and Breuer 1955). Although hysterical states involve dissociation and dramatised simulation of suffering, they nevertheless constitute serious defence mechanisms against unbearable mental pain. The phenomenon of hysteria in the nineteenth century can therefore be thought of as a kind of instinctive, acted-out protest against a chauvinist, paternalistic culture that repressed not only women but everything to do with emotionality and spontaneity. One of the principal driving forces in the development of Jung's psychology was his concern about the ultra-rationalism at the end of the nineteenth century, which he felt, was reflected in Freud's desire to make psychoanalysis "medical" and "scientific". Marie-Louise Von Franz, probably C. G. Jung's most celebrated colleague, herself grew up in the region Freud came from and observed that it was probably the most ultra-paternalistic and chauvinist area in that part of Europe at the time. Jung himself came from another bastion of bourgeois artificiality, Zurich, which almost certainly played its part in his developing such unconventional and radical ideas about psychosis. Bourgeois respectability is exclusively concerned with appearances and requires anything embarrassing or irrational to be repressed and denied. A polemical comment on this can be found in the autobiographical book *Mars* by Fritz Zorn ([1976] 2000). Zorn is a pseudonym (it is the German for "anger"), and the book is all about the fact that the author is dying of cancer, which he believes to have been caused by the stifling effect of bourgeois Swiss culture he experienced as concentrated in his family.

Psychoanalysis came into being in response to the neuroses and existential angst caused by the widening gap in the human psyche as humankind got progressively out of touch with itself. The historian Norman Davies, in his 1300 page history of Europe is only able to devote one paragraph to psychoanalysis, summarising the essence of Freud's and Jung's theories. He concludes with the observation that by 1938 "psychoanalysis (...) had established a new, uneasy dimension in people's perception of themselves: 'the Ego is not master in its own house'" (Davies 1997: 861). This is, indeed, the heart of the matter in a nutshell. The real, ground-breaking realisation of psychoanalysis, however, is that the only remedy lies in promoting *understanding* of the unconscious forces at work and learning to *cooperate* with them. Simply reinforcing the Ego to enable it to impose its will on the unconscious forces, regardless, is an intra-psychic version of trying to crush a mutiny or an insurrection without any attempt to understand what gave rise to it in the first place.

It is here that psychoanalysis finds itself on the horns of the ultimate dilemma. The principal – almost the only – medium of communication of the "Talking Cure" is that same written and spoken language that is so big a part of the problem. Words in their logical, lexical form can prove black is white, confound meaning and generate confusion, just as much as the reverse. Freud was acutely aware of this, and whatever aspirations he may have had for psychoanalysis to be "scientific", he was always clear that the essence of it was a human relationship, as opposed to a medical procedure as evidenced in his letter to Jung in 1916 in which he defined it as essentially "a cure through love" (McGuire 1974: 12–13). Central to this, too, was his realisation about the "dangerous method" that led to the crucial discovery of transference: that setting up a situation where the patient apparently fell in love with the doctor was actually the re-experiencing or recreating of the unresolved Oedipal dynamic, which was usually at the heart of emotional dysfunction. There was no way around this if real emotional development was to occur. Theoretical discussion or mind games would not only fail to have any impact on the underlying problems but were actually likely to exacerbate them by creating an illusion of understanding. Real learning and maturation could only occur to the extent that the patient could recognise and abandon the attempt to control the analyst/parent by seduction. Only through a genuine appreciation of the parent's love and resources could the child start to develop them himself/herself.

The other key issue in the question of representing the un-representable is the difficult issue of symbolisation. It is important, here, to be very clear at the outset about there being two somewhat conflicting (even diametrically opposite) uses of the word "symbolic". At the everyday level, anything that stands for something else can constitute a symbol, and words are probably the most common example. The basic principle here is summed up by the expression "Let X equal the unknown quantity", which underscores the arbitrary nature of this use of symbols. When traffic lights were first invented, an administrative decision was taken to use the colour amber to alert the road-user to the fact that the lights were about to change.

By contrast, the use of the word symbol in Object Relation theory and particularly in Jungian psychology, concerns attributes, characteristics and truths about the nature of the world, which are connoted or inherent in human being's perception of their environment. So, for example, the colour red has always been the colour of blood and fire and has consequently had lively or stimulating connotations. The sky and sea are only blue when the weather is calm, and hence blue has a universal connotation of stillness or calm. If the blueness is excessive this may extend to the experience of being becalmed, "having the Blues": in other words being depressed. If any human being from any culture or ethnic group is made to contemplate a pure red screen, his or her pulse will speed up perceptibly, and the opposite will occur with a pure blue screen. Art therapists who work in hospices and people like me who have studied colour symbolism are familiar with the way in which seriously ill adults and children will reflect in the spontaneous choice of colour in their artwork both their emotional experience and unconscious awareness of their medical conditions.

All the cultural achievements of civilisations down the ages make use of this sort of symbolism in the way that they express profound truths and aspirations of the human condition, which, by their very nature, cannot be precisely defined or summed up. They can only be symbolically connoted. The symbols are packed with meaning that can only be partially accessed. It can never be definitively explained or translated. This is how a play by Shakespeare, a piece of music by J. S. Bach or a picture by Leonardo da Vinci has an almost unlimited scope for reinterpretation and being re-experienced.

In the personal experience of individuals, the same is true of the symbolism of dreams. The dream mind expresses itself mostly in visual images that cannot be explained or translated, only contemplated. Perhaps the most serious of all Strachey's mistranslations of Freud into English was the title given to his key work *The Interpretation of Dreams*. The German word *Traumdeutung* was actually coined by Freud and derived from the word *Sterndeutung* which means Astrology, or strictly speaking "scanning the stars in search of meaning". According to Bettleheim, Freud wanted to evoke in his reader's mind the idea of the possibility of extracting some important meaning from mysterious data (Bettleheim 1985). When an analyst interprets a patient's dream he or she is not explaining or reproducing it in words, like someone interpreting from one language to another, but trying to enable the patient to access what is locked up in the symbols. This is much more akin to the interpretation of a piece of music where there is a correct sequence and value to the notes involved but most of the effect of the music comes from the *way* it is played.

Insight is seldom, if ever, achieved as a result of intellectual understanding. Moreover, intellectual understanding is very prone to lending itself to an illusion of insight. A woman social worker patient of mine came one day to a session in a completely distraught state. She explained tearfully how she had begun to realise how damaging it must have been for her children to ship them off to be looked after by relatives for long periods when they were very small. Part of her distress was caused by the fact that she felt she had no excuse for being so psychologically unaware because she had studied Attachment Theory and vividly remembered seeing the films made by the Robertsons about the effects of brief separations. I was able to console her that she had at least learned something very important, namely the uselessness of purely intellectual understanding of a psychological issue.

The mixed blessing of logical thinking and intellectual understanding has a very long history and dates back beyond the Enlightenment to the point where Descartes sought the proof that he existed in the act of thinking rather than the experience of feeling. There is, however, a much more serious threat to emotional insight and real understanding, which has massively increased in the last 50 years and that is the menace of fraudulent and delusional thinking. The problem here is that the un-representable becomes misrepresented.

In the 1960s, long before the concept of Virtual Reality was coined or even conceived of, pioneers in widely different schools of psychoanalytical thought were all beginning to recognise and describe an increasing tendency towards chronic self-deception. Winnicott produced his seminal paper on the aetiology of the False Self (1979), Meltzer produced his paper on Projective Identification (1966), and von Franz her book of lectures on the Problem of the Puer Eternus (1970). All three were, from their different perspectives, addressing the problem that more and more people who – despite being intelligent and sane (from a psychiatric point of view) – were living in a delusional, fantasy world that completely disconnected them from emotional reality, despite apparently functioning in the outside world. The spectacular impact all three of these publications had on their respective readerships testified to the fact that they were all vividly identifying (and in some way, managing to represent) a phenomenon of vital importance. It was, however, the Kleinian tradition with its detailed understanding of the developmental processes in the Inner World – through the work of Bion, and elaborated by Meltzer – that was ultimately to provide a comprehensive understanding as to what was going on. Winnicott's object relations approach places little emphasis on the infant's unique individuality and temperament with the resultant implication that children are somehow created or formed entirely by the mother's treatment and attitudes. Consequently the False Self problem tends to be presented almost as a product of conditioning rather than something the patient is unconsciously keeping going. By contrast, Jung had absolutely no interest in early infantile development and consequently offered no account of how the early emotional development of the infant might be affected by the relationship with the parents.[1] By taking psychoanalysis back to the starting point of birth (and even before) Melanie Klein focused attention for the first time on how mental and emotional functioning develops. It was only as a comprehensive picture began to be formed of how the baby develops its mind through the relationship with that of the mother that it began to be possible to see how the Virtual Reality phenomenon of projective identification resulted from a kind of pathological simulation of healthy developmental processes. It is important to recognise here that what we are talking about is nothing less than the core processes through which knowledge *qua* relationship and knowledge *qua* understanding the world takes place. Mother's mind constitutes a kind of start-up disk, which the baby has to be able to access in order to "download" its own capacity for thinking and relating. If this process is seriously obstructed – mother is physically or emotionally unavailable, or her own mind is seriously disturbed – the baby may have no option but to fabricate a fantasy mother on which to base its understanding. The result, in varying degrees, is likely to be that the individual that results is someone who is play-acting being a person and has little in the way of authentic feelings, beliefs or even understanding about the way the world works.

Bion provided further understanding of the way this process could work and also how it could malfunction (see 1984). He conceived of the infant having mental and emotional experience, which at the start of life it was completely unable to process. He labelled the content of this experience, Beta elements. He suggested that good interaction with the mother's mind gradually provided the baby with the capacity to process its experience, a facility he called Alpha function. Bion's account has a number of advantages. First, it provides a way of understanding how normal development takes place in the mother-baby interaction. Second, it offers an account of how the baby's emotional capacity develops and also how difficulties with that can continue to occur in adult life.

Perhaps Bion's most inspired and revolutionary contribution to our understanding is his concept of Love, Hate and Knowledge (L, H and K) (Bion 1984). The basic premise is that knowledge of the world, as well as knowing another person, results from a state of total engagement where maximum feelings of Love and Hate are experienced. The degree of true knowledge possible is seen as proportional to the degree of engagement. Bion's stroke of genius was to conceive of a negative version of this – minus Love, minus Hate and minus Knowledge – all of which centred round avoidance and non-engagement. Thus, minus Love is not Hate, but the avoidance of Love and desire: perhaps characterised by puritanism. Similarly, minus Hate is not Love, but the avoidance of Hate as is found in sanctimony. The more minus Love and minus Hate are present, the more there is likely to be minus Knowledge: avoidance of understanding, the "don't-want-to-know mentality" such as we see in the denial of critical issues like climate change or indifference to poverty and famine.

Donald Meltzer, with whom I worked for over 20 years, not only managed to digest the dense and difficult writings of Bion (whose supervision groups he attended), but also elaborated the whole phenomenon of projective identification further. He realised that the model on which the psychic retreat of projective identification was unconsciously based was the fantasy of the inside of mother's body as imagined by the baby, according to the perception it had of different parts of her. Thus, the eyes and the breast are the source of a blissful and exhilarating experience so that the illusion (through projection) of being inside that part of the mother produces "heady" delusions of being infinitely wise, inspired and "above it all".Thus someone in this state of mind is described as "living in the Head/Breast" (Meltzer 1992: 72). Secret fantasies of being an undiscovered genius, or the new Messiah, usually occur and flourish when people are in this state. If the experience of the Head and the Breast are Heaven, then Hell and the Underworld are to be encountered at the other end: mother's Rectum. Life in this state is vividly described by Kafka, especially in *The Trial*. Life seems to go on, but there is no escape from the unspoken accusations and persecution of an invisible police state where everything and everyone is corrupt and the only relationships are sleazy, sexual fumblings.

The paranoid experience of Kafka's world arises from a deeply buried awareness that the manoeuvre of projective identification is essentially an illicit one in that it involves a kind of stowaway operation to get inside the Object and thereby magically acquire its qualities. The beauty of mother's smile and the blissful experience of her breast, as portrayed in thousands of paintings of the Madonna, *is* a representation of heaven, but it can only be genuinely experienced through a real, dependent relationship with a Mother.

It seems likely that more often than not when people are diagnosed with depression – particularly when they are suicidal – what is actually happening is that they have unconsciously fallen into the Rectum, psychically speaking. Genuine depression is characterised by a feeling of unworthiness and humility, whereas people in suicidal states are usually insisting that life *must* go the way they want it or else they will take themselves hostage and kill the hostage. In the Middle Ages, evidently, there were epidemics of people getting into this mind-set as whole monastic communities were affected. There were even specialist monks – sort of mediaeval, group analysts – who were called in to deal with the problem. The way it was viewed suggests that the mediaeval Church had a better grasp on psychology than modern psychiatry, as the diagnosis that was usually made was Acedia, one of the Seven Deadly Sins that is usually defined as Pride, in the form of denial of the Love of God (Norris 2008). In other words, they realised that what was happening was not that the brothers were being mysteriously afflicted by something happening to them but that they were indulging in a sinful attitude that was making them feel they were in Hell.

The key to all of this lies in the recognition that the main problems occur whenever someone creates an illusion of being someone or something else by using the mechanisms of projection. Once there is confusion about the boundary between internal fantasy and external reality of emotional experience it is literally true to say that all hell breaks loose in the mind. A vivid, visual portrayal of the kind of hell that threatens can be seen in the painting *The Garden of Earthly Delights* by Hieronymus Bosch, where one detail portrays the Prince of Hell simultaneously eating people and excreting them. A more modern portrayal of the confusion of zones and boundaries is that which occurs in Peter Greenaway's film *The Cook, the*

Thief, His Wife and Her Lover (1989) where a Mafia Godfather-style figure presides over torture scenes in a kitchen that somehow seems to be also a bathroom-cum-toilet while an angelic choirboy sings in the background. What is being so vividly represented here is both the conflicting images of heaven and hell as well as the geographical and zonal confusions into which is the viewer is plunged.

Meltzer's detailed description of the various forms of Virtual Reality into which people unconsciously plunge themselves, which he called the Claustrum (Meltzer 1992), is of vital importance in understanding the most common psychological and relational problems that take up most of the time of the helping professions. Probably one of the most paralysing and debilitating forms of this is anxiety states (often referred to under the generic heading of "Stress"), which in the analytical consulting room almost invariably turn out to be caused by the strain of the patients' trying to keep up the chronic performance of pretending to be what they are not. They feel as if they are undercover agents who are permanently terrified that they are going to forget their cover story and reveal their fraudulent identity.

Over the last 20 or 30 years psychoanalysis has produced a massive amount of evidence that this is what actually lies behind most problems of panic, phobias and particularly claustrophobic states. I have come to believe that a significant factor in global warming is the claustrophobic anxiety behind the millions of frantic, unnecessary airline flights and car journeys by which people are actually trying to escape from the fantasy safe-house in their head which has become a prison. This explains, too, why it is so common for people to be endlessly trying to fit themselves into some kind of preconceived idea of what they ought to be or what ought to be happening, rather than to respond spontaneously to life. Clearly when this is operating in supposedly personal relationships there can be no emotional contact, only play-acting and delusion.

This was, of course, anticipated by Ibsens's play *Et Dukkehjem* (*The Doll's House*). Helmer is in the Claustrum where he does not see that he is play-acting being a husband. Nora is no longer in the Claustrum. She is in touch with her feelings and sees their marriage is a farce – but it could change! If only they could both change!

NORA: *Da maate baade du og jeg forvandle os saaledes at...* [Then both you and I would have to change ourselves so that ...]
HELMER: *Nevne det!* [Name it!]
NORA: *At samliv mellom oss to kunne bli et ekteskap. Farvel.* [So that the relationship between us to could be a marriage. Adieu!] (Ibsen 1962: 114)

To my English ears, the Danish word for marriage – *ekteskap* – is particularly relevant since it is made up of two words: *ekte* which means "real" or "actual", and *skap* which means "creation". Thus, the word for marriage literally means something like "the real thing" or "the genuine article". In a more everyday and much less surreal manner than Hieronymus Bosch's painting or Greenaway's film, Ibsen's drama manages to represent vividly the misrepresentation of a relationship.

Finally, there is another form of representing that plays a central part in psychoanalysis and that concerns the way in which the analyst represents something for the patient in the sense of being a *representative*. In this kind of representation the demands of the contributions of one person or group of people cannot be directly expressed unless they have a representative to act for them. In society and in politics we are familiar with the idea of a particular interest group or minority needing to be represented. This kind of situation is almost always present in psychoanalysis in the way in which either the patient's real interests have never had a voice that was heard, or else the patient has not encountered representatives from the world of good parenting. In such cases, the efficacy of the analyst depends on how far he or she can be a satisfactory representative, either in giving a voice to the un-heard emotional needs of the patient or being an authentic representative of parental concern and reliability, which the patient may not even be able to imagine. It often seems to be necessary – perhaps particularly in Jungian circles – to establish the fact that the world is not peopled by mothers and fathers, devils and angels, but by ordinary human beings through whom it is possible to have angelic or diabolical experiences. Thus, the analyst is always representing something, but the resultant experience the patient can have is nonetheless potentially a real one. The analyst sitting in the chair behind the patient's head is just an ordinary person, probably a bit older than the patient, who is simply listening and trying to understand. Patients can know this but nevertheless have a genuine emotional experience of the analysts as if they were actual, loving parents.

Returning for a moment to the question of the limitation of language, it has often been observed that what the analyst actually says is probably far less important than is popularly supposed. As with the child's experience of its actual parents, it is their character and what they genuinely stand for that has the most influence. Having talked to hundreds of children about the adults in their lives, I have often been struck by how acutely aware children are of the true nature of their parents and teachers. A super-efficient adult who is basically cold and calculating is going to have a far more negative effect on the child than a genuine, warm-hearted parent who is a bit disorganised. In the case of psychoanalysis it is impossible for someone to have the undivided attention of another person two or three times a week for years without being able to form a pretty definite impression of what his or her true character is and be influenced by it.

What distinguishes psychoanalysis from virtually every other therapy is that it is essentially about core values. It has no agenda, magical solutions, quick fixes or messianic message. As far as I can see, it inevitably shares the basic truth of Christianity about the centrality of love and the capacity for concern. In order to develop and cultivate this, the destructive part of the personality must be recognised and the battle joined to keep it in check. Therapies that are preoccupied with feeling better, coping or success do not have this. The spiritual father of psychoanalysis I have always believed was not Freud, but Socrates who summed it up by saying "the unexamined life is a Life not worth living" (Plato 1960: 132–133).

Note

1 In a personal communication (1994) to me shortly before he died, Michael Fordham described how he had had a conversation with Jung's wife, Emma, in which she said, "The trouble with Carl is he doesn't understand anything about children. He is only interested in archetypes".

References

Bettleheim, B. (1985) *Freud and Man's Soul*. London: Fontana Paperbacks.

Bion, W. R. (1984) *Learning from Experience*. London: Heinemann.

Davies, N. (1997) *Europe a History*. London: Random House.

Freud, S. and Breuer, J. (1955) Studies on Hysteria (1893–1895). *The Standard Edition of the Complete Psychological Works of Sigmund Freud, Volume II (1893–1895): Studies on Hysteria*. Ed. and trans. James Strachey. London: Hogarth.

Ibsen, H. (1962) Et Dukkehjem. In *Nutidsdramaer (1877–99)*. Oslo: Gyldendal.

Kafka, F. (1984) *Der Prozess*. Berlin: Fischer Taschenbuch Verlag.

McGilchrist, I. (2012) *The Master and His Emissary*. New Haven and London: Yale University Press.

McGuire, W. (ed.) (1974) *The Freud/Jung Letters: The Correspondence between Sigmund Freud and C. G. Jung*. Princeton: Princeton UP.

Meltzer, D. (1966) The Relation of Anal Masturbation to Projective Identification. *International Journal of Psychoanalysis* 47: 335–42.

Meltzer, D. (1992) *The Claustrum: An Investigation of Claustrophobic Phenomena*. Strathay: Cluny Press.

Norris, K. (2008) *Acedia and Me: Marriage, Monks and a Writer's Life*. New York: Riverhead Books.

Plato (1960) *The Apology*. London: William Heinemann Ltd.

Von Franz, M-L. (1970) *The Problem of the Puer Eternus*. New York: Spring Publications.

Winnicott D. W. (1979) Ego Distortion in Terms of True and False Self. In *The Maturational Processes and the Facilitating Environment*. London: Hogarth.

Zorn, F. ([1976] 2000) *Mars*. Frankfurt: Fischer.

Filmography

The Cook, the Thief, His Wife and Her Lover (1989) Directed by Peter Greenaway. UK: Allarts Cook, Erato Films, Films Inc.

PART V
Wounds and suture

12

RETHINKING THE PRIMAL WOUND, TRAUMA AND THE FANTASY OF COMPLETENESS

Adopted women's experiences of meeting their biological fathers in adulthood

Elizabeth Joyce

Introduction

This chapter draws from an in-depth qualitative interview with a female subject to give a psychoanalytic and discursive reading of adoptive women's experiences of meeting their biological fathers in adulthood. It relates the narrative data to three principle discursive constructions of the "reunion" experience: first, the themes of "truth", subjectivity and belonging in relation to notions of loss and wounded subjectivity; second, discourses of eroticism and desire; and finally, the entanglements of cultural and familial politics in respect to "selfhood". I argue that adoptive subjects have been widely constituted by an irreparable "primal wound" caused by the trauma of maternal separation (Verrier 1993). The figure of the wounded adoptee is bound up in discourses of erasure and repression, loss and longing and the idealisation of "real" parents rooted in biology (see Freedgood 2013; Schuker 2013; Schwartz 2013). As Andrew Cooper puts it, "The emotional realities of abuse, neglect and abandonment experienced by so many of the children who are placed for adoption are almost unthinkably painful" (2008: xiii). The adoption experience, symbolised by the "unthinkably painful" trauma of disconnection, then raises complicated questions about representing the "unrepresentable".

The construction of the adoptive subject as being immersed in a fantasy of incompleteness and longing for the birth mother closes down the space for imagining the birth father's role. It is only in juxtaposition to the all-encompassing maternal that his figure is brought into being. Indeed, as Tabitha Freeman writes, "psychoanalytic theory recreates the fundamental paradoxes of patriarchy by giving central place to the father as a symbolic figure of authority while eclipsing men's relationships with their infants under the shadow of the omnipresent nurturing mother" (2008: 115). The peculiar tension between the "symbolic presence and substantive absence of fathers evident in patriarchal thought" more broadly raises questions significant to this research about the absent presence of the birth father in adoption (ibid.). That he has hardly been spoken about directly does not imply that he is invisible. Rather, it would seem that his absence shores up the potentiality of biological discourses that reinforce normative conceptions of belonging. The birth father is often uncharted territory and can therefore only vaguely be imagined. This gap, which defines his position, arguably reflects the lack that constitutes the wounded adoptee and biological father alike. Something is missing that cannot be named. The missing biological father might then become symbolic of a deeper notion of loss associated with adoption overall. This implies that the dearth of knowledge surrounding the biological father may perpetuate an already present deficit within the adoptee, which is linked to the original grief. Lifton illustrates this point when she says:

> An adopted daughter who looks in the mirror hoping to see her birth mother's face has no way of knowing if it is her father who looks back at her. She is linked to her mother through fantasy and longing, but her father is lost in the void with no mooring. (1994: 193)

From this perspective, then, the story of the adopted subject begins with the story of an internal split between the adoptee and her "real" mother, as well as the adoptee and her "real self". The "outside" figure of the birth father remains the "shadowy figure" of adoption (see Clapton 2008), his indiscernibility marking a non-place within adoption theory and practice. By interrogating these constructions, this research attempts to set up a discussion about how we might bring the "shadowy" father into focus and how, by representing the predominantly unrepresented, we might challenge static ideas about adoption trauma and the possibility of ever recovering an essential self. In creating space for thinking through the father's position, this work undermines culturally normative representations of the maternal bond, asking instead questions about what the birth father represents; why he has widely remained overlooked; and how this thinking can challenge essentialist ideas and allow new stories and subjectivities to emerge.

Trauma culture

Before moving on to analyse the narrative material, it is worth passing comment on a wider cultural discourse onto which the notion of the traumatised adoptive subject can effectively be mapped. If we interpret the primal wound idea in isolation, apart from general discourses of self, we might assume that the issue of trauma uniquely determines adoptive subjectivity. But if we interrogate wider discourses, then we find a range of accounts of trauma, which in some ways construct *all* human subjects as wounded. Indeed, Fassin and Rechtman argue that "trauma has become a major signifier of our age" (2009: xi). Against this backdrop, one could think about the wounded adoptee in terms of our cultural fascination with what Mark Seltzer names as "suffering, states of injury and wounded attachments" (1997: 4). Invoking the intersection between private desire and the public sphere, the primal wound could be contextualised temporally as a product of trauma culture, responding to collective internal fantasy and desire, emotional damage and psychic pathology, as well as being located outside with the exposition of confession and vulnerability. "The notion of trauma", Seltzer argues, has "come to function as a switch point between individual and collective, private and public orders of things" (ibid.: 5). This idea that "the wound" is everywhere in Western culture has been taken up by other theorists, notably, Roger Luckhurst, whose influential essay "Traumaculture" puts forward the thesis that "a new kind of articulation of subjectivity emerged in the 1990s organised around the concept of trauma" (2003: 28). Following Seltzer, he recapitulates the notion that "the wound opens the inside to the outside (and vice versa), eliding boundaries and confusing subject and object" (ibid.).

In a world in which pain is eroticised and "the torn and exposed individual" has become a "public spectacle" (Seltzer 1997: 3–4), trauma and loss, stress and pain are now widely accepted terms in the language of everyday life. It is possible then to construe a relationship between these discourses and suggest that the primal wound is a product of trauma culture. But this analysis would be inadequate. Throughout adoption discourses, adoptive subjects are widely constituted by a different kind of trauma: something that goes *beyond* the trauma capturing our cultural imaginary and outlined in the above text. It is a complex, developmental trauma, resulting in deep-rooted attachment problems and requiring a particular understanding and approach in order for its victims to be healed. The Reverend Keith Griffith, quoted widely across websites and popular adoption literature, summarises, "Adoption loss is the only trauma in the world where the victims are expected by the whole of society to be grateful" (2013). Here again we are reminded not only that adoption implies loss, but also that there is no way out of this loss. The complexities of lived experience are reduced to narratives of suffering, and its subjects are located in immovable positions of permanently repeating psychic pain. Referring to the trauma controversy, Lambek contends, "Trauma lays out unambiguous victims and villains; it thus serves as a morality play [...] a kind of local and contemporary witchcraft scenario" (2009: 255). If we look at the language used in this discourse, we find terms such as "healing", "reunion", "homecoming" and "closure" being attributed to the adoption experience, giving readers the sense that adoptive subjects are "survivors", engaged in a trajectory of recovery. Equally, we find accounts of on-going trauma that resist notions of restoration and in doing so bring into existence the definitive victim bound by "lifelong expense/ pain/ torture ..." (Athan 2010).

Here I shall touch briefly on a critique made by a biological mother in her blog, Adoptioncritic.com. The author levels her charge against the idea that adoptees can ever gain "closure" from the "continually compounding" loss in which "every birthday apart, every moment separated, all the years and minutes apart… and the ties that are not ties, family that is not family". Recalling Lambek's (2009) notion of the "morality play" of trauma culture, adoptive subjects and their "natural parents" become the victims of exploitative adopting families and societal institutions and are rooted in subject positions of "unresolved grief, ongoing pain" and "ongoing loss". They are the walking wounded, permanently disturbed by their psychic pain. It was Freud who "cemented the idea of psychic trauma" (Hacking 1996: 76), and the limits of giving it expression are tied up with Freud's notion that it manifests as "an experience which within a short period of time presents the mind with an increase of stimulus too powerful to be dealt with or worked off in the normal way" (Freud 1963: 275). This raises questions about the authority we allow ourselves in attempting to represent the unrepresentable. Turning now to the narrative of one female adoptee, which has been drawn from a larger sample of 15 interviews, the following analysis seeks to rethink well-documented notions of maternal separation trauma (see Horowitz 2013) and the primal wound, by creating space for an exploration about the marginalised paternal figure.

The participant

Mary, a 45-year-old white American female subject, made contact with me by responding to an advertisement I placed on an online adoption forum seeking to recruit volunteers to take part in research on adopted women's experiences of meeting their biological fathers in adulthood. I chose Mary's account from the pool of other stories because of the ways in which it relates to the limits of representation. She had been in contact with her biological father for about a year at the time of our two interviews, which were both conducted via Skype. She was adopted in infancy by a couple who had lost one baby during childbirth, and another two of their biological children had been institutionalised due to severe disabilities. Mary was a biological mother herself, having given her son up for adoption 24 years prior to the interview. Around the time she placed him for adoption, she obtained papers from the court regarding her own biological history. These records detailed the name of her birth mother and a short commentary about her birth father. This information enabled her to find her birth mother quickly as well as offering her clues about the identity of her birth father. She initially established contact with her birth mother for about a year and a half. She learnt that her birth mother had been married to her birth father when she was born and that she had siblings on both sides, but they had since separated, and her mother never remarried. Her biological siblings had been led to believe that they all came from the same parents, so her mother had kept Mary's birth a secret. In Mary's words:

> [My mother] wasn't able to tell anybody about me and so eventually she wrote and said she couldn't have contact. She wasn't able to have contact. It was just emotionally too hard for her, and it was the second worst decision

she'd ever made in her whole life, umm, 'cause she'd walked out on my brothers when I would've been about seven years old, and so, umm, that was, I mean that was a very hard rejection at that point, and, umm, I have not had any contact with her since.

Speaking to the difficulties of representing the silence and shame surrounding exclusion and the politics of stigma, a similar story emerged in relation to her biological son, whom she had put up for adoption then met during adulthood. Maintaining that she had felt adoption "was the proper thing to do" at the time because "nobody had stepped up and said I'll help you take care of him" and she "didn't want the influence of his father", she said her attempts to prevent her son's father's involvement had since "backfired" on her, angering her son and turning him against her. Stressing the fluidity and complexity of these relations, she said that when she had first met her son, she "went through the whole, umm, regression thing with him where he regressed back and contact was incredible". Describing an intoxicating period in which she was in contact with her son all the time, she explains, "I was on the phone with him for over sixty hours a week and made seventeen or eighteen hundred text messages and he still, he said he still wasn't getting enough of my time and attention". This ended when "one day he just walked away". Although still maintaining a link with Mary's husband and other children, and most significantly with his own birth father, he refused to engage with her at all. Her son's adoptive father was in prison, and so she said, "the adoptive family has put the birth father in more of a fatherly position – they don't care if he has contact, he's not a threat to them. And, umm, they look to me as more of a threat to the mother, so, umm, they pretty much told me to take a hike." Set against this narrative of alienation with regard to her position in these kinship structures, it seemed that Mary initially found consolation in the figure of her biological father, accrediting him with the ability to say exactly what she needed in order to "make [her] feel okay".

But this was complicated terrain. Mary had only known her biological father for a year at the time she gave her account and as with the story she told about her birth mother and son, the narrative could not be read as static or fixed. Indeed, shifts can be traced between the first and second versions, given only a month apart, in which her experiences were initially described as "really healing" and in the latter account became "confusing". As she said in her second interview, "I'm still trying to wrap my brain around it all," saying that she could provide an outline of the story but had trouble filling in the gaps or reconciling "the whole disconnection around my emotions". Following Freud's analyses of trauma, Cathy Caruth links the difficulty of representing psychically overwhelming experiences with the idea that "the experience of trauma, the fact of latency, would thus seem to consist, not in the forgetting of a reality that can hence never be fully known; but in an inherent latency within the experience itself" (Caruth 1995: 8). The "disconnection" in Mary's text emphasises a failure to make sense of her reality and put it into words. This raises ethical issues about the researcher's role in the narrative construction of another's experience and the ways in which it speaks to temporality. Setting up a dialogue about the complex dimensions of multiplicity that form the layers of the adoption "reunion" experience, I want to reinforce Jones' idea that the "interviewer as writer/storyteller emerges later in the (narrative inquiry) process through his/her retelling of the story as a weaver of tales, a collage-maker or a narrator of the narrations" (Jones 2003: 61). This also opens up a space for thinking about the licence we give ourselves to speak for the other and how this relates to the problem of representing the unrepresentable. I will turn now to the themes of "truth", subjectivity and belonging that are interspersed throughout Mary's account.

"Truth", subjectivity and belonging

The theme of the relevance of biological fatherhood is fundamentally linked to positionality: namely, his position within the discursive framework and the adoptee's position in relation to that. Here the theme of belonging, which permeates Mary's discourse, is discussed in relation to "truth" and subjectivity. Returning briefly to the source of data from which this narrative has been drawn, it is notable that, in some accounts, the biological father was constructed as presenting a challenge to the adoptee's feeling of security and belonging; whilst in others his position was hailed as aiding self-acceptance and an experience of being genealogically linked to the world. A few narratives pointed to a longing for connection that was not formed, whilst some emphasised the importance of belonging to wider networks such as culture, religion and myriad kinship groups. Taking as a starting point the idea that the birth father is constituted as a potential challenge to the female adoptee's subjectivity and belonging, Mary related as an example the notion that her birth father was the first person she ever felt accepted by just for being herself. But she followed this with an admission of fear that he would one day abandon her:

> … but in the back of my head I'm always, you know like when am I going to say something, you know when is something going to happen and he's just going to walk away, and you know that's my fear because I feel like a lot of times you know I'm just walking on eggshells because I'm scared something's going to happen even though he's given me no reason to.…

Crediting her biological father with the power to both "make [her] feel okay" and deprive her of security indicates a paradox in relation to what the encounter can offer.

Suggesting that narrative is constantly on the move and that there is no end point to be reached, the tension between the instability of this flow and the subject's desire to "know", to "understand" and by implication, to fix, is developed when she talks about her fear of the uncertainty of where her relationship with her biological father will lead. Relating this uncertainty back to the biological father's lack of definition or place within existing discourse, we can make links to the possible wider ramifications of his absence and its influence on the creation of adoptee subjectivity. Here the birth father's presence evokes anxiety about his imagined absence, which is always imminent, and which dismantles the notion of "reunion" as being some kind of harmonious, uninterrupted state. The fear of loss that is fundamental to Mary's account of finding her biological father also invites us to think about the ways in which the theme of loss is organised in adoption "reunion" discourse generally. If we understand the dominant discourse as that which formulates adoption in terms of trauma created by the child's loss of the biological mother, then we get an idea about how the "healing" process is mapped. Loss then produces its counterposition of gain, but the initial gain – of the child's adoptive parents – is overlooked in favour of a future imagined gain, that is "reunion" with the lost mother and the achievement of psychic integration. This discourse then raises questions about what it does to the adoptive subject who inhabits the space of loss or lost space. Configured by loss, the adoptive subject is divided within this binary field of loss and gain, real and unreal, biological and social, and thus the "healing" which is imagined by "reunion" is somehow always unreachable and the "self" unknowable. The sense of gain that comes from finding is constantly vulnerable to the threat of losing and the subject continually in danger of coming apart, or as Mary puts it, her foundation reduced to "eggshells".

But before coming to the conclusion that Mary's story should be read as an account of a split subject that reinforces the pervasive trope of the adoptee's abnormality, it is important to rethink the ways in which dominant discourses of adoptive life function to produce notions of psychic disturbance. Mary's narrative draws attention to the complexity of 'adoption trauma', as her fear of loss raises questions about how this experience might differ in a subject who has been brought up by her parents or with full knowledge of who her parents are. To contextualise the subject's anxiety that 'something's going to happen' and that her father will leave, simply within the framework of her adoption, is to give too much significance to the kinship system in which she is located. As the text suggests, she is fearful that something is going to happen, even though she has been given no reason to be so concerned. While this might be interpreted as a form of attachment anxiety rooted in the original parental separation and unconscious wounding, this forecloses other possible readings about the limits of certainty and stability in all relational processes and the fragmentation of subjectivity. The introduction of the biological father also marks a radical departure from the normalising discourse of the mother–child bond and the idea about trauma resulting from this moment of separation. As I argue, he is still constituted as the unknown and forgotten figure of adoption. Mary's narrative troubles this by opening up a space, not just creating new possibilities for thinking about him but also disrupting the power surrounding naturalising notions of mother–child unity. Naming their "reunion" experience as "pretty amazing" and "healing" produces a portrait of the idealised father, far removed from the indeterminate, neglected "shadowy figure" constructed by leading discourses. Her narrative enters into questions concerning fatherhood generally and the potential for comparisons between adoptive and biological fathers. For Mary, her adoptive father was "very caring, very attentive", the "polar opposite personality of [her] natural father". But this was not imagined by her as a good thing. She aligned herself more with her "opinionated, strong-willed" biological father and attributed difficulties in forming a bond with her adoptive father to these personality differences: "I have this very strong-willed personality, and [until I met my birth father] I didn't have anybody to sort of help me process it or deal with it in any way".

This example of reciprocity in their personalities might be flatly interpreted as an affirmation of her sense of being seen and valued by her birth father and the idea of belonging to blood, as opposed to "fictive" kin. But a deeper reading emphasises ambiguities and uncertainties, as her descriptions of not knowing who her father is or how he and she might fit into each other's lives, along with her fear of what might happen, signify the fluidity of "reunion" as not just a singular event as the word implies, but a relation that is open-ended and complex: challenging to restrain or pin down. Peppered throughout her story we find traces of anxiety, turmoil and the feeling of being overwhelmed, as well as a longing for meaning and perhaps certainty. In Mary's words:

> Like if I don't keep busy then my anxiety levels will go up and I'll start being very, you know, tense and, umm, scared, you know it's that whole, umm, baby in me again saying "oh he's gone again" or he's umm, you know, he can't do this anymore, you know the emotions are just too hard, and so then it's a lot about dealing with the emotions myself, reassuring myself, and, you know, talking to myself about, you know, he's been very clear he's not going, but you know this is all very new and raw and so, what does not going anywhere look like?

The anxiety and rawness sketched out in Mary's text speak to the limits of representability. Apparently seeking to give form and certainty to the uncertain: 'what does not going anywhere look like?' leads to questions about eroticism and desire, roles and expectations which will be unpacked in the following section.

Discourses of eroticism and desire

Developing the point about Mary's identification with her birth father's temperament, she also noted a likeness with his appearance: "[Before meeting him] we got his pictures and I looked at him, he was, umm, he looked so familiar to me, and it was very, umm, soothing, it was like I already knew him". Although this text could be tied in with any theory of the unconscious desire of daughters vis-à-vis their fathers, what makes adoption stories unique is the subject's experience of holding two fathers in mind. This narrative has recourse to genetic discourses of comparison but also to a magnetic appeal he represented, which she extended to the allure of men generally who reminded her of her birth father: "the men I've been attracted to [...] are very similar to my father". Indeed, she was straightforward about the connection between what her biological father meant to her and erotic discourse but unsettled this with reference to other people's construction of what was going on between them: "I mean, it looks a lot like an affair, because my age and the amount we communicate and the interaction between us, you know because we don't, to the outside, depending on the eyes that you look at the relationship through. Does that make sense?" Her account of the ambiguity of other's perceptions of their relationship seemed to motivate her to close down any potential concerns as she said firmly:

> ... the relationship is, well, it is a love relationship, I mean, that's what it is, I mean, it must look so weird to the rest of the world now, because you know, I'm an adult now, because, and what I say to people is consider what you feel about an infant and you know, how hard it is to leave, you know, what it feels like to leave that child, and you know, just having him hold me is a beautiful thing, you know, it just kind of calms me, because I'm like, I just want a hug, I just want him to hold me, just hold my hand, you know, just hold me, and umm, he just wants to be with me. ...

The regressive imagery within the discourse of her biological father's capacity to soothe her may be interpreted as being homogenous with the notion of the mother-child union presented in the Primal Wound theory. But more than that I think there seems to be a strong sense of rationalisation and eroticism here. This raises pertinent questions about representability and the licence I give myself to interpret differently the respondents' intentions, since despite Mary's protestation, her description of longing to be held by her birth father does on some level read like an erotic encounter. Affirming her position as an adult forming an adult (as opposed to a parent-child) relationship with her father, she remarks on the particularity of their bond, which she acknowledges looks unusual through a societal lens. But it is perhaps this distinctiveness that gives it unique and compelling significance.

This point, which will be expanded upon in the next section, also lays the ground for another dimension about her role – or lack of – within his field. She suggested that her biological father expected her to be nothing other than herself, and more than that, enabled her to surrender any performance of a "self" role.

> I think the other thing I've realised is all my relationships, well, all's not quite the right word, in most of my relationships, umm, I have a job to do, [...] whether it's with my adoptive parents and fulfilling the role of the daughter they couldn't have, and, you know, and he's the first one who has just loved me because I'm me, you know, just because I'm his child, you know, he

claimed me, he wanted me, he came to see me, [...] so the fact that he is able to speak my love language and be able to just be there for me has been pretty amazing to me, because, he's just kind of known what he needed to say and do just to make me feel okay, without knowing it.

Here Mary's narrative puts into question the normative assumptions around the natural, caring mother, as it was her birth father who seemed to possess these instinctive qualities; mothers, on the other hand were portrayed as "Needy... needy... you know, the world revolves around them, it's not about me". Her biological father's ability to speak her "love language" can be interpreted as her experience of having formed an intimate connection with him, which validates her, enabling her to feel safe and cared for. But this reading again pushes up against the limits of representation since her account of being fully "met" by her birth father conflicts with her portrayal of the newness of their relationship, her anxiety that it will fall apart, and the difficulties she expresses about locating her "self" in relation to others. It is to this latter point that I will now turn.

Cultural and familial politics in respect to the "self"

As has been suggested, Mary's story raises some compelling questions about truth, subjectivity and belonging, eroticism and desire, and their representability. In all of this, however, her narrative reveals paradoxes as she grappled with the uncertainty around what the relationship was to her and to others, and how it could be defined: "but what is everybody else thinking? You know, I still can't get past what everybody else thinks. [...] you know, it's not a natural kind of relationship". In order to avoid jealous reactions from his wife, Mary said he would only contact her when his wife was away from the home: "but, he still calls me a couple of times a day. Umm, he just chooses to do it, around, when she's not home. So in that regard it feels like that whole affair thing... you know, like you're the other woman". Following popular scientific theories such as the notion of Genetic Sexual Attraction (Greenberg 1993), Mary's text might be used to set up a discussion about the erotic symbolism of the father. She was the "other woman" involved in an illicit "love relationship". But I think an alternative reading would shift the lens away from Mary's desire and focus instead on the implications this has for the social.

The relationship, she says, is not "natural". It is something society views with suspicion. In all her other relationships, she has "a job to do," in that their function has been naturally determined and transmitted. Naming and speaking about the biological father thus challenges our assumptions about what is natural, offering instead a quite radical position in relation to normative kinship dynamics. So whilst on the surface Mary presents a portrait of an idealised and eroticised father figure, she asks, "what does everybody else think?" In some ways, the notion of mystery surrounding her relationship and the questions she raises about how others perceive it could be part of the erotic excitement. We may take her uncertainty as a representation of the greater drama about what the biological father-daughter bond might entail. For Mary, her relationship was hidden from the world, and that closed, secretive space offered a sense of danger and intoxication. Her intrigue about what others were saying and thinking about her intensifies the particularity of her exclusive involvement with him. Together, they were cut off from the world, defying certain norms and arousing suspicion and jealousy in others. But equally by bringing the birth father out of the shadows in this way she raises important questions about what this relationship, which is not recognised or valued by the social order, might be when it has not been essentialised or fixed. Similarly, it asks us to think about whether it is this non-foundationalism that makes the birth father in this case so apparently compelling. The biological determinist ideas about original trauma that have been socially and culturally impressed upon us are therefore being subverted, and the most peripheral figure of adoption is no longer an empty category. Troubling sociocultural notions of binding and relationality, this discourse implies that the "reunion" relationship with the father is sometimes experienced as something novel and co-constructed through a mutual engagement that is not recognised or validated by the social world.

This analysis recovers various subjects and voices, all of which may be interpreted as unique and singular, but also constitutive of the multiplicity of practices, discourses and conditions determining them. The tension between singularity and plurality generates a set of questions about how these different strands can be brought together. I suggest that in some ways these questions are unanswerable since what they do instead is to expand the boundaries of what the adoptive female's encounter with her birth father might be about. In this sense, rather than close this inquiry down to limiting endeavours of finding cohesive and universal "truths", it complicates what can be known about this experience and opens up a space for more voices to emerge. In relation to their functionality, narratives such as this help redefine the boundaries of normative ideologies concerning the naturalised maternal bond by foregrounding the hitherto overlooked position of the father and presenting detailed accounts about what he meant to them. For some in the data sample, meeting the father was framed as a transformative, even erotic experience: one that has been misconceived or discounted by the social world but is nonetheless supported by powerful discourses about ideal love and "rescue" fantasy.

For instance, when Mary remarks that the kinds of men she has been attracted to are very similar to her father, and the post-"reunion" relationship she has built "is a love relationship", that "must look so weird to the rest of the world" she is producing statements that recast the power of the object under study, creating room for saying what has previously remained unsaid. This throws new light on the limited existing body of literature on birth father "reunion", going beyond the binary constructions of the visible and longed-for mother and invisible/ignored father. And it articulates notions of eroticism as well as the idea of falling in love with the father and how to cope with disappointment. That these issues rarely get discussed – the biological father-daughter relationship "must look so weird to the rest of the world" – illuminates the capacity of the participants' discourse to disrupt existing power relations and add new content to our understanding. This links in with the first function performed by this analysis, which relates to the notion of "truth". In speaking about that which has previously been silenced, this work exposes some of the "regimes of truth" that pattern forms of thought about the birth father's role. Through finding him – which in various cases implies a process of "self"-transformation, falling in love with him, rejecting or being rejected by him – accounts emerge that pertain to ideas of "truth" and "self"-discovery, resisting dominant models of what the adoptive subject's "reunion" experience *is*. This points instead to a process of unfolding rather than drawing a line under the adoptee's experience and shutting it down.

Summary

Intersecting between registers of the internal and external, private and social, Mary's complicated and nuanced narrative makes trouble for the kind of totalising identity politics that gives rise to fixed and static notions of wounded adoptive subjects traumatised by the broken mother bond. Focusing instead on the neglected figure of the birth father, her representations of their emerging relationship are often disjointed, emphasising their precarious subject positions and lack of recognition from others about how they both "fit" in the order of things. Questions about "truth" and meaning are interwoven between notions of belonging and the limits of knowing. And notions of eroticism and love come up against problems surrounding the representation of desire and the impossibility of imposing an integrated totality. The difficulty of adequately speaking for another's experience raises questions, following Butler (1993), about giving an account of oneself. Oscillating between the poles of loss and gain, within or outside of which the fantasies of fragmentation and wholeness seem continually to play out, this story interrupts the dominant narrative of the primal wound, giving us a new sense of how we might read and understand adoptee subjectivity in the present time. Opening up the connection between subjectivity and inter-subjectivity, the account invites us to pay attention to the fractional and multiple representations of addressing the question of what it could mean for an adopted female to meet her biological father for the first time in adulthood. This is a question that takes in ideas about finding "truths", filling "gaps" and engaging in quests for identity, relationality and meaning.

And going beyond this, it is also an issue about kinship and what it means to have a family. It speaks for an indistinct family system, constituted by disunity and indeterminate domestic roles. The fractures that symbolise this ill-defined kinship form might also reflect the fractured subjectivity that purportedly characterises the adoptee's internal world, as she deals with issues of loss, a quest for belonging and the desire to return to a different time and place. Thinking about this within the wider context of postmodern family discourses – telling the story of a shifting form marked by discontinuity and splits – we can recognise the production of different groups, subjectivities and identities co-existing in various contexts throughout history. The adoptee-biological father "reunion" then raises a range of issues about space and temporality, in that what may be spoken about in the present (the centrality of the maternal bond and the notion of the primal wound) and what remains largely unsaid (the secrecy surrounding the biological father as well as the durability or "success" of adoption as a family form), is continually in flux. Thus the kinds of adoptee subject positions that may be taken up are in part constituted by disparate methods of erasure, made complex by the introduction of new narratives. What we are left with is a multiplicity of stories about adopted women's experiences of meeting their biological fathers, which problematise taken-for-granted ideas about the adoptee's need to find her "original" mother in order to fill the gaps created by separation and become a unified whole. On the one hand these narratives unfold within a family discourse suggesting that kinship is important to the participants in terms of the ways in which it offers a sense of biological continuity, identity and a feeling of belonging. But they also exceed this framework in their descriptions of disconnection, disappointment, alienation and the perpetual quest for something apparently out of reach. It is here that a new conversation is needed about the limits and potentialities of kinship identification and how "selves" emerge beyond the boundaries of these already unstable dimensions.

References

Athan, L. (2010) *Adoption Critique*. Available at: http://adoptioncritic.com/tag/adoption-separation-trauma/. [Accessed 14 January 2012].

Butler, J. (1993) *Bodies That Matter: On the Discursive Limits of Sex*. London: Routledge.

Caruth, C. (1995) *Trauma: Explorations in Memory*. Baltimore: The John Hopkins University Press.

Clapton, G. (2008) *Birth Fathers and their Adoption Experiences*. London: Jessica Kingsley, Publishers.

Cooper, A. (2008) Forward. In D. Hindle and G. Shulman, *The Emotional Experience of Adoption: A Psychoanalytic Perspective*. New York: Routledge.

Fassin, D. and Rechtman, R. (2009) *The Empire of Trauma: An Inquiry into the Condition of Victimhood*. Princeton: Princeton University Press.

Freedgood, B. (2013) Loss and Resilience Form a Family: An Adoption Story from a Relational Point of View. *Psychoanalytic Perspectives* 10(1): 20–41.

Freeman, T. (2008) Psychoanalytic Concepts of Fatherhood: Patriarchal Paradoxes and the Presence of an Absent Authority. *Studies in Gender and Sexuality* 9(2): 113–39.

Freud, S. (1963) Introductory Lectures on Psycho-Analysis (1916–1917). *The Standard Edition of the Complete Psychological Works of Sigmund Freud, Volume XV-XVI (1916–1917): Introductory Lectures on Psycho-Analysis*. Ed. and trans. James Strachey. London: Hogarth.

Greenberg, M. (1993) Post-Adoption Reunion – Are We Entering Uncharted Territory? *Adoption and Fostering* 17(4): 5–15.

Griffith, K. C. (2013) *Adoption Healing*. Available at: http://www.adoptionhealing.com/Trauma/Chapter%200.html. [Accessed 7 November 2013].

Hacking, I. (1996) Memory Sciences, Memory Politics. In P. Antze and M. Lambek (eds.) *Tense Past: Cultural Essays in Trauma and Memory*. New York: Routledge.

Horowitz, S. (2013) Loss, Insecurity, and Uncertainty: The Impact of Adoption on the Developing Selves of a Birthmother. *Psychoanalytic Perspectives* 10(1) 10–19.

Jones, K. (2003) The Turn to a Narrative Knowing of Persons: One Method Explored. *NT Research* 8(1): 60–71.

Lambek, M. (2009) Terror's Wake: Trauma and Its Subjects. In B. G. Bergo and K. B. Golden (eds.) *The Trauma Controversy*. Albany: SUNY Press.

Lifton, B. J. (1994) *Journey of the Adopted Self: A Quest for Wholeness*. New York: Basic Books.

Luckhurst, R. (2003) Traumaculture. *New Formations* 50: 28–47.

Schuker, E. (2013) Comments on Reading the Adoption Roundtable. *Psychoanalytic Perspectives*: 10(1): 136–38.

Schwartz, D. (2013) Adoption News: Heterosexual Parents Helped by Gay Man. *Psychoanalytic Perspectives* 10(1): 139–48.

Seltzer, M. (1997) Wound Culture: Trauma in the Pathological Public Sphere. *October Magazine, Ltd. and Massachusetts Institute of Technology* 80: 3–26.

Verrier, N. (1993) *The Primal Wound*. Baltimore: Gateway Press, Inc.

13

EMBODYING TRAUMATIC GRIEFSCAPES

Per Roar

Over the last decade, in the artistic research project *Docudancing Griefscapes* (Roar 2015), I have explored choreographic strategies for embodying traumatic contexts of grieving by using ethnographic tools and documentary material in order to construct performances relating to such socio-political realities. Hence, I have dealt with issues that are often claimed to be unrepresentable. In this chapter, I will look at one of these projects, entitled *An Unfinished Story* (2006), which was developed based on my enquiries into the socio-political reality of loss and grieving brought about by the disintegration of Yugoslavia and the Bosnian War.[1] Without going into the larger discussion about the unrepresentable quality of trauma, or the details and conflict leading up to the Bosnian War, I will mainly focus on my approach to addressing the lived experiences of this socio-political context of grieving and how I dealt with representing its unrepresentable matters in this project.

In an interview in *Vagrant*, Hal Foster argues that terms such as "experience", "the lived" and the "experiential" have "come back with a whole other meaning" in the arts at the turn of the twentieth century. These concerns with "the real" have returned "in an absentee way," that is, fuelled "by the authority of the traumatic" (Foster, French et al. 1997: 5–6), which he states "throws over any simple scheme of before and after, cause and effect, origin and repetition" (Foster 1996: 29). Foster refers to this move within the arts as a "the return of the real" by drawing on psychoanalysis and the psychoanalytic concept of "deferred action" and its complex relay in which "one event is only registered through another that recodes it" (ibid.).[2] This psychoanalytic understanding, even though not always explicitly made, fundamentally and implicitly shapes my strategies and reflections here on embodying traumatic griefscapes. By drawing on this understanding and insights from psychoanalysis and Judith Butler's reading of Levinas (Butler 2004),

I will end this article by discussing the relationship between trauma and performance and hence reconsider the notion of what it means to represent the unrepresentable.

Griefscape and communal grieving: from organized violence to a socio-political wound

Trauma is here understood as a historical embedded discourse and experience, which, I consider, despite its being perceived experientially and subjectively, can be intersubjectively understood and shared (Cvetkovich 2003; Gordon 1997; Taylor 2006). The concept of *griefscape* evolved from a visceral intuition to become a research-based construct through my artistic research enquiry and can ethnographically be seen as a "messy text" (Marcus 1994; Denzin 1997; Heaton 2002), that is, being composed of several and disparate, often incommensurable, sources of information. Here it included ethnographic fieldwork, choreo-somatic explorations, psychoanalytical thinking combined with a focus on trauma and traumatisation and post-traumatic stress syndromes, to issues related to Human Rights and the struggle against impunity and for political justice. In sum, these issues brought about fundamental and existential questions related to body and identity, loss and grieving, memory and historical narrative. Through the multiple voices and the aesthetical-ethical paradoxes I encountered, my understanding of this specific communal griefscape was refined and defined.

For me the notion of "communal" does not necessarily refer to the numbers of casualties involved, but rather to the social impact of a traumatic event on a community or a large group of individuals.[3] For me the concept of communal grieving therefore relates to the spectral and affective nature of these collective experiences, that is, the raw feelings of aggregated grieving, which are not to be confused with mourning, the publically shared rituals we may apply for mourning traumatic events, often administered by the religious communities and the funeral industry (Hope 2007: 172). Nevertheless, I assume that there is certain correlation between the scale of the traumatic event – in terms of lives lost and/or damage suffered – and the socio-political importance that shared mourning rituals may play in a situation of communal grieving. However, I think that there is substantial and qualitative difference when the trauma is a result of a premeditated action and, as in the context of communal grieving here, brought about by organized violence on the level of states, or groups of equivalent coherence and level of organization (Schauer, Neuner et al. 2005: 7; Sveaass 1994: 54–61). In addition to having to confront their losses, these circumstances force the bereaved also to face the horror that the suffering endured was deliberately intended and committed. As stressed by both Maggie Schauer and Nora Sveaass, the deliberate intention to inflict pain on the civil society has severe traumatic consequences. The impact of such organized violence will not end with its operations, as Anita Schrader McMillan demonstrates in her case study on the maltreatment of children in post-war Guatemala (2005), but, as Schauer points out, "reach far into the future of a society" (Schauer, Neuner et al. 2005: 7). In situations of impunity, like many in Bosnia-Herzegovina experienced, this impact becomes especially exacerbated, because the survivors have to live on in a constant fear of having to face the perpetrators of the organized violence and their informers – and sometimes without even knowing who they were (HCHRS 2005; Fischer 2007). Even in cases where lawsuits have been filed to hold the perpetrators responsible, the traumatic impact might be further amplified.[4] These ordeals however are often needed for re-establishing any sense of social order and justice. As Piotr Kuhiwczak poignantly observed, with regards to developments in Poland after communism and South Africa after apartheid: "the ghosts of the past will not be properly buried until those responsible for breaking the law are brought to justice" (1999: 176). In this way grieving becomes not only a matter of the grief stricken in a traumatised culture, but it enters the complex economy of body politics. This trajectory adds layers of political overtones and mistrust, from which there is no easy way out; they rather complicate the process of grieving and can often result in prolonged and complex grieving processes (Herman 1997 [1992]: 119). Through looking at the Bosnian griefscape as a context of communal grieving, I wanted to investigate the consequences of living under such conditions. With a socio-political perspective on trauma, my aim here was to construct a performance that could embody and thereby convey a sense of this context, its embedded cultural memory, as an inter-subjective reality that could be shared with others and communicated across socio-political divisions.

The Bosnian War (1992–1995)

Bosnia-Herzegovina was known as the most ethnically diverse of the former Yugoslavian republics – where different ethnic groups lived side by side as in a composite mosaic (Judah 2000: 293, 344). When the war broke out, after Bosnia-Herzegovina declared independence from the former Yugoslavia in March 1992, warmongers targeted their geo-political and cultural assets. This had dramatic and tragic consequences. When the war ended in December 1995 nearly half of the population was on the run, fleeing from their homes, and close to 100,000 people had been killed, this is, without including the many who died of secondary reasons, like starvation, exhaustion, or illness due to lack of medicine etc. during the war. Eighty-three per cent of the civilian victims were Bosniaks, that is, Bosnians with a Muslim background (RDC 2007: 91–95). According to the census of 1991 for Bosnia-Herzegovina, this percentage is nearly double what the demographic statistics would suggest, whereas the opposite is the case for civilian victims with a Serbian Orthodox and a Croatian Catholic background. This statistics testifies to the dark and grim horrors of the Bosnian War: a civil war fuelled on xenophobic fear and mistrust, ideas of religious and cultural superiority that resulted in pogrom-like situations of ethnic cleansing, culminating with the genocide in Srebrenica where more than 8000 young boys and men were killed in July 1995.

According to the International Committee of the Red Cross (ICRC), there were still 17,000 people unaccounted for and considered "missing" in 2008, 13 years after the war had ended (ICRC 2008). This situation alone produces what can be called "the conditions for an unfinished work of mourning" in a society (Azoulay 2001: 4). Even though the destinies and experiences hidden in these numbers are hard to comprehend – as they seem to slip into a void, which seems to resist containment and reductive summaries, the accumulated effect of these numerous absences retains both a painful void and the dead weight of the loss suffered. The impact of these absences is a social figure that for me constitutes what Avery F. Gordon (1997) calls *ghostly matters,* which can traumatically haunt both society at large and the individual on a personal level for decades.[5]

FIGURE 13.1 Audience watching. Photo by Fuco Fuoxos – Vijećnica, Sarajevo 2006.

On a personal level, I find this succinctly expressed in the eyewitness accounts of Emir Suljagić, a survivor from Srebrenica. When writing about the thousands killed, he simply states: "There is no difference between their death and my survival, for I remained to live in a world that has been permanently and irreversibly marked by their death" (Suljagić 2005: 11).

Many in Bosnia-Herzegovina are, like Suljagić, caught up in a painful and affective loop where they repeatedly have to face the return of the real, the seething presence of the multiple losses and blows that this brutal and ethnically driven war caused. (In addition to Suljagić, see, for example, accounts by Drakulić 1996, 2004; Ugrešić 1998, 1999; and by Warsinski 1998; Woodhead 1999; Zbanic 1997, 2006). This haunting experience ruptures the temporal divides of past, present and future and leaves them in a state of trauma. As Suljagić alludes, the war disrupted all aspects of life. It tore up the very fabric of civil society and divided people according to cultural and ethnic affiliations;[6] this contributed to blurring the borders between private and public spheres and making the grieving process far more complex and indecipherable. The high figure of missing people further exacerbated this situation by depriving large numbers of individuals and families of a closure. Altogether, this creates a messy composite of intersected grieving processes that is hard to contain, emotionally as well as politically. The grieving seemingly seeps out and affects society as such – as a traumatized culture – not only within the national borders of Bosnia-Herzegovina, but also in the diaspora of Bosnians at large.[7] This contextual complexity of grieving is what I address as a communal griefscape here. I call it "communal," simply because I believe that the impact of this embodied non-verbal grieving on society at large is more than the sum of the individual pain experienced. Like Barbie Zelizer stresses in her photo-journalistic study of the trauma of the Holocaust: "No single memory reflects all that is known about a given event, personality, or issue. Instead, memories resemble a mosaic, where they generate an authoritative vision in repertoire with other views of the past" (1998: 3–4). By using the notion of a mosaic, Zelizer points to the way shared memories are formed and built in a society. I find this viewpoint especially relevant with respect to my project of embodying communal grieving as a griefscape here, even though this griefscape, its mosaic, is not of a fixed or static character, but constituted in a state of flux, like the ever-shifting formations of migrating birds in the sky, or the somatic state of a living organism.

In my attempt to grasp this griefscape, as what Marita Sturken would call "cultural memory" (1997), I approached trauma from a bodily and socio-cultural angle, like Ann Cvetkovich (2003) does in her book *An Archive of Feelings,* by treating it "as a social and cultural discourse that emerges in response to the demands of grappling with psychic consequences of historical events." Hence, like Cvetkovich, I sought to hold on to trauma's historical embeddedness as a historical phenomenon (2003: 17–18).

This included taking into account my role as an "outsider" and the fact that I worked in the stretch between the Bosniak and Serb dominated areas, which added additional layers of challenges to the project. Issues I have discussed at lengths elsewhere (Roar 2015) and will leave aside here, but in short, the context offered no even ground to dance on in this project, rather an emotional minefield, which intrinsically was a part of the griefscape itself.

I constructed the performance *An Unfinished Story* based on the multifaceted pool of data collected from ethnographic fieldwork and background research about the war and the social reality in the region.[8] In collaboration with the performers involved, the collected inputs were processed through bodily speculations and imaginary questioning. In essence, the artistic challenge was about how to explore, intertwine and merge such multiple sources of information we faced about this socio-political and traumatic reality and, with the help of an imaginary speculation, turn this insight into a choreographic body.

In her article "The Site of the Memory," Toni Morrison expands on what such an imaginary speculation leaves open for her to do artistically by stating: "My job becomes how to rip that veil over proceedings too terrible to relate" (1990: 302). This challenge resonates with my struggle here to embody what resists being silenced and forgotten but silently "speak" through traumatic reminders that evoke past horrors. According to dance scholar Mark Franko, this traumatic and psychoanalytic dimension is largely left untouched in dance studies, despite the fact that it "opens onto memory and how the body remembers," as well as how it forgets (2006: 13).

Constructing an unfinished story

An Unfinished Story was devised in collaboration with performers and artists from Oslo, Belgrade and Sarajevo and produced on location in the area of the former Yugoslavia, partly in Belgrade and mainly in Sarajevo where the performance also had its premiere at Vijećnica, the former national library. It lasted approximately 50 minutes and was made to fit any larger assembly or congregation hall where the audience could share the floor with the performers: Slaven Vidak (Sarajevo), Peder Horgen, Kristianne Mo, Terje Tjöme Mossige (Oslo), and Marija Opsenica (Belgrade).[9]

The performance was developed with the performers over a period of nearly five months from June 2005 to September 2005 and built on my extensive background in the region, which included first-hand experiences of the former Yugoslavia, the Bosnian War in 1993 and the post-war situation in Kosovo and Serbia after 1999 with the decline and fall of Slobodan Milošević. The turning point in the artistic research process was the participation in the annual commemoration of the victims of the Srebrenica Genocide, the worst war crime committed in Europe since the Second World War, at the Srebrenica-Potočari Memorial and Cemetery in July 2004. On 11th July each year, since 2003, the remains of newly identified victims, found in mass graves all over the area, have been buried there. The ceremony gathers tens of thousands of people and is broadcasted nationally in Bosnia-Herzegovina.

In 2004, 380 caskets were buried, each in its individual grave, by the effort of family and friends present. The practical effort involved in organizing these burials manifested in itself the scale of this communal griefscape. The impact of witnessing this traumatic event made it clear to me that the performers involved in my artistic-research project, and then especially those from outside the region, had to experience this event first-hand. In 2005 I returned with the performers to this traumatic epicentre of communal grieving and witnessed 610 caskets being buried. The burials release a flood of pain, raw and unbearable. For the performers and me, these experiences gave the Bosnian griefscape and communal grieving a body – composed of a tactile mosaic of personal encounters with survivors and the remains of the war in the landscape where the horrors once were committed. These encounters left a multitude of imprints of faces, expressions, voices, smells, sounds and other sensuous observations (for more about our encounters, see Roar 2011, 2015).

When my collaboration with performers started, the damages caused by the war were visible everywhere; these physical scars made me wonder about the extent of the invisible wounds that the survivors of this traumatic horror might have and led to the core question of this artistic enquiry: What does it take to maintain a sense of equilibrium and balance under such circumstances – on such an uneven psychological ground? Through the fieldwork in this composite artistic research process, I hence also identified the physical or corporeal approach to the traumatic in this project by probing into movement explorations of the physiological functions of the vestibular system, that is, our physical sense of balance and the psychobiological

FIGURE 13.2 Circle. Photo by Fuco Fuoxos – Vijećnica, Sarajevo 2006.

or somatic strategies for coping with post-traumatic stress. The outcome of this exploration provided the base for the choreographic material used in the construction of the performance, and also explains the subtitle of the performance: "a study in the neurology of grieving."

Probing into the bodily consequences of trauma

Since falling is the ultimate consequence of losing one's balance, our investigation of balance expanded to include a more detailed physical study of the mechanics of falling from an upright position to lying on the ground. I expanded our explorations by introducing the element of will or willpower, the ability to control one's impulses and actions, which augmented our probing. Because the falling is conditional on the dynamic range of the willpower in play within us, the pull of gravity will meet various degrees of resistance or compliance affecting it (Plevin 2007: 107). At this point in our enquiry, we were exposed to an upsetting video shot during the war. The video had circulated in closed circles as part of heroic memorabilia among the hard-core nationalists but surfaced as evidence in the trial of Slobodan Milošević in The Hague in 2005 (Judah and Sunter 2005).[10] Its release had aroused international attention and caused a public outrage in Serbia after it was broadcast on national television.[11] The video depicts how a group of young Bosniak men, bruised and beaten with their hands tied behind their backs, are ordered off a truck and summarily shot from behind. To view the unedited video was horrifying, but the close-up footage also revealed bodily states of falling not normally seen; the images of falling, dying bodies added crucial insights into what we were physically exploring. They brutally demonstrated for us the mechanics of mass surrendering to the pull of gravity, that is, how the body without willpower to keep it upright succumbs to the laws of physics. Whereas the violent intent causing the final surrenders captured in the video speaks of a brutality that is difficult to comprehend, the bodily mechanics of its consequences are conceivable in part and can be conveyed bodily. Concretely, in deconstructing the physical mechanics involved in falling movement-wise, I found a tool for approaching the wounds that the war had inflicted. This was not a mimetic but a physical task for the performers: to kinaesthetically explore and re-explore falling and surrendering to the pull of gravity by probing into its inherent logic. With this approach and in collaboration with the performers, I wanted to embody some core aspects of this communal griefscape that we together strived to grasp and convey in our performance work.

By this time in the process, I had already used the diagnostic criteria of post-traumatic stress disorder (PTSD)[12] as raw material for our movement explorations of the bodily consequences of trauma. Here, I focused on the most common categories – or clusters – of the symptoms of PTSD: intrusive recollections, avoidant/numbing symptoms, and hyper-arousal symptoms (Friedman 2010: 1).[13] I was particularly interested in looking at their bodily consequences, the physicality produced by these traumatic reactions.

In this way I tried to devise a physical approach to deconstruct highly emotional states that also enabled the performers to keep a critical distance from the material, without confusing it with the intoxicated seduction that a narcissistic mirroring or "reductive over-identification" could produce (Foster 1996: 203). This strategy became important as the totality experienced from meeting people, visiting places, being exposed to mass graves, watching documentary films, attending seminars and talks, and so on, was simply too much to contain and comprehend. Though this distress was simultaneously what made the process of rehearsal profound for the performers, it also created a strong need amongst them to connect their "personal journeys" to the process of making the performance itself; they literally wanted to utilize their personal stories and their own associations in the development of the movement material. In contrast, I was convinced that these emotions were better channelled into the sensorial and neurological psychobiological investigation of bodily balance and reaction-patterns related to PTSD symptoms and traumatic experiences. I therefore based the choreographic work on a succession of small tasks questioning the basic conditions for our being in the world, like "falling" as I already have discussed. In this way, the choreography was pushing forward a whole series of highly existential issues to be explored. They appeared nearly as Zen-like *koans*,[14] that is, as paradoxical tasks: the action of transferring weight and falling into walking, running, floating in a vertigo of off-balance or struggling between surrendering or fighting against the pull of gravity, all while exploring the combinations of willpower and the "fight", "flight" or "freeze" impulses in the body. These concrete tasks might at first seem removed from the complexity embedded in the communal griefscape we constructed. However, in developing a higher degree of precision concerning the psychobiological and physical premises for executing these movement tasks, I will argue that such an approach offered a tool for conjoining the personal and the interpersonal interests of the performers.[15]

Consequently, a large part of the remaining choreographic work process was spent on clarifying the bodily specificity and the foundational physical premises underlining the movement tasks used in the choreography. From my point of view, it became important to stress that we did not work with the traumatic event itself but with its post-traumatic manifestations – the tension levels in these traumatic reaction patterns and their deposits – through addressing how such traumatic experiences are embodied physically and kept alive long after the traumatic incident itself.

From traumatic reaction patterns to choreographic structure – in search of a common ground

An example of this post-traumatic perspective can be seen in the use of latex gloves in the performance, which in this respect became a minor but important gesture to highlight this temporal perspective here. The fortuitous accident that led to this usage stemmed from the old varnished floor at our first rehearsal space in Belgrade, which was difficult to clean and therefore felt sticky and dirty. This made one of the performers touch the floor rather unwillingly and gingerly. This particular cautiousness fascinated me, and I decided to try solving the performer's issues with the dirt, as well as enhancing the quality of cautiousness added through accentuating this touch with the help of a visual marker; I therefore introduced the gloves as an auxiliary tool. However, as I noted after our first public work-in-progress showing for an audience in Belgrade in December 2005: "The clinical touch of the surgical gloves provided a minor gesture, which allowed us a visual reading that drew attention to the past in the present through establishing a 'now' that clinically deals with the emotional scars and the consequences of the past on our present flux. Thus, the gloves served as visual reminders of the temporal factor involved in our performance."[16] In triggering images known from forensic investigators in television crime series, the gloves signalled and hence indicated that we entered the story from a post-traumatic position, as someone dealing with the debris left behind. They provided a clinical touch and a distance from the trauma we were dealing with that made it clear that we were recalling something that had already taken place. The tragedy had already happened; the performers were just tracing the ghostly but affective remains – the griefscape. The gloves were redirecting the focus towards the present-day challenges and hence reminding the performers of their entrance point.[17]

Another example of this retrospective perspective in the staging can be seen in the entrance of the last performer, who first enters the centre stage in the second half of the performance, after having spent its first half in the role as an audience member in a wheelchair. His first actions after rolling to centre stage were to put on latex gloves, step out of the wheelchair and push it over to the other side of the stage, where he resumed his role as a paraplegic sitting in the wheelchair but now as a performer starting a duet with one of the other performers on stage. For me, not only did his entrance mark a shift in the performance, but his actions also pointed to the difference between the "real-real" and the "stand-in" in our staging, as his actions created a Brechtian *alienation effect*. His actions literally freed me as a viewer – and the general audience as well – from a more sentimental bonding of pity or identification of the paraplegic character as a "victim." Instead, his actions as a performer allowed us as viewers to stay focused on grieving while critically questioning the definition of victimhood: as a role as well as how we can all feel paralyzed at times, regardless of our physical condition. In this state, we might feel left without a clue about how to move on, enmeshed between roles assumed and ascribed – whether as a survivor or as a bystander – overwhelmed with a feeling of shame or guilt for what one did or did not do.[18]

Trauma and performance: unrepresentable and ephemeral, or repetitious and citational

In my attempt to embody the performance of trauma, both on an individual level and on a societal level as in the example above, I mainly tuned in to the presence of the dead among the living and thereby the presence of what is absent. This focus made me question the divide between the living and the dead[19] and recall the possibility that Butler in her reading of Lévinas points to when discussing what it might entail to face the other. She states,

> the human is not identified with what is represented but neither is it identi-fied with the unrepresentable, it is, rather, that which limits the success of any representational practice. The face is not "effaced" in this failure of represen-tation, but is constituted in that very possibility.
>
> *(Butler 2004: 144)*

What Butler identifies with this possibility has for me a parallel potential in this study of representing the unrepresentable: it illuminates for me what is at stake when I try to pursue both the presence of the absent and how to make choreog-raphy through embodying griefscapes.[20] However, as a choreographer-researcher, it is challenging to grapple with this possibility she describes. Butler's emphasis on "that which limits the success of any representational practice," calls therefore on conceptual and critical attentiveness. Here, in part, this relates for me to how juxtapositions can create coimpossible situations and frictions compositionally,[21] which in their "failures" can constitute the very possibility of facing the other, like in the example above with the use of the wheelchair. In exploring a connection between my interest in this potential and my questioning of the divide between the living and the dead, as also articulated in the quote of Suljagić that I mentioned earlier, I find Tracy Davis' notion of performative time necessary and useful (2010: 153). Her notion harbours this failure in its cross-temporal perspective, in contrast to the notion of theatrical time that is framed by a beginning and an end, precisely because performative time "recognizes the simultaneity, difference, separation, over-lap, and pretences of citation through, as, and across temporalities to build upon and multiply the experience of theatrical time's doubling of represented and durational time" (ibid.). This also means as Davis stresses "performative time may reverberate indefinitely" (ibid.). This cross-temporal perspective allows me to conceptualize how artistic works or interventions, like trauma, can rupture the continuum of lin-ear time and transgress the theatrical time frame through entering the economy of circulating representations, while revealing also their failures. In this way, the artistic works (as interventions) may continue to have an impact (cross-temporally) as long as new readers are reimagining them. Moreover, as Davis argues, I also believe that this "[c]itationality ... complicates [Peggy] Phelan's contention (...) that perfor-mance is ephemeral," and that trauma is unrepresentable. Likewise does this cita-tionality open up for new questions, such as: "What gets to count as citational, and for how long?" (Davis 2010: 155). From this perspective, "performative time [also] calls attention to who has agency to convey history, as well as how evidence for history is generated, and gives a rationale of what, by other criteria, is vulnerable to accusations of missampling" (ibid.: 161). Without going further into historiography,

FIGURE 13.3 Crawling. Photo by Fuco Fuoxos –Vijećnica, Sarajevo 2006.

my main point here is to draw attention to how an artistic intervention or performance can in a performative time frame have a cross-temporal impact that resembles how a traumatic event can live on in an individual or a society as a trauma. For as long as an event can be re-evoked, through traumatic reminders as in the case of trauma, it calls into question what constitutes the present. In this interstice, trauma and performance are communing, and the presence of what is absent blurs the divide between past and present, living and dead. This possibility constitutes for me a potential for addressing grieving and being human.

In paying attention to the performance of trauma with its traumatic repeats in this project, I have experienced it at times as if I was listening to the past in the present while engaging with futurity. For me this is about an empathetic tuning in to "rememories" of those absent and dead. As Phelan poignantly remarks in her *Mourning Sex: Performing Public Memories*: "We bury more than bodies" (1997: 19). In the performance *An Unfinished Story*, I wanted therefore to listen to what this surplus might have to convey to me and about us as a society. This meant to be attentive to what emerged from these "unclaimed experiences" and how those absent and dead might perform through the living in the present. In the process of making *An Unfinished Story*, relating to the context of communal grieving and the Bosnian war, I experienced that the dead may still arrest us, the living, in unresolved dilemmas or disputes related to the political and social responsibility caused by their deaths. In the context of the Balkans, Sophocles addressed this arrest already in his tragedy *Antigone* at 442 BC through pointing to the dilemmas and difficulties that the dead's claim on the living might bring upon us (2003).[22] As his *Antigone* demonstrates, listening to the dead performing in the present is not necessarily pleasant but may challenge the listener to the core of his or her being. However, the challenge of perceiving this presence of absence and how it impacts the present is at the heart of what I tried to pursue artistically in embodying this griefscape.

In a cross-temporal perspective, I perceive our history of "improperly buried bodies" (Gordon 1997: 16) as a continuum of cries, wounds and losses that stretches from the past into our time. This includes unknown destinies, such as those behind Sophocles' story about *Antigone* to the many who vanished unaccounted for in Treblinka, Sobibor and Belzec (Gilbert 1987)[23] and more recent losses like those voiced by the members of the association called the Women of Srebrenica or by the faceless refugees drowned in the Mediterranean Sea in 2015. These cries are haunting, but as Gordon stresses, such haunting can draw us affectively into "a transformative recognition" of a reality of experience (Gordon 1997: 8). In paying attention to the particular way of knowing that haunting is, this "can lead to that dense site where history and subjectivity make social life." Hence, it can transform our recognition of what constitutes social life.

Through constructing and embodying contexts of grieving like griefscapes, I attempted, "to enact and mimic the losses that beat away within them," and as Phelan adds here: "In this mimicry, loss itself helps to transform the repetitive force of trauma and might bring about a way to overcome it" (Phelan 1997: 12). For me, this potential can come about with the help of a transformative recognition (Gordon 1997: 8).

In a theatrical time frame, performance is by many scholars defined as an act of disappearance and, like trauma, it is considered as an inaccessible and unclaimed experience of the past. In contrast, in a performative time frame trauma and performance can both be viewed as performative acts, which through reiteration and citationality can transgress and have an impact beyond the definite boundaries set by theatrical time. I will conclude this article in this intersection of perspectives in which I identify a framework for reviewing trauma and a potential for choreography as a critical and socio-political aesth/ethical practice.[24] With the support of Butler's reading of Levinas, I believe as Cathy Caruth: "By carrying that impossibility of knowing out of the empirical event itself, trauma opens up and challenge us to a new kind of listening, the witnessing, precisely *of impossibility*" (Caruth 1995: 10, original emphasis). This outlook situates both my artistic aim and my approach as I constructed and embodied this griefscape of communal grieving.

Notes

1 The article builds on my doctoral thesis *Docudancing Griefscapes: choreographic strategies for embodying traumatic contexts of grieving in the trilogy Life & Death* at the University of the Arts Helsinki (2015).
2 In unpacking this claim, Foster advocates for another reading of the avant-garde than those raised by disparate arts critics such as Peter Bürger (see 1996: 29). In short, as the art scholar Charles Harrison renders it: "Foster's argument is that the traumatic effect of

avant-garde activity is only fully registered in subsequent workings out" (Harrison 1996: 1). Hence, the expression "the return of the real", which also is the title of Foster's book. For me this argument is pertinent and grounds my outlook as an artist-researcher here.

3 As Ann Cvetkovich has pointed out, can the experience of traumatic events create "'trauma culture'– public cultures that form in and around trauma" (2003: 9).

4 Not only because the court proceedings themselves can easily draw out in time, and often are intertwined with the mesh of political agendas involved in any liability claims, but also because they come with the need to go into minute details about the atrocities committed again.

5 Gordon especially discusses the haunting quality of the legacy of slavery in the contemporary United States. Her arguments have been picked up among others by the performance studies scholar André Lepecki in his discussion of the relationship between colonialism and choreography, which he understands as "predicated on a politics of the ground [that] reveals those movements initiated by 'improperly buried bodies of history,'" by referring to Gordon and how she views those bodies "as haunting epistemology, as powerful ethical and critical forces" (Lepecki 2006: 18). My reasoning in this project builds on a similar understanding of Gordon's "improperly buried bodies of history."

6 As in the case of Mostar, see reports by Daria Sito-Sucic (2012) and Ian Traynor (2004).

7 The many Bosnians living in exile that I met during my fieldwork – either while they visited Bosnia or in their new countries – told me more or less the same story. The situation seemed, however, to be hardest for those who had reached adulthood prior to 1992 and remembered everyday life before the war began, as adults.

8 In this process I combined my knowledge of choreography and somatics with my background from social sciences and history with a tacit knowledge about qualitative research and from performance studies the emphasis on the performative and a socio-cultural understanding of trauma.

9 In addition to the sound artist Jørgen Larsson (Bergen), the composer/producer Ivan Vrhunc and the costume designer Samina Zajko (Sarajevo). Other central collaborators and partners included Hamo Muhommod (Sarajevo) for his compilation of traditional folk dances from Sarajevo – taught us by Mersiha Zembo and Kolo Bosansko at Bosnian Cultural Centre (Sarajevo); the local project coordinators Dušica Parezanović (Belgrade) and Sandra Sandbye (Oslo); set designer Silje Kiise (Bergen); movement advisor Ingunn Rimestad and Gindler practitioner Gro Torgersbråten (Oslo). The project was co-produced with the Dansens Hus – the national stage for dance in Norway, the Oslo National Academy of the Arts, the Rex cultural centre in Belgrade, and the MESS in Sarajevo. Funded by the Arts Council Norway, the Ministry of Foreign Affairs in Norway, Fond for lyd og bilde, the Programme for artistic research Norway, and the Intermedia at the University of Oslo.

10 Recorded by members of the infamous Scorpions, a feared paramilitary unit that operated during the war. For excerpts of the video, see United States Holocaust Memorial Museum's interview with Nataša Kandić: http://www.ushmm.org/confront-genocide/cases/bosnia-herzegovina/bosnia-video-gallery/eyewitness-testimony-natasa-kandic [Accessed 6 September 2015].

11 The video was shown on Serbian television on 1st June 2005 and caused an outrage (Judah and Sunter 2005).

12 On PTSD and diagnostics, see Friedman (2010), APA (2000), and Foa et al. (2009) and the International Society for Traumatic Stress Studies (www.istss.org) and Psychiatry Online (www.psychiatryonline.com) [Accessed 10 May 2015].

13 Therefore, the criticism and discussion concerning details and functions of these diagnostic criteria had less relevance for my uses of the clusters of symptoms of PTSD in this project. For more about this discussion, see Herman (1997: 31–32), Spitzer et al. (2007) and Summerfield (1999).

14 Koans are paradoxical statements or tasks given by a Zen master to his student that transcends rational thought. Hence, they are used for opening up to new insights (see Kadowaki 1989: xi). In this case, I refer to the paradoxical in focusing on simple physical tasks as a way to address complex socio-political issues.
15 Trained dancers and plastic performers may through their bodily insights and tools consciously access and work with the unconscious layers (the deposits of movements accumulated through living) within us and at times even make art out of this complicated mesh with skilful precision.
16 Source: Fieldnotes 21 December 2005 in Belgrade. Here, our first test audience picked up on and commented on this use of gloves in the Q&A session after our first work-in-progress showing.
17 That is, they were not representing the totality of the traumatic event personally, but just retrospectively exploring aspects of its psychobiological consequences in being receptive and paying attention to the bodily reverberations they might experience as they executed the physical tasks in the choreographic construction. While leaving me as the first viewer feeling as if "bumping into a rememory that belongs to somebody else" (cf. Toni Morrison's notion of "rememory" [1987: 35–36] and Gordon [1997: 164–5]).
18 Based on my fieldwork observations in combination with support from trauma studies and clinical research, I decided that I did not want to spend time on "fetishizing" the perpetrator. Leaning on Hannah Arendt (1994 [1965]) and her telling description of "the banality of evil" and supported by the accounts of Drakulić (2004) and Seierstad (2004), I decided to leave the perpetrator as a closed category that I would not spend time speculating on here.
19 A phenomenon common among mourners: see Walter (1999: 17–116) about "Living with the dead."
20 For me choreography can at its utmost a/effectively induce permeable and transmutable propositions in which sensory awareness, aesthetic sensibility, and traumatic repeats blend together in a contextual setting that engage my bodily and cognitive memory. This impact might ripple beyond the delineation of its temporal theatrical framework.
21 Cf. Lepecki (2004: 137).
22 In *Antigone*, Sophocles portrays through his characters and the plot how the dead may impact the living. When the play is experienced as relevant today, it demonstrates how it across centuries and in different socio-political contexts has been able to speak to involved actors and audiences. According to Loraux (2002), the play was written in a time of imperialistic ambitions and extensive wars, which emphasized civic duties at the expense of loss and mourning suffered by the citizens.
23 To name some of the extermination "camps" made by the Nazi regime, made solely for killing Jews and other "unwanted." Few stayed alive here more than a few hours upon arrival, hence leaving few stories behind (Gilbert 1986: 425).
24 As a choreographer, I work primarily to meet the challenges imposed by theatrical time, but as a choreographer-researcher I do this with an awareness of the coexisting multiple temporalities that are set in motion with any choreographic project.

References

APA (2000) *Diagnostic and Statistical Manual of Mental Disorders (DSM-IV)*. Washington, DC: American Psychiatric Association.

Arendt, H. (1994 [1965]) *Eichmann in Jerusalem. A Report on the Banality of Evil (Revised and enlarged edition)*. New York: Penguin Books.

Azoulay, A. (2001) *Death's Showcase*. Cambridge: MIT Press.

Brown, L. S. (1995) Not Outside the Range: One Feminist Perspective on Psychic Trauma. In C. Caruth (ed.) *Trauma: Explorations in Memory*. Baltimore: John Hopkins UP.

Butler, J. (2004) *Precarious Life. The Powers of Mourning and Violence*. New York: Verso.

Caruth, C. (ed.) (1995) *Trauma: Explorations in Memory*. Baltimore: John Hopkins UP.

Cvetkovich, A. (2003) *An Archive of Feelings: Trauma, Sexuality, and Lesbian Public Cultures*. Durham: Duke UP.

Davis, T. C. (2010) Performative Time. In C. M. Canning and T. Postlewait (eds.) *Representing the Past: Essays in Performance Historiography*. Iowa City: University of Iowa Press.

Denzin, N. K. (1997) *Interpretive Ethnograpy: Ethnographic Practices for the 21st Century*. Thousand Oaks: Sage Publications.

Denzin, N. K. (ed.) (2003) *Performance Ethnography: Critical Pedagogy and the Politics of Culture*. Thousand Oaks: Sage Publications.

Drakulić, S. (1996). *Cafe Europa: Life after Communism*. London: Abacus.

Drakulić, S. (2004). *They Would Never Hurt a Fly. War Criminals on Trial in The Hague*. London: Abacus.

Emerson, R. et al. (eds.) (1995). *Writing Ethnographic Fieldnotes*. Chicago: University of Chicago Press.

Fischer, M. (ed.) (2007) *Peacebuilding and Civil Society in Bosnia-Herzegovina: Ten Years after Dayton*, 2nd edn. Münster: LIT Verlag.

Foa, E. B. et al. (eds.) (2009) *Effective Treatments for PTSD: Practice Guidelines from the International Society for Traumatic Stress Studies*, 2nd edn. Part IV, Treatment Guidelines. New York: The Guildford Press.

Foster, H. (1996) *The Return of the Real: The Avant-Garde at the End of the Century*. Cambridge: MIT Press.

Foster, H., French, L. et al. (1997) Hal Foster interview. *Variant*, 1–8.

Friedman, M. J. (2010) Posttraumatic Stress Disorder: an Overview. Available: http://www. ptsd.va.gov/professional/pages/ptsd-overview.asp. [Accessed 15 March 2014].

Ghassem-Fachandi, P. (ed.) (2009) *Violence. Ethnographic Encounters. Encounters: Experience and Anthropological Knowledge*. Oxford: Berg.

Gilbert, M. (1987) *The Holocaust: The Jewish Tragedy*. London: Fontana Press.

Gordon, A. F. (1997) *Ghostly Matters: Haunting and the Sociological Imagination*. Minneapolis: University of Minneapolis Press.

Hackney, P. (1998) *Making Connections: Total Body Integration through Bartenieff Fundamentals*. London: Routledge.

HCHRS (2005) *Human Rights and Collective Identity - Serbia 2004*. Belgrade: Helsinki Committee for Human Rights in Serbia.

Heaton, D. W. (2002) Creativity: Between Chaos and Order or My Life as a Messy Text – A Case Study and a Challenge. *American Communication Journal* 6(1).

Herman, J. L. (1997 [1992]). *Trauma and Recovery: The Aftermath of Violence - from Domestic Abuse to Political Terror*. New York: Basic Books.

Hope, V. (2007). *Death in Ancient Rome: A Sourcebook*. London & New York: Routledge.

ICRC (2008) Missing Persons on the Territory of Former Yugoslavia. *Field Newsletter (25.04.2008)* Available: http://www.icrc.org/eng/resources/documents/field-newsletter /serbia-missing-newsletter-010408.htm. [Accessed 15 March 2014].

Judah, T. (2000) *The Serbs. History, Myth and the Destruction of Yugoslavia*. New Haven: Yale UP.

Judah, T. and Sunter, D. (2005) How Video That Put Serbia in Dock Was Brought to Light. *The Observer*. Available: www.guardian.co.uk/world/2005/jun/2005/balkans.warcrimes [Accessed 6 June 2010].

Judah, T. and Sunter, D. (2005). Srebrenica Massacre Tape Forces Belgrade to Face Truth. Bosnia Report, 45–46. Available: http://www.bosnia.org.uk/bosrep/report_format.cfm ?articleid=2993&reportid=2168. [Accessed 10 June 2010].

Kadowaki, K. (1989) *Zen and the Bible*. London: Arkana.

Kuhiwczak, P. (1999) Justice or Retribution? *The Cambridge Quarterly* XXVIII(2): 174–78.

Lepecki, A. (ed.) (2004) *Of the Presence of the Body. Essays on Dance and Performance Theory*. Middletown: Wesleyan UP.

Lepecki, A. (2006) *Exhausting Dance. Performance and the Politics of Movement*. New York: Routledge.

Loraux, N. (2002) *The Mourning Voice: An Essay on Greek Tragedy*. Ithaca: Cornell UP.

Marcus, G. E. (1994). What Comes (Just) after "Post"? The case of Ethnography. In N. Denzin and Y. Lincoln (eds.) *The Handbook of Qualitative Research*. Thousand Oaks: Sage.

McMillan, S. A. A. S. (2005) *Circles of Trust: Parent Education and the Reversion of Child Maltreatment in Post-War Guatemala*. PhD Thesis, Institute of Latin American Studies, University of Liverpool.

Morrison, T. (1990) The Site of Memory. In R. Ferguson (ed.) *Out There: Marginalization and Contemporary Cultures*. Cambridge: MIT Press.

Phelan, P. (1997). *Mourning Sex: Performing Public Memories*. London: Routledge.

Plevin, M. (2007) Journey in Between Will and Surrender in Authentic Movement. A Personal and Clinical Perspective. In P. Pallaro (ed.) *Authentic Movement: Moving the Body, Moving the Self, Being Moved. A Collection of Essays. Vol. 2*. London & Philadelphia: Jessica Kingsley Publishers.

RDC (2007) *Human Losses in Bosnia and Herzegovina 91–95*. Sarajevo: Research and Documention Center Sarajevo.

Roar, P. (2011) An Unfinished Story: On Ghostly Matters and a Mission Impossible. In J. Birringer and J. Fenger (eds.) *Tanz und WahnSinn / Dance and choreomania*. Leipzig: Henschel Verlag.

Roar, P. (2015) *Docudancing Griefscapes: Choreographic Strategies for Embodying Traumatic Contexts in the Trilogy Life & Death*. Helsinki: Acta Scenica.

Schauer, M. et al. (2005) *Narrative Exposure Therapy: A Short-Term Intervention for Traumatic Stress Disorders after War, Terror, or Torture*. Göttingen: Hogrefe & Huber Publishers.

Seierstad, Å. (2004) *Med ryggen mot verden. Fremdeles. Portretter fra Serbia*. Oslo: Cappelen.

Sito-Sucic, D. (2012) *Mostar: One Family, Three Armies, a Divided City*. Available: http://www.reuters.com/article/2012/04/02/uk-bosnia-mostar-idUSLNE83102N20120402. [Accessed 15 March 2014].

Sophocles (2003) *Antigone*. Cambridge: Cambridge UP.

Spitzer, R. L. et al. (2007) Saving PTSD from Itself in DSM-V. *Journal of Anxiety Disorders* 21: 233–41.

Sturken, M. (1997) *Tangled Memories: The Vietnam War, the AIDS Epidemic, and the Politics of Remembering*. Berkeley: University of California Press.

Suljagić, E. (2005) *Postcards from the Grave*. London: Saqi Books.

Summerfield, D. (1999) A Critique of Seven Assumptions behind Psychological Trauma Programmes in War-Affected Areas. *Social Science & Medicine* 48(10): 1449–62.

Sveaass, N. (1994) The Psychological Effects of Impunity. In N. J. Lavik, M. Nygård, N. Sveaass, and E. Fannemel (eds.) *Pain and Survival: Human Rights Violations and Mental Health*. Oslo: Scandinavian University Press.

Taylor, D. (2006) Trauma and Performance: Lessons from Latin America. *PMLA* 121(5): 1674–77.

Traynor, I. (2004) *Bridge Opens but Mostar Remains a Divided City*. Available: http://www. theguardian.com/world/2004/jul/23/iantraynor. [Accessed 15 March 2014].

Ugrešić, D. (1998) *The Culture of Lies. Antipolitical Essays*. London: Phoenix.

Ugrešić, D. (1999) *The Museum of Unconditional Surrender*. London: Phoenix.

Walter, T. (1999) *On Bereavement: The Culture of Grief*. Maidenhead: Open University Press.

Zelizer, B. (1998). *Remembering to Forget: Holocaust Memory through the Camera's Eye*. Chicago: University of Chicago Press.

Filmography

After After (1997) Directed by J. Zbanic. Bosnia and Herzegovina: Deblokada.

Crime and Punishment: Witnessing the Massacres in Srebrenica (1998) Directed by M. F. Warsinski. Norway: Speranza Film.

A Cry from the Grave (1999) Directed by L. Woodhead. UK: BBC2/PBS.

Grbavica: The Land of My Dreams (2006) Directed by J. Zbanic. Austria and Bosnia Herzegovina: Coop 99 / Debolkada / Jadran Film.

14

SUTURE AND GUS VAN SANT'S *MILK*

Richard Rushton

One of the striking things about Gus Van Sant's 2009 film on the life of charismatic gay political activist Harvey Milk (Sean Penn)—the film is called *Milk*—is that it is not an overtly gay or queer film. Rather, the film focuses primarily on political struggles and aspects of political life, of campaigns for political office and legislation in San Francisco during the 1970s. The film raises questions like: What strategies are necessary for gaining political office? Or, In what practical ways can social change be brought about? Or, How can political alliances be forged? From such a perspective, *Milk* can be considered a film that sidesteps questions of gay relationships and gay sex to instead focus on aspects of politics.

In doing so, what does this film achieve? I would like to propose that what *Milk* achieves is something that psychoanalysis has for a long time called *suture*. This approach entails re-thinking the notion of suture as it has primarily been theorized in Film Studies and psychoanalysis more generally.[1] As a point of departure, I want to begin with three propositions that will guide my approach to the notion of suture.

1. Cinema has the potential to tell stories that suture audiences. Suture, therefore, is less a matter of cinema technology, technique or apparatus and much more a matter of constructions of subjectivity at the level of narrative and story situations. For the spectator, then, suture functions in order that the spectator can be positioned in relation to the story of a film, as well as to the characters, situations and events that are part of that story.
2. Processes of suture occur by way of what Film Studies has for a long time called *identification*. More specifically, suture occurs as the articulation of a situation or set of relations. Thus, for example, a spectator, when sutured, identifies

less with a specific character than with a set of relationships between characters. At the cinema, therefore, the spectator identifies less with characters than with what characters do in relation to other characters, with decisions characters make or actions they perform in relation to other characters and to the story world more generally.

3. As a result, these positions of identification will be constantly shifting and changing throughout a film. If suture was for many years defined as a way of "fixing" the attitude of the spectator or of producing the spectator as a "total" or "unified" subject, then these conceptions have to be rejected. Rather, suture will fix the spectator *at certain points* in the unfolding of a film's story—suture is, after all, a matter of freezing or arresting the subject—but such fixing will never be definitive or totalizing. It will instead always be temporary and will adapt from moment to moment.

These, then, are the three points I wish to set out from. There will be different processes of suture—Stephen Heath convincingly argued such a point (1981: 100)—so that it is both impossible and unproductive to point to a definitive, "one size fits all" account of suture. I want to set out from two historically important approaches to suture in the cinema. Each of these approaches adapts, in its own way, the fundamental conception of suture first theorized by Jacques-Alain Miller: that psychoanalysis gives us a conception of the human subject in which a "zero" assumes the status of a "one" (1977/8: 30). For the traditional conception of suture and cinema—first put forward by Jean-Pierre Oudart (1977/78), and then strongly backed up in an essay by Daniel Dayan (1985)—this sutured human subject who assumes the status of a "one" is utterly fraudulent. The unified conception of the sutured subject, exemplified by the unified view of the spectator at the cinema, is explained famously by way of classical cinema's typical use of shot/reverse-shot set ups: the absence (and thus the *zero*) indicated by the first shot of an alternating couplet is "filled in" and unified by the second shot, thus giving rise to a conception of suture in which a *one* (the answering shot) takes the place of a *zero*. Suture, from this perspective, merely produces a unified subject in ways that go hand-in-hand with conceptions of cinema's ideological apparatus, especially the apparatus articulated by Jean-Louis Baudry (1985). Thus, this conception of suture, prominent during the 1970s and 1980s (see Silverman's brilliant summation [1985: 194–236]) was a key element in explaining the ways in which cinema spectators were duped by the imaginary operations of the cinema and the psyche.

Slavoj Žižek has, since the 1990s, offered a convincing alternative version of cinematic suture. He is satisfied that suture produces a one in place of a zero, but he accepts this formulation only on the proviso that the zero will never be completely covered over: the *one* is never unified or self-contained. Rather, a remainder or leftover is produced by any and every suture (see Žižek 2012: 587). Žižek provides a range of cinematic examples, from Hitchcock's *The Birds* (1963) (see Žižek 2001:

38–39), Kieślowski's *Three Colors: Blue* (1993) (Žižek 2001: 169–71) and others, before delivering a summative declaration: "We can see how", he writes, "in this precise sense, suture is the exact opposite of the illusory self-centred totality that successfully erases the decentred traces of its production process". To which he adds, "Suture means that, precisely, such self-enclosure is a priori impossible, that the excluded externality always leaves traces within" (Žižek 2012b: 157). Suture can never fully be closed; it always leaves an excess or remainder, and it is this excess that is most fundamental to it.

What does Žižek's analysis allow us to achieve? For a film like *Milk* the answer might appear obvious: if, in this film, suture occurs at the level of the political, then the excess or remainder that is left out of this political suture is rather obvious: what is ejected is sex. As countless commentators argued, the film's logic, as well as the faithfulness of its representation of Harvey Milk, was compromised by the avoidance of gay sexuality (see Erhart 2011: 158–60). And yes, we can surely accept such a criticism: *Milk* manages to suture the political field only insofar as it excludes issues of gay sexuality.

But might there be something more to be said other than simply admitting that "what is included will always contain what is excluded", that "the excluded externality always leaves traces within"—such are Žižek's claims—with the result that there can never be a full or unified totality, that any totality can never be fully closed? I certainly believe we can say a good deal more than that. Therefore, I want to examine several ways in which the topic of suture might be expanded, with the overall aim of considering how such a theory of suture might contribute to an understanding of the politics of cinema.

What is missing in the traditional theory of cinema and suture put forward by writers like Oudart and Dayan, but also elided in the process of suture proposed by Žižek? What is missing is *a way out*: either one is trapped by suture, or one can merely endlessly confront the repressed remainder that is produced by suture. In contrast with these theories, I would like to propose something of a way out, for I believe this is what a film like *Milk* shows us.

I've never been entirely convinced by the Lacanian focus on subjective lack, of a subject defined by a lack that consigns humanity to a life of misery and frustration. From that perspective, the only overcoming of the subject's definitive lack will be a fraud, an illusion, and this is pretty much what the traditional theory of suture tells us: there can only ever be subjective consistency if that consistency is based on an imaginary that is mired in illusion.[2] And this is the conclusion posed by the commentaries on cinema and suture put forward by Oudart and Dayan. An alternative, proposed by Žižek, is to declare that for the subject there will always be a remainder, a blind spot, a gap or lack; whatever the term, the subject is destined to fail and will do so repeatedly. Any victory will invariably be shallow and illusory, a mere construction—a fantasy—that covers over the true Real lurking beneath it. At the end of the day, this offers no way out, as though the definitive conclusion to be drawn from psychoanalysis is that human existence is inherently unsatisfying and disappointing.

I remain unconvinced by such constructions, and there are places in Lacan where notions of suture and the Imaginary are not merely matters of covering over a lack, nor of the potential remainders that will spill out of that covering over. As Lacan claimed in *Seminar XI*, "Only the subject – the human subject, the subject of desire that is the essence of man – is not, unlike the animal, entirely caught up in this imaginary capture. He maps himself in it" (1977: 107). Lacan thus argues that the human subject *can* and often *will* be caught up in imaginary capture but also that the subject is capable of mapping herself in this imaginary: the Imaginary does not automatically lead to illusion or ideological distortion. Following up on the ramifications of all of this for a theory of suture will require going beyond Lacan to some degree. What follows, therefore, is a three-part inquiry that proposes another theory of suture. The models for this theory are based on the psychoanalytic notions of sublimation and the "joke-work" as well as the notion of "hegemonic suture" taken from the field of political theory.

Lacan's concise definition of sublimation, "the raising of an object to the dignity of the Thing (*das Ding*)", can immediately bring us onto the terrain of suture (1992: 112). Sublimation takes an object that is nothing, a zero—Lacan tells us that "in every form of sublimation, emptiness is determinative" (ibid.: 130)—and raises it to *something*, a something that brings with it a transcendent allure. "The Thing", Lacan writes, "will always be represented by emptiness precisely because it cannot be represented by anything else" (ibid.: 129). The sublimated Thing will be empty, "nothing", but it is precisely in this emptiness that it thereby attains the capacity to act or stand in for *something*. This superimposition of something in place of nothing can provide the subject with a certain promise of consistency, with a project that can be considered potentially fulfilling and worthwhile. Most pointedly, the example of sublime allure is related by Lacan to the medieval rituals of courtly love, and there should be no need to declare here that the ritual of courtly love is futile, a quest that will end in nothing; rather, the satisfaction lay in the *pursuit* of the beloved ideal, in the project of possible love. It is here that sublimation provides its promise, and Lacan assures us that sublimation is nothing less than a "way out": "One thing only alludes to the possibility of the happy satisfaction of the instinct and that is the notion of sublimation" (1992: 293). While there is certainly no promise of satisfaction here, Lacan goes so far as to acknowledge its possibility.

Why, however, might this notion of sublimation have anything to do with the theory of suture? I believe we can place suture and sublimation in the same general orbit by virtue of the ways they articulate the relationship between nothing—emptiness, zero—and a something that will enter into the place of that nothing in order to fill it, to give it consistency. Traditional theories of suture will declare that this "something" will be illusory or fraudulent; Žižek too will tell us that even if something enters the place of nothing in this function, it will nevertheless leave a remainder, that a repressed leftover will invariably return. By contrast, the notion of sublimation gives us an object and a form in which there is, according to Lacan, "satisfaction without repression" (1992: 293).

Crucial here in Lacan's approach to sublimation is the transformation of the aim of the drive. Typically (as with Freud) this is conceived in terms of a transformation of the drive from a sexual aim to a non-sexual one. And yet, as Lacan makes clear, *any* aim of the drive will always-already be a transformation, for there can never be a "pure" drive. Additionally, Jean Laplanche in his seminar on sublimation emphasizes that it is difficult if not impossible to clearly separate a sexual aim from a non-sexual one in cases of sublimation (1980: 111). What is ultimately at stake for the theory of sublimation expressed here is a satisfaction of the drive without repression.

If, therefore, we can consider sublimation as providing a way in which the subject can find satisfaction in the pursuit of an object—such as the pursuit of the idealized object of courtly love—and if additionally we can consider the hypothesis that suture can likewise be considered to operate in such a manner—as positing for the subject a relation to an object that can deliver "satisfaction" or "happiness"— then we can at least begin to chart some of the events of *Milk* in these terms.

First and foremost, we can consider the film's shift from the sexual to the non-sexual, from sexuality to politics. Following a prologue in which we are shown the assassination of Harvey Milk and the then Mayor of San Francisco, George Moscone (Victor Garber)—thus delivering to us the event towards which the remainder of the film will build (and noting too that Van Sant here follows the structure of Rob Epstein's documentary on *The Times of Harvey Milk* [1986])—the film focuses on the preceding years of Harvey's life. He is something of a drifter, and on his 39th birthday we see him pick up a younger man, Scott Smith (James Franco), in a New York subway station. This sexual fling quickly turns into a relationship and, in the hope of giving his life new direction, Harvey moves with Scott to San Francisco where they open a photographic store. Harvey soon becomes something of a community organizer: he sets up a mailing list of customers and provides a meeting place and safe haven for homosexuals in the area around Castro Street.

Many in the community tolerate the gay subculture, and the businesses there appreciate the additional trade that the gay community brings. Some members of the public actively support the work Harvey does, but there is still a widespread intolerance and antipathy towards the gay community. Such intolerance very much applies to the police whose tactics are oppressive and often violent. The film charts these tensions in clear ways that make the opposition between pro-gay and anti-gay the centerpiece of the film's plotting. It is specifically in response to police oppression that Harvey turns to politics: he decides to run for election as a city supervisor (i.e., a member of the city council) and is adamant that the gay community needs a leader and organizer in order that the discrimination and violence perpetrated against the gay community can be addressed.

What thus happens in the first 20 minutes or so of *Milk* is a transformation from sexuality to politics. What the film offers is a process analogous to sublimation.

(To be clear, the film does not *sublimate* nor does it *represent* sublimation; rather, it provides a shape or process akin to sublimation.) Certainly, we could argue that Harvey himself transforms his sexual passions into political striving. But I would also want to declare that this is what the film's "drive" does: the film itself changes its emphasis from sexuality to politics.

This movement from sexuality to non-sexuality, from a life of drifting and trying to find one's feet to a life that discovers something akin to a purpose or project is, as I have tried to insist, analogous to sublimation. But I would also like to insist that it can be conceived in terms of suture. In his passing comments on suture Lacan effectively refers to it as a process that freezes movement, as something that "arrests" the subject, especially of a subject fixed by the gaze of another (or the Other) (1977: 117–18). And so too might the situation Harvey finds himself in be seen as something akin to an arrest, but only insofar as this arresting or fixing can be seen as fixing on a project. The Harvey we have seen so far in the film is restless and ungrounded; he looks for brief, evanescent encounters; he shifts from New York to San Francisco until he finally fixes on a political quest. He discovers something—an aim, no less, that, as Lacan would say, will put him in a relationship with the *Thing* (see 1992: 119). This might even be a sure way of defining suture: the invention or discovery of a something that fixes one's life or actions in a particular direction, as that which imbues life with a substance and outside of which life would be imbued with a kind of nothingness. And it will come as no surprise that Lacan's theorization of the gaze—it is there that he mentions suture—is very much a reconfiguring of many of Sartre's points from *Being and Nothingness*. And perhaps that is all the theory of suture is concerned with, the conviction that there can be *something* rather than *nothing*.

Notions of sublimation can tell us a good deal more about what is at stake in *Milk*. Those who fail or refuse to sublimate their sexuality come off rather badly in *Milk*: Harvey's long-term lover, Scott, eventually walks out on him because he feels Harvey is spending too much time and energy on politics: their sexual life has been smothered by Milk's political obsessions. The other lover depicted in the film, the flamboyantly over-emotional Jack Lira (Diego Luna), goes so far as to commit suicide, again because Milk's political commitments have led him to neglect their relationship. Harvey Milk, we might say, is himself a model of political sublimation: he knows how to transform his sexual drives into political practice.

But such a conclusion is rather too hastily made. The issue of sublimation will need to be considered in a little more detail. Jean Laplanche, in a long seminar devoted to the topic, was led to question the all-too-easy dismissal of sublimation as the transformation of sexual libido into a non-sexual aim. First of all, as Laplanche makes clear, the object of sublimation will always be imbued with sexual energy. And what are the political aims of Harvey Milk if they are not also sexual? His campaign is ultimately one that aspires to champion the right for gays to have sexual relations freely and equally. Thus, in *Milk*, politics is not so much a refusal or denial of sexuality as it is a way of achieving sexual satisfaction in a free and safe way. The aim changes from sex to politics, but in the end, politics is a way of achieving the goal of sexual freedom. Sublimation here is more a matter of giving consistency to a "something" that can imbue a life with a purpose or project. It is a way of potentially satisfying the drives, that is, of finding or discovering or inventing something in conscious life that will provide satisfaction for drives that are otherwise unconscious.

Sublimation is not capitulation or repression. For Harvey, no criticism is strong enough of those in the gay community who wanted to fly "underneath the radar": there are several meetings in the film between Harvey and two other San Francisco gay rights power-brokers, David Goodstein (Howard Rosenman) and Rick Stokes (Stephen Spinella), who try to counsel Harvey against running for public office on the grounds that a gay man running for office will be too public and open and that it will incite hatred towards the gay movement. Milk rejects such a strategy and instead urges his fellow homosexuals to make their sexuality public. Here, privacy, playing politics behind the scenes and staying in the closet are declared enemies. Repression is not an option.

Sublimation is not suture, and yet, as I have tried to argue here, sublimation can provide human subjects with projects that are worthwhile and can offer the possibility of "satisfaction without repression". The conception of suture I am proposing here offers a similar possibility of satisfaction. With this in mind, does psychoanalysis posit other modes of experience in which, like sublimation, there is a translation of impulses from the unconscious into the system of consciousness, which gives rise to a satisfying outcome? Freud certainly posits such a process in his 1905 book on *Jokes and Their Relation to the Unconscious* (1976). Jokes, Freud argues, rely on the effect of transforming something that is unconscious into a form that is at one and the same time acceptable to conscious thought but also satisfies the unconscious in one way or another. Methods of condensation and displacement come to the fore as unconscious material is reworked—by the "joke-work"—in order to be acceptable to conscious thought, but also to give some access to the kind of unconscious wish-fulfillment similarly performed by dreams under the influence of the "dream-work". In writing specifically of what he calls tendentious jokes (those that have an "aim"), Freud writes that, "They make possible the satisfaction of an instinct (whether lustful or hostile) in the face of an obstacle that stands in its way" (1976: 144). Thus, like sublimation, the joke functions in such a way as to subject unconscious drives to conscious revision but achieves this in a way that does not amount to repression. On the contrary, these processes provide modes of expression of unconscious drives, the "satisfaction of an instinct".

These formulations allow the process of suture to be approached from a somewhat different angle. Again here, as was achieved above with sublimation, it is not a matter of declaring that jokes work in the same way as suture, but rather that the form or process of jokes functions in a way that is analogous to suture. If traditional suture theorists proposed suture as an illusion of unity that covered over and thus repressed a hidden truth, while Žižek, for his part, emphasizes the repressed or excluded remainder that always accompanies suture, then examining the logics of sublimation and jokes instead focuses on modes of transformation that express the unconscious in some way. Might it be possible to conceive of suture in such a way?

Freud emphasizes that tendentious jokes are particularly designed to combat social restrictions and moral codes in a manner that can induce a psychical discharge. What is normally repressed in everyday life can be accorded a conscious outlet by way of jokes. In short, jokes offer a feeling of freedom from repression (1976: 145). At another point Freud argues that the best jokes happen spontaneously; we can't see them coming: "We have an indefinable feeling, rather, which I can best compare with an '*absence*', a sudden release of intellectual tension, and then all at once the joke is there – as a rule ready-clothed in words" (ibid.: 225). The mechanism here is one in which there seems at first to be a nothing—an *absence*, Freud tells us—only for that nothing to suddenly be replaced with a "something": the punch-line of the joke. It is this sudden filling up of the absence that creates the satisfaction of the joke, and I don't think I am going too far to suggest that the filling up of the absence is precisely a functioning of suture: the punch-line "sutures" the joke, as it were.

If we examine closely the propositions on suture put forward by Jacques-Alain Miller, then we will see that what is essential to suture is what he calls the "identity function". Miller argues that, in order to be an identity, a "one", any identity must therefore distinguish itself from that which is not identical: a *zero*. "It is this decisive proposition", he writes, "that *the concept of not-identical-with-itself is assigned by the number zero* which sutures logical discourse" (Miller 1977/8: 29). The zero is thus that which is "ejected" from identity: the zero is definitively outside the terrain defined by the one, and it is only by drawing that border that the identity of the one is established. However, Miller then takes an additional step: the zero is *not nothing*. Rather, in order to be effective—and thus to enable the possibility of identity—the zero must be *taken for* a one: it is a non-representable that must nevertheless function in the guise of a representation. Why? Because a zero is not nothing; rather, it is part of the series of numbers without which the notion of number, beginning with one, would not be possible. To continue the rhetoric, Miller then goes on to tell us that the notion of the "zero as one" is a fundamental logical proposition of psychoanalysis: it is a non-identity that functions as an identity, a non-truth that functions as a truth. Such a non-identity, Miller will finally tell us, is none other than what psychoanalysis calls the subject (ibid.: 33).

A zero that is taken for a one: might we not see here, alongside a logic designated as suture, also those processes of sublimation and jokes that I have alluded to? Sublimation takes something sexual from the unconscious and transforms it into something intellectual or artistic (or political, as occurs in *Milk*). Laplanche puts it more forcefully: sublimation is a matter of the symbolization of objects that would otherwise have no symbolic existence—nothing less than a transformation of a "nothing" into "something" (1980: 60–61). And do not jokes also transform something forbidden and unspoken into a discourse that is spoken? "What these jokes whisper", Freud tells us, "may be said aloud: that the wishes and desires of men have a right to make themselves acceptable alongside of exacting and ruthless morality" (1976: 155). In short: what should have remained a zero can, by way of sublimation or jokes become not nothing; what should have remained silent can be said aloud.

A further step is necessary. By far the most significant re-theorization of suture occurred in the field of political theory. This interjection is of course that of Ernesto Laclau and Chantal Mouffe's conception of "hegemonic suture", as defined in their *Hegemony and Socialist Strategy* (1985: 47). Perhaps what is most remarkable about Laclau and Mouffe's formulation is that it conceives of suture from both the inside and the outside. This means suture has to be approached in a dual manner. First, from the inside, what are the processes that enable a suture to be produced; how is a social field brought together or "sutured" in such a way as to form a totality or identity? Second, from the outside, what is it that is excluded from the identity that suture produces? That is, if suture brings together certain elements of a social field in order to form an identity, upon what exclusions is this identity formed?

For Laclau and Mouffe, one final determinant is necessary, and that is to answer the question, What is politics? Laclau and Mouffe offer a very clear definition of what politics is: it is "a type of action whose objective is the transformation of a social relation which constructs a subject in a relationship of subordination" (1985: 153). Where a group or community fights against its subordination: there we have politics.

If the conditions of hegemonic suture are to be met, then, two operations need to occur. The first, which Laclau and Mouffe call *articulation*, involves the bringing together—the suturing, no less—of a social field. What this means in straightforward terms is that, if disparate groups of scattered individuals are in positions of subordination—if they are exploited, discriminated against, and so on—then some expression of that subordination must be articulated in order for it to be acted upon. In short, if an exploited community is fragmented and powerless—say, a group of factory workers has been asked to work longer hours with no increase in pay, and none of the members of the workforce quite knows how to express his or her feelings of subordination at such a request—then a way must be found to bring together and articulate those feelings of subordination. Only then can political action begin to take place. Articulation is the prime mover: it is only by articulating the concerns, hopes, needs and desires of a subordinated social field that a suturing of that field can emerge. "The social *is* articulation", Laclau and Mouffe declare, "insofar as 'society' is impossible [without such an articulation]" (1985: 114).

In *Milk*, what the character of Harvey Milk expresses above all are the articulations that make the suturing of a social field possible. He unites the gay community of San Francisco, many of whom had not wanted to be involved in politics and political activism. In doing this, Milk then makes it possible for a social field to act with a view to the transformation of the political field. And such is the major concern of the film: to chart the political transformations that are achieved as a result of the political activism Harvey Milk inspires. Perhaps the key character in this respect is Cleve Jones (Emile Hirsch). Jones is initially skeptical of political activism; he considers politics vacuous and dismisses elections as shallow, bourgeois sideshows. Jones, by contrast with the notion of hegemonic suture, offers a prime example of how potential members of a social field can be defined by fragmentation and difference: in this instance, by a monistic individualism that prioritizes private enjoyment (sexuality, no less) above public issues. As the film makes clear, however, in the end, Harvey was eventually successful in rallying Jones to the cause, and Jones becomes one of his chief allies throughout the film. Jones thus becomes an excellent example of the way in which what was previously not a social field comes to be articulated as a social field, for Jones becomes sutured into the social field defined by Milk's political activism.

At one point, Milk hits upon a masterful tactic of articulation: "dog shit". When, having been elected to the San Francisco board of supervisors, Milk proposes a gay rights ordinance for the city that will protect homosexuals from discrimination in the workplace, he tries to conjure up a way that he can garner more general support from the electorate. He figures that if he wins the general favor of the people of the city, then they will be more likely to support his gay rights ordinance. Therefore, he comes up with the idea that it will be a prosecutable offence if an owner fails to clean up the "dog shit" left by his or her dog. Milk and his aides decide this issue is the number one problem for most people living in the city. The signifier "dog shit" here performs perfectly the operation of articulation that brings about a suturing of the social field: it is something that brings together a range of different interests in a community and "articulates" those interests as a matter of defining a community. In this instance, it matters little whether those who are enraged by dog shit are similar or even sympathetic to issues of gay rights. The fact that these different fields are brought together—sutured—is precisely what is at stake in political formations. It also matters little here what the *contents* of this articulation are: it can be any manner of things, as it is, here in *Milk*, a matter of dog shit. This articulation brings about a suturing of the social field, so that those who are incensed by dog shit might also come to be allied with those seeking gay rights: this demonstrates quite precisely how hegemonic suture operates.

We will recall that this notion of hegemonic suture has a second dimension. If the first of these dimensions shows us suture from the inside—that is, of how a social group or community is brought together—then the second aspect shows us suture from the outside: it is a matter of what is excluded from the social field in order that it may operate as a unity or identity (even if such unity or identity can only ever be temporary). Laclau and Mouffe call this second dimension *antagonism*. "Dog shit" performs this second function, and thus it demonstrates the two dimensions of hegemonic suture. Dog shit clearly comes across as being a bit of a joke in the film, and Milk hams up the publicity opportunities by stepping in some dog shit in full view of television cameras while campaigning. But it is by way of this joke that the similarities between jokes and suture can be pinpointed.

Jokes, Freud tells us, perform a *social function*, especially tendentious jokes. Such jokes require three people: a first who tells the joke; a second at whom the joke is directed; and a third who "gets" the joke (Freud 1976: 143). Suture could be said to function in a similar way: the teller of the joke and the third person who gets the joke are, by way of the joke, sutured in such a way that joins them together; they "share" the joke, as it were. This is analogous to what above I have called suture "from the inside": those who are "in" on the joke are sutured, brought together. The second person in the joke—the butt of the joke—is akin to that which is excluded in the operation of suture, and Freud tells us that such jokes are often fueled by antagonism and a desire to demean the object of the joke. Thus, the person who is the object of the tendentious joke functions in a similar way to the excluded object of antagonism in operations of suture.

For "dog shit", therefore, the butts of the joke are those citizens of San Francisco who fail to clean up after their dogs; they are the "enemies" of the suture invoked by the dog shit joke/law. And the community is thus brought together by their united disapproval of such enemies. Dog shit thus achieves both functions of suture: it brings a community together from the inside—those who are "in" on the joke—while at the same time constructing a barrier against those who are excluded from the suturing process, the enemies who are left "outside" the suture.

This enemy from the outside that is necessary for the operation of hegemonic suture is defined very clearly by Laclau when he declares that "it is through the demonization of a section of the population that a society reaches a sense of its own cohesion" (2005: 70). Politics—and suture—requires the construction of an adversary that is opposed to and thus excluded from the society that is being articulated. In politics, not everyone can win, nor is it desirable that everyone win. Rather, politics is essentially a matter of division, argument, difference. Thus, for one identity to be formed, other identities must be excluded from that identity-formation. For *Milk*, the stakes of such antagonism are clear: one cannot be both pro-gay and anti-gay. Thus, those in favor of gay rights find their antagonistic adversaries in a range of anti-gay lobbyists and politicians: Christian campaigner Anita Bryant, conservative politician John Briggs (Denis O'Hare) (he introduces "Proposition 6")[3] and also one of the other members of the San Francisco board of supervisors, Dan White (Josh Brolin): the only member of the board to vote against the gay rights ordinance, and furthermore the figure who will eventually murder both Harvey Milk and George Moscone. What these figures represent are exclusions from the field of "gay rights supporters", and they are thus external to the community of supporters that Milk manages to suture. That group of supporters is, by being brought together, also actively placed in opposition to these external antagonists. Just as the process of articulation is essential to suture, so too is the process of antagonism fundamental to the political stakes of hegemonic suture.

*

What can the notion of suture contribute to Film Studies? As we have seen, during the 1970s and 1980s processes of suture were most often allied with modes of subjective, ideological illusion at the level of the Imaginary. Since the 1990s, Žižek has attempted to realign notions of suture with the Lacanian Real, thus making an "excluded remainder" central to a new notion of suture. By way of contrast with each of these approaches, by following a different path of investigation on the notion of suture, I have here relied on psychoanalytic conceptions of sublimation and the mechanism of jokes, while I have also taken a great deal from Laclau and Mouffe's theorization of hegemonic suture. I have done this in order to propose an unashamedly positive notion of suture, one that provides a "way out" of the deadlocks proposed by previous notions of suture.

By way of conclusion, I will return to the three propositions with which this paper began. First of all, that *cinema has the potential to tell stories that suture audiences.* Thus, it is less the cinematic techniques employed by films—such as shot/reverse-shot—that are important for conceptions of suture in the cinema. Rather, suture is a matter of the story world evoked by film. If a film like *Milk* focuses on the suturing of a social field in support of gay rights, then it is assumed it will also be attempting to suture cinematic spectators into a similar social field, one that is sympathetic to gay rights issues. In this way, processes of spectatorship are central to operations of suture in the cinema.

Second, *processes of suture occur by way of identification.* Identification is crucial to Laclau and Mouffe's conception of hegemonic suture (see Laclau and Zac 1994), but I would also claim that identification is central to a theorization of cinematic suture. What the cinema spectator identifies with, however, are not specific characters in a cinematic fiction (what Metz termed "secondary identification"). Rather, what is identified with are *sets of relations between characters*; that is, what the spectator identifies with is akin to what Laclau and Mouffe call a "social field". (The origins of such a conception of Film Studies go back to Elizabeth Cowie's classic formulation of "Fantasia" [1997].) Thus, identifications in *Milk* are not solely a matter of identifying with Harvey Milk. Rather, identification will be a matter of identifying with the procedures and actions—as well as the dreams and hopes—undertaken by Milk and other characters in relation to one another. Thus, it will be the relationships between Milk and Scott Smith, between Milk and Cleve Jones, between Milk and Dan White that come to articulate a position or positions of identification in the film.

Finally, positions of identification shift and change throughout a film. Significantly, too, functions of suture will always be shifting and changing. These positions of identification shift and change in *Milk*. For example, early in the film, Cleve Jones rebukes Milk, while later he is sympathetic: the relationship between them changes, and so too will our spectatorship of these relationships change. First of all, Jones is something of an enemy, a person who seems to be excluded from the hegemonic suture; while later he accepts and joins Harvey's campaign, and thus the dimensions or emphasis of the suture change. Conversely, Dan White at first befriends Milk only later to turn against him, and these changes can be considered functions of suture whereby spectators shift and change their sympathies. This is one way of saying that there can never be any stable or permanent position of identity that any spectator will adopt. Any identification and thus any suture will only ever be temporary and thus always open to the possibility of change. Such processes of identification and identity will also never be fully totalizing. Rather, they are contingent and always open to the possibility of further transformations.

Milk provides a rather too convenient explication of these modes of suture, and I fully admit that a film that advocates the political coming together of an oppressed community will offer a rather convenient example of "the political coming together of an oppressed community". And if this might be a definition of suture or hegemonic suture, then I would like to believe that it could also offer a starting point for a definition of cinematic suture. Such a definition fits with some films I have written about in the past (Rushton 2013)—such as *Marked Woman* (Bacon and Curtiz, 1937), *Mr. Smith Goes to Washington* (Capra, 1939) or *On the Waterfront* (Kazan, 1954)—but it might also open up possibilities for future research on other films (such as *Norma Rae* [Ritt, 1979] or the Dardenne brothers' recent film, *Two Days, One Night* [2014]).[4] In short, I would like to believe that there is a future for the notion of suture.

Notes

1 I have gone same way towards trying to redefine suture in *The Politics of Hollywood Cinema* (Rushton 2013: 108–129).
2 See Robert Samuels (1993: 59–74).
3 This was a 1978 'name and shame' proposition for the state of California that would have allowed homosexuals (and anyone who supported them) to be fired from teaching in State schools. The battle against Proposition 6 provides one of *Milk*'s key episodes.
4 I delivered a paper on this topic at the *Radical Film Network* conference at Birmingham City University in February 2015.

References

Baudry, J.-L. (1985) Ideological Effects of the Basic Cinematographic Apparatus. In B. Nichols (ed.) *Movies and Methods Volume 2*. Berkeley: University of California Press.

Cowie, E. (1997) *Representing the Woman: Cinema and Psychoanalysis*. London: Macmillan.

Dayan, D. (1985) The Tutor Code of Classical Cinema. In B. Nichols (ed.) *Movies and Methods Volume 2*. Berkeley: University of California Press.

Erhart, J. (2011) The Naked Community Organizer: Politics and Reflexivity in Gus Van Sant's *Milk*. *Auto/Biography Studies* 26(1): 156–70.

Freud, S. (1976) *Jokes and Their Relation to the Unconscious*. Trans. J. Strachey. Ed. A. Richards. London: Pelican.

Heath, S. (1981) *Questions of Cinema*. London: Macmillan.

Lacan, J. (1977) *The Four Fundamental Concepts of Psychoanalysis*. Ed. J.-A. Miller. Trans. A. Sheridan. London: Hogarth.

Lacan, J. (1992) *The Ethics of Psychoanalysis: The Seminar of Jacques Lacan, Book VII*. Ed. J.-A. Miller. Trans. D. Porter. London: Routledge.

Laclau, E., and Mouffe, C. (1985) *Hegemony and Socialist Strategy: Towards a Radical Democratic Politics*. London: Verso.

Laclau, E., and Zac, L. (1994) Minding the Gap: The Subject of Politics. In Laclau (ed.), *The Making of Political Identities*. London: Verso.

Laplanche, J. (1980) *Problématiques III: La sublimation*, Paris: PUF.

Laplanche, J. (1984) To Situate Sublimation. Trans. R. Miller. *October* 28, 7–26.

Metz, C. (1982) *Psychoanalysis and Cinema: The Imaginary Signifier*. Trans. C. Britton et al. London: Macmillan.

Miller, J.-A. (1977/8) Suture (Elements of the Logic of the Signifier). Trans. J. Rose. *Screen* 18(4): 24–34.

Oudart, J-P. (1977/8) Cinema and Suture. *Screen*, 18(4): 35–47.

Rushton, R. (2013) *The Politics of Hollywood Cinema: Popular Film and Contemporary Political Theory*. Basingstoke: Palgrave Macmillan.

Samuels, R. (1993) *Between Philosophy and Psychoanalysis: Lacan's Reconstruction of Freud*. London: Routledge.

Silverman, K. (1985) *The Subject of Semiotics*. New York: Oxford University Press.

Žižek, S. (2001) *The Fright of Real Tears: Krzysztof Kieślowski Between Theory and Post-Theory*. London: BFI.

Žižek, S. (2012a) *Less than Nothing: Hegel and the Shadow of Dialectical Materialism*. London: Verso.

Žižek, S. (2012b) "Suture," Forty Years Later. In P. Hallward and K. Peden (eds.) *Concept and Form, Volume Two: Interviews and Essays on the Cahiers pour l'Analyse*. London: Verso.

Filmography

Marked Woman (1937) Directed by Lloyd Bacon and Michael Curtiz. USA: Warner Bros.

Milk (2009) Directed by Gus Van Sant. USA: Focus Features.

Mr. Smith Goes to Washington (1939) Directed by Frank Capra. USA: Columbia Pictures.

Norma Rae (1979) Directed by Martin Ritt. USA: Twentieth Century Fox.

On the Waterfront (1954) Directed by Elia Kazan. USA: Columbia Pictures.

The Times of Harvey Milk (1986) Directed by Robert Epstein. USA: Black Sand Productions.

Two Days, One Night (2014) Directed by Jean-Pierre and Luc Dardenne. Belgium/France/Italy: Les Films du Fleuve.

PART VI
Auto/Fiction

15
UNNAMEABLE

Anna Backman Rogers

You asked me once
What it is that I fear
The inchoate endless
Drip drip drip of something
That wracks my brow
And shakes my right palm …
The tremor your brain, and your father before you
Gave to me.
I can tell you now that
It is your obliteration that troubles me.
The secretive and insidious ways
That you have
Seeped out of
This moth eaten and inadequate
Brainhole of mine.
The way that you have become
A character in a narrative
That makes no sense at all.
That I speak around you
Because I cannot reach you.
I recall all the details.
The red birthmark on
The little toe of your right foot.
The meatiness of your hands.
The way you say

"As they say",
When they never do.
The cold clayness of your clasp
As you gripped my hand
And they wheeled you backwards
Down the corridor
Like a film in reverse.
Transformed in your hospital gown,
Your mouth hemorrhaged anger
That I never heard you speak before.
And your disregard for all
The tiresome rules
And the people who follow them.
Because around all of that,
We drew the curtain.

With all of these things,
I am left with nothing to navigate the distance
Between us.
Or to understand
The imprint you so fervently
Squashed down into
My heart that all too often
Pulsates with pain.
The minutes
The hours
The weeks
The months
The years
That now separate us.
A time frame I cannot fathom.
When even did you die?
It was when I wore
Red sandals in the Scottish rain …
And you said
"You never will dress appropriately, will you".
With all of these things,
That are left after you …
What am I to do?

I often see you
Standing on that bridge
And waving to me
Beneath the dark, sunken and sodden skyline

Of Durham.
You had come across Europe
To tell me
That there are things in life that
I cannot control.
And I was only twenty one.
Perhaps you already knew
About the things I have in me
That make me graze up against the
Bodies and brains
That trouble me
In order to feel anything at all.
And to make those things
A part of me.
You taught me then already
That I could not steal your death from you,
However much I wanted to.

So, years later
When your words cut through the stale air
Of the last room you slept in
To ask me if you were dying,
I knew it was because you
Feared that it would not end.
And I have always shared that fear with you.

16
EACH DAY AT A TIME – A DAILY INTERVENTION INTO LOSS[1]

Myna Trustram

When something seemingly unbearable happens
a person is told to *take each day at a time*,
as though their future has been washed clean away.

On 2 August 2012, I started to write a diary. I was at Vejle in Denmark, and on that day I took a walk to Jelling, an ancient Christian place, and passed along a straight road edged by verges of wild flowers; beyond these lay sweeping fields of wheat and barley. I was bored with the landscape; it was too much like the English scenes of my childhood. Only the style of the houses and their particular yards and gardens told me I was in this country called Denmark.

I focused on the flowers rather than the terrain, and I had the idea that each day for a year I would pick and describe a different flower. My hope was that the rhythm of doing this would bring me back to keeping a diary. It was an experiment in how to recover my impulse to write. This was something I had lost two years before when a disaster made my life un-writable. I could no longer find *the words to say it* (cf. Cardinal 1975). The grief of each day was seemingly unbearable and so un-representable in a diary; flowers are bearable, and they repeat each year.

I grew up knowing the names of flowers in the fields, woods and water-meadows of the chalk plain of Wiltshire in the south of England. My mother grew more flamboyant flowers than these in her garden and turned them into stiff arrangements in our house. There were jars of wilting wild flowers on the tables at my infant school after a nature walk, and this division between garden and wild was repeated at the church fair and the Women's Institute competition where you could submit an arrangement of one or the other but not the two together. And now I grow both garden and wild and on the grave of the one I lost in the disaster.

I faced the hazard of sentimentality and whimsicality, but from that day, every day, I looked for a flower, picked it and described it in a diary. August was the easiest month; March the hardest.

I call it *Each day at a time* because the common advice to those who have suffered a great loss, when nothing more can be said, is to "take each day at a time". As though it is too much to consider the future without the lost one, in our case a lost child. I suppose I took the advice, despite feeling contempt for the giver: have you nothing more than clichés for me?

I set myself a task that risked becoming a punishing small feat of endurance. Perhaps that was the point: to punish myself for living on. Equally, it was an assumption of the responsibility of the living to live and record life through small acts that notice what simply exists. I don't normally set myself tasks or tests. Was it a denial of what I really needed to do, a roaming around the surface of grief looking for beauty, rather than a mining into it? There's little to be gained from mechanical acts of will that remove one from desire and imagination. This was no Olympic feat of emotional or botanical stamina in either intention or actuality, though I did begin during the London Olympic fever of summer 2012. In fact, I failed since there were a few days when I forgot to look for a flower and one when I could not find one. I didn't pick 365 flowers.

Monday 3 September 2012

A pink lychnis from a self-seeded clump in the garden. It has a long grey stem and delicate, simple pink flowers. The petals are shrivelled, ragged. The sepal is fluted with high ridges. Two tiny leaves an inch or so from the bottom. Rabbits ears – the grey, furry stem and leaves remind me of a plant from childhood called rabbits ears that I never liked much. The petals are sad, floppy and torn.

I picked the flowers whilst moving about the day: in my own and in neighbours' gardens, in public parks, in allotments, on waste ground, in the countryside, in cities. In England, in Wales and in Scotland, Denmark and Norway. In Stockport, Manchester, Cheshire, Derbyshire, Cumbria, Cornwall, London, Llangollen, Yorkshire, Shetland. I made the diary entries in the evening, often the last thing at night when I was tired, so some are reports of a dutiful mourner rather than studied descriptions of the flower or my mood.

20 November 2012

This is becoming mechanical: the search in the daytime for the flower and in the evening coming up here to record it. There's satisfaction in the slow accumulation. I've done 118 now. Today's flower is tree mallow (lavatera or malva) from a garden on Palatine Road. It's an inch and a half long the flower, with a double calyx and pink veined petals in a trumpet. The ends of the petals are turning inky blue-black.

In her introduction to the new Penguin translation of Freud's *Mourning and Melancholia*, Maud Ellman says, "In order to be lost the object must be looked for; it is the seeking that establishes its absence". She goes on to say, "Art is the means by which we lose the object in order to call it back in a new form" (Ellman 2005: xxii). I think she means that the loser needs to look for the lost object, not to find it but to establish its loss. This is mourning: looking and then knowing the loved one is gone.

The diary was in part a melancholic response to loss in that it was a repetitive search for beauty and its decay. Mourning's longevity means it has plenty of scope for tipping into melancholia. But an absolute distinction between the two, as in the title of Freud's classic text (2005 [1917]: 201–218) isn't helpful. The mourner can rarely be absolutely distinguished from the melancholic.

Freud writes, "In mourning the world has become poor and empty, in melancholia it is the ego that has become so" (2005 [1917]: 205). The daily search and collecting of a flower was a kind of re-entry into the world: an attempt to make it once again rich and satisfying. And it helped to prevent my lapsing into a poor and empty ego; by which I mean it buoyed me up, gave me a job to do. For Freud "the disorder of self-esteem" distinguishes melancholia from mourning (2005 [1917]: 204). Certainly at times my self-esteem was in disarray. It was in part to confound the emotional disorder that my life fell into that I embarked on the diary: a set of simple instructions in sympathy with my inner life (the need for order) and therefore likely to be achievable. If it isn't to drift into melancholia mourning requires one to find not what has been lost but what has been lost within oneself. The loss of the object must be established in order to integrate it into oneself in a new form. Hence the paradox that in losing you find something, a new circumstance, a new object. And in losing you *make* something: a collection, a garden, a diary, a grave.

The shortcoming of the flower diary was when it held me in a mere list of flowers like a curator's catalogue or a naturalist's species list, rather than the resonance of a particular beauty internally. It did have the air of a punishment, a year's sentence, a collusion with an instinct for atonement. But then again, like punishment it contained seeds of rehabilitation in its daily reminder of beauty and love, or what simply exists.

I was living in the same place with the same things around me, but each thing had a new resonance. I breathed disaster and knew of things I didn't want to know. I was surrounded by what I had lost, although there was no actual evidence: no bombed city, no flooded plain, no fallen trees, no mangled bodywork. I want to say that the flowers I picked trembled with this knowledge. Of course they didn't. I simply projected the trembling I felt inside onto those sweet things. Here flowers – you feel and show it, not me!

Sunday 13 January 2013

I think this is chaenomeles speciosa (Japanese quince). It's from the car park by the swimming pool. Cup shaped red flowers. Five petals from a substantial almost succulent calyx. Yellow stamens untidily inside. Just one living flower on this stalk and a dead one. I like it when the flowers come before the leaves on deciduous shrubs.

The diary felt like a rather literal act, a move to root myself in each day, rather than a poet's giving in to not knowing what might be found (see Heaney 2002: x). It came from a curator's impulse to find and record: curating used to be my trade. Though I was inconsolable and didn't want to be part of a literature of consolation, I was seeking consolation as well as insight. I wasn't gathering specimens for a museum's herbarium. I was aligning myself with a living beauty in the hope that it would revive a taste for living. There was a pathos in the act of collecting whereby I speeded the decay of each flower, put it in a box with the others and made a collection of dried and dead flowers. Each flower in a herbarium is laid out on a piece of paper, identified and dated, whilst my flowers are tangled up in boxes.

Sunday 24 February 2013

If we "dream ourselves into existence" (Christopher Bollas, Being a Character 1992), what am I trying to dream into existence in this diary? I walked around the garden this afternoon. The only things in flower are witch hazel, pulmonaria, kerria, polyanthus and winter-flowering jasmine. I have attachments to all these plants, good and bad, but my rule is to find a different one each day. I haven't done that. Nothing.

FIGURE 16.1 Collection of flowers. Photographer: Mary Stark.

The diary is no blithe "take each day at a time". The flowers wither and bring to mind each day's dying; they will continue to fade, like the artist Anya Gallaccio's gerberas in her gallery installations. As one critic of her work has said, "Discrete experiences of beauty and art are pinpricks in large areas of time. Flowers are slowly grown, and then, in one quick moment, cut – and at their very prime" (British Council 2009). They then add, "the 'unbearable' nature of beauty [as Albert Camus describes it] is the offer of 'for a minute the glimpse of an eternity that we should like to stretch over the whole of time'" (ibid.).

The narrator of Ali Smith's *Artful* (2012) has lost her lover but nevertheless talks to them and asks, what will happen next? The diary told me what would happen next. Each day I would find a flower and describe it. It was a holding on to what's known. Ali Smith describes giving in to loss, lying down with it and allowing it to do what it wants, allowing the imagination to work. I wanted the diary to be a recovery of imagination. This imagination thing is where it faltered because some entries were perfunctory, more fitting for a herbarium catalogue than poems. The flowers lost their symbolic power when the diary became simply the last thing I did at night. I chose a pedantic form to release something more flowing. The diary's formula is its attraction. Each day a job is done. But it's the recovery of the capacity to imagine another kind of life that signals development. The dreaming of the lost one in imagination is the work that the diary performed. Later, I came to read in Richard Mabey's *Nature Cure* that it wasn't the splendour of nature that cured his depression but the imaginative acts he undertook in his exploration of it (see 2006: 224).

> When something seemingly unbearable happens
> a person is told to *take each day at a time,*
> as though their future has been washed clean away.
> The days go by and the suffering settles in.

Saturday 1 June 2013

> *After a week away I open the kitchen door and the garden overflows. Pink campion and aquilegia are adrift, pouring over the edges. And there's a promise of more to come, forgotten plants wait to appear in this glorious spring and summer. I hate the ivy-clad sycamores that lour over the garden but someone pointed out that they are habitats for birds, and the birds do sometimes sing and sing throughout the day as though there is no past, no lost hovering thing.*

I was nervous of becoming bound up in the cliché of flowers as symbols of loss and dying. It seemed to work, though. Just think of the simplicity of this: in Herman Hesse's unfinished novel, *Haus der Träume* an old man removes himself into his garden to tie up his roses and prepare to die (see Lindqvist 2012: 9). I call upon a canon in order to turn this common experience into something greater. I open Roland Barthes' *Mourning Diary* (2011) and find:

> July 18, 1978 To each his own rhythm of suffering.
> (…)
> July 20, 1978 suffering … it's an essential, an intimate part of yourself …
> (2011: 162, 163)

And Margaret Atwood:

> not just some, but *all* writing of the narrative kind, and perhaps all writing, is motivated, deep down, by a fear of and a fascination with mortality – by a desire to make the risky trip to the Underworld, and to bring something or someone back from the dead. (2003: 140)

My diary wasn't a risky meditation on suffering but a keeping on through a daily recording of beauty that actually entailed a shortening of that beauty. It was a daily *intervention* into loss. If an intervention is a coming between, then I was squeezing something in between my self as the subject of grief and the object of my grief. I had lost the one who came between me and my own death. Loss demands ritual and daily practices. The diary was a kind of slow, controlled collecting, an enactment of the impulse to search and find.

I chose a device for writing about loss, a diary, that has time at its heart. David Grossman's book about parental loss is called *Falling Out of Time* (2014) and Denise Riley's book about losing her son is called *Time Lived, Without Its Flow* (2012). Our daughter fell out of our time, or rather she shot out of it. I have to get it accurate, these metaphors and verbs, and make the links with others but preserve the excruciating exactitude of what happened in our particular case. I lost a unique part of my life and so attempt to keep what makes me like no other one on Earth.

> When something seemingly unbearable happened
> I was told to *take each day at a time,*
> as though my future had been washed clean away.

Postscript

Following the accident one of my earliest thoughts was: but this happens all the time to people across the world, how can something so common be so obliterating? And besides, the psychoanalysts say that every one of us is in mourning (or perhaps melancholic) because as infants we all felt a profound loss of attachment to our mothers. The answer to my question of course is that you have to feel loss and death for yourself; there is no preparation. But I still turned to others' presentations of death in literature and music, for a link to the wider human experience, for some preparation after the event. In my performance of this text, I presented these two things – my personal response interspersed with others' reflections. And here was my difficulty: how to present the unpresentable and have it heard, without simply appealing to a sympathy vote.

I've been asked by listeners to the text: what kind of response do you want? For these people it seemed to hang somewhere, to be *in a kind of suspension* between an evocation of suffering and a narrative examination of that suffering. The one being raw and not much mediated and the other an analysis, or art even. When I perform the text, it's interlaced with my emotional embodiment. It's different if I give it to you as a piece of writing to read.

So how to present both my experience, something I am deeply connected to and that might therefore engender compassion, anxiety, tears, *and* an intellectually and artistically driven enquiry? How might these two go hand in hand? One answer seemed to be to align myself in some way with art and with nature. When I cry at Schubert or the moonlight on the sea I cry with the ache of the beauty, I am not suffering. Perhaps something similar could go for my audience – not suffering but waving recognition. The flowers are presentable and representable; they are not suffering.

When I write I sometimes have D. W. Winnicott's deceptively simple question in the back of my mind: what makes life worth living (1988 [1971]: 76)? And in my case I have to add *again*. What makes life worth living *again*? In her book *Dust,* Carolyn Steedman says that Winnicott is "trying to understand those situations in which people are free, *in a kind of suspension* between the constraints of external and interior compulsions and dictates" (2001: 81, my italics). I think there is no actual freedom, just a greater access to spontaneity and creativity. Accidents cast one adrift from such things. Winnicott's answer to his question is "creative apperception" (1988 [1971]: 76). I think he is talking about what Patricia Townsend has called the endowment of "the outside world with elements of our own experience" (2013: 154). Perhaps I was loading onto the flowers my sorrow but mingling it also with elements of the flowers, their commonplaceness, their charm, their Latin name.

In *The Artistic Turn: A Manifesto* the authors quote Jorge Luis Borges: "I think we can only allude; we can only try to make the reader imagine" (Coessens, Crispin, and Douglas 2009: 156). My piece was an allusion to an experience, not a representation but an allusion and a presentation. I'm looking for my lost object and making something new, something that isn't the lost one but that contains elements of her. And then repeating that over and over again.

This thing I am experiencing isn't actually mourning, melancholia, grief, sadness, trauma. It's death. Those other things suggest a passing state. This state I am in will never pass, this knowing of death. It doesn't need to be graced by ritual, it is simply here with me now. The flower diary was divorced from conventional ritual because I wanted to stay with the knowing of death, I didn't want to move into an easier state of mind. It was a settling into a new state, the repetition of everyday life, rather than a working through. It was an attempt to organise the chaos of mourning and to move into the "preliminary chaos" (Milner 2013: 169) of the creative process.

> The point is that this wasn't *the usual order of things*:
>   In the usual order of things, lives run their course like rivers. The changes and metamorphoses of a life due to vagaries and difficulties, or simply the natural unfolding of circumstance, appear as the marks and wrinkles of a continuous, almost logical, process of fulfilment that leads ultimately to death.
> *(Malabou 2012: 1)*

So begins Catherine Malabou's *Ontology of the Accident*. Our young daughter's *process of fulfilment* was halted by an accident. To use these words of another, of a philosopher, to describe her death is strangely and alarmingly exhilarating. I am drawn to this book because it links her accidental death to some wider philosophical enquiry; it elevates a stupid failing of attention into something else. It was an accident. Blame can be apportioned, but I cannot place my grief within some larger narrative of warring humanity, psychotic episodes or natural destruction. So I am left with a narrative of vulnerability, of death and life; it is this that flowers lend themselves to, exquisitely.

Note

1   This is a slightly revised version of a text (without the postscript) that I first performed at the Nordic Summer University in Ulsteinvik, Norway, 2013. I later performed it at the Month of Performance Art in Berlin, May 2014, and it is the basis of a sound-art piece (with Helka-Maria Kinnunen) made for the Finnish Broadcasting Company (http://www.helkamariakinnunen.fi/aaniuniversumi.html).

References

Atwood, M. (2003) *Negotiating with the Dead: A Writer on Writing*. London: Virago.

Barthes, R. (2011) *Mourning Diary*. London: Notting Hill Editions.

Bollas, C. (1992) *Being a Character: Psychoanalysis and Self Experience*. London: Routledge.

British Council (2009) *Preserve Beauty (New York)*. Available from: http://visualarts.british-council.org/collection/artists/gallaccio-anya-1963/object/preserve-beauty-new-york-gallaccio-19912003-p7871. [Accessed: 19 August 2015].

Cardinal, M. (1975) *The Words to Say It*. London: Picador.

Coessens, K., Crispin, D., and Douglas, A. (2009) *The Artistic Turn: A Manifesto*. Ghent: Orpheus Instituut.

Ellman, M. (2005) Introduction: Bad Timing. In *On Murder, Mourning and Melancholy*. Trans. S. Whiteside. London: Penguin.

Freud, S. (2005 [1917]) Mourning and Melancholia. In *On Murder, Mourning and Melancholy*. London: Penguin.

Grossman, D. (2014) *Falling Out of Time*. London: Jonathan Cape.

Heaney, S. (2002) *Finders Keepers*. London: Faber and Faber.

Lindqvist, S. (2012) *The Myth of Wu Tao-Tzu*. London: Granta.

Mabey, R. (2006) *Nature Cure*. London: Pimlico.

Malabou, C. (2012) *Ontology of the Accident*. Cambridge: Polity.

Milner, M. (2013) Winnicott: Overlapping Circles and the Two Way Journey. In J. Abram (ed.) *Donald Winnicott Today*. London: Routledge.

Riley, D. (2012) *Time Lived, Without Its Flow*. London: Capsule Editions.

Smith, A. (2012) *Artful*. London: Hamish Hamilton.

Steedman, C. (2001) *Dust*. Manchester: Manchester University Press.

Townsend, P. (2013) Cultural Experience and Creativity: An Introduction. In A. Kuhn (ed.) *Little Madnesses: Winnicott, Transitional Phenomena and Cultural Experience*. London: IB Tauris.

Winnicott, D. W. (1988 [1971]) *Playing and Reality*. London: Pelican.

17
THE SCENT OF PHILOSOPHY

Birthe Tranberg Nikolajsen

Suddenly I could smell the same scent as in my grandmother's house.

I have been at the summer school a few days. When I entered my hotel room the scent was intense, and I was torn back to wonderful holidays. In my grandmother's home I was allowed to read books, and she gave me books to enjoy during her afternoon nap.

The scent is a bridge to my past, a bridge to my early beginnings, to my desire and to my emotions. The days at the summer school provide a sense of belonging and freedom and open me up to the underlying sources of emotions and a state of well-being.

The bridge leads me over a swamp where no emotions exist and where the core of well-being is drowned in rough seas. From this the only flight available is into nothingness. Under the bridge is the shame over my family's neglect and failure.

In my mother's home I was not allowed to read.

...

I have studied philosophy for 13 years now.
I didn't tell my mother until half a year ago.

Her reaction was, "What will you use that for?"
I told her, I want to do research about what knowledge is important when you bring up children. Immediately she started a story that was meant to tell me that the only important thing is to be stiff and tough. Otherwise the children will not know the difference between right and wrong, she said.

She only noted herself and was not interested in anything about my study and me. She didn't mention anything about herself or what she meant, but then she was only arguing to justify her own abuse and neglect of my siblings and me.

I lost myself while she spoke.

Perhaps that was the main reason I had not told her before. I could not bear to see that she is not interested. That the feelings of other people are simply beyond her.

Early in my childhood I learned that I had to hide my feelings and my need to avoid activating her anger. Now that she is older, her anger does not turn on so easily any longer.

Previously she would have belittled me and ridiculed me, even in front of the other people. My experience was that if I caused her anger, it would bring about her rage. She would be unable to control herself; sometimes she locked one of us in a dark room for half a day or more.

Now I understand her anger and neglect were due to her inability to see and understand other people. It depends neither on my feelings nor on me.

The face

Her small feet entered into the grass
The straws touched her hands
The seeds flew through her fingers

The wind gently touched her cheek
The sound of the grasshopper's tingling reached her ears
And the song of the lark

All of it was like mother's gentle voice

Summer went
Autumn and winter

The small feet were cold in the snow
Always looking for mother's voice
She heard the sound of it
in the sky above and in the earth below

Her steps became stronger
Her body stretched up
She is walking on her father's fields
Her mind made up, as nothing else matters

A desire

Every breath is pushed in with mother's breath
Every word is spoken with mother's voice
Every question is answered with mother's words

Even "Yes" in the church
Is mother's "yes"
The divorce was a shame against mother

The cows had made the path
It leads to the far corner of father's field

Clouds gather in the sky
It darkens

Nothing can stop her steps
The wind blows on her back
The lake appears ahead

The meadow grass cuts the feet
And the earth is flooded with water

She jumps from tuft of grass to tuft of grass
Not to touch the water
The surface of the lake gathered
The wind made ripples on the water
The thunder rolled across the sky

The water in the lake is rough
Gathered to be shaped as her mother's face

Mother's face was all over the lake
Enticing and intimidating
It will leave nothing behind

Suddenly she stopped
Her soundless scream went into one with the thunder
She gave up

Hanging between the thunder and the face
As a soap bubble
Without an inner life
And without an outer

It is not possible to study without an inner life and without an outer.

Your ability to learn and your way to knowledge are linked to your emotions and your senses.

My feeling of being nothing, the emptiness of the inner life has followed me everywhere. It had made it difficult to form my own life, think my own thoughts and speak my own words.

However, the scent in the hotel room gave me a connection to my senses and to my inner world, where the capacity to recognise senses, emotions, desires and intellect can take place. At the summer school I was in a safe place, where I was accepted and recognised for the person I am, and I'm given a common interest.

It gave me a connection to my outer life. The summer school gave me possibilities to manage my fear of what would happen, if I speak out, and if I share my feelings and emotions.

I decided to give a presentation at the summer school.

The trial

Actually this is not a presentation it is a picture.
In fact it is not only a picture it is a bit of a film.
Come to that, it's not a film either it is a part of...
Well, you will see.

It is about all that stuff about resolution of feelings.
It is about all that stuff about construction, how we make our understanding of the world.
It is about all that male and female power.
And it's about the necessity to be in contact with your emotions to be able to break through to knowledge.

My picture:

We are in a courtroom. A man is on trial.

There are a number of chairs along the wall at the back.
I arrive first. I go to the far corner.

The prosecutor comes in.
She is a beautiful young woman with long blond hair.
She is wearing a thin and fine silk shirt, elegant black trousers and small tiptoe shoes.
Her movements are easy, and she has a pretty smile.

The accused comes in, and his lawyer. They are both men.
The lawyer is wearing the typical formal clothing of a lawyer with heavy shoes.
The accused looks down at his feet.

Two men sit in the back in the other corner.
"Don't go there", they had texted the day before.
"If you do anyway. It will only be for your own amusement".

When the judge enters, everybody stands up. It's a female judge.
The trial starts.

The young woman is full of words. She speaks and speaks,

shows pictures.
All those words.
All these things, which had been done.
People come and go.
A lot of words.

The accused just sits there. His clothes are simple, and dirty, his hair is long.
He is overweight and unkempt.
His face closed.
After the first session he looks around and catches my eye. He looks shifty.

Every word was meant to judge him
and they did.

Then during the session a transformation of him begins to occur.
It is as if he is collapsing into something else. A kind of breaking down.
His movements, his attitude, his words, all of him.
Slowly he begins to look like my father.

Suddenly he points at me.
"She is my sister, she was the only one who helped me, when I needed
somebody to stop all this."

Now I couldn't remain hidden anymore. It is my brother.

He got two years in prison for sexually molesting his stepdaughter

....

All this is my family.

Now, the transformation of my brother in the court scene was exactly what
I experienced happening with my father during my childhood. My mother
was the beautiful young judge.
All her words damaged my father until he ended up humiliated and
accused.

It didn't amuse me being there
as my brothers had said it would.

It had been the explanation I always have had in my head, but never spoke
aloud.
Now the court has announced it,
the judgement had been pronounced on my family.

Now I'm free.
I'm free to speak.
My mother's words are not in my mouth anymore.

This is one of the pillars supporting the bridge between my early beginnings and my being able to study, to speak, a beginning of new life as a free human being. This is my possibility to study philosophy.

If it had been left to me to judge my family, I would have done the same as my mother: only judging.

This has been my picture. My picture presented in words.
Now it is yours, and you can read into it what you like.

*

What is it about, describing the worse part of my life?

To tell my story:
To obtain so much courage.
To sit face to face with people that I admire and respect for their intellectual capacity and then tell them the most shameful part of my life and my family.
This was a struggle.
My struggle against the effect of my coping mechanisms in my family life.

This was a kind of redemption
from a single idea
that my only possible way to live in the world was to be silent
whilst hiding and supressing my emotions.

Now I'm free to speak.

INDEX

abjection 61, 76–7, 127
Abraham, N. 81
accidents 24–8, 222–9
Acedia 165
"acousmêtre" 64–7
adoptee-biological father reunion 171–83
Adoptioncritic website 173
affects 41, 143
aggression, youthful rebellion 59
"All Those Sleep Shapes" 116
Alpha function 164
already-no-more 114
Althusser's model 102
Altman, Robert 62
Alzheimer's disease 21, 22, 26, 34
amans amare 137
Amour 20–36
An Archive of Feelings 189
"an idea emerges as one speaks" 100
Antigone 196–7
An Unfinished Story 185, 190–2, 196
A Passage to India 76
"Aphantasia" 145
aphasia 144–6
Apocalypse Now 62, 63
"appetite comes while one eats" 100
appreciation, victims showing 173
Arendt, Hannah 40, 46
Aristotle (philosopher) 29, 94, 95
Arnheim, Rudolf 66
Artful 226
articulation 211–12

art of the impossible 130–8
The Artistic Turn: A manifesto 228
Asimov, Isaac 79
assassination 43
As You See 57
Atemwende 116
"A Throw of the Dice" 116
Attachment Theory 163
Atwood, Margaret 227
"auditory experience of self and place" 59
aural objects, materiality of sound 67–8
Aus der Geschichte einer Infantilen Neurose 98
automaton 29–30
awkwardness, aesthetics of 137

Bach, J.S. 162
bad acid trip 63
Balso, Judith 124
Barthe, Roland 227
Bataille, Georges 61
Baudry, Jean-Louis 204
Bauman, Zygmunt 61
Beckett, Samuel 23
Beguine Hadewijch d'Anvers 137
Being a Character 225
Being and Nothingness 208
belonging, adoption 176–8
Belting, Hans 60
Benjamin, Walter 58, 60
Benny's Video 24, 26
Bermudez, Jose Luis 145
Beta elements 164

Bettelheim, B. 162
Beyond the Pleasure Principle 27, 36
big Other 100–1
binding 153, 181, 223
biological father reunion
    experience 171–83
Bion, Wilfred Ruprecht 40, 46–7, 163–4
The Birds 204
birth father's role 171–83
"black milk" 115
Black Skins, White Masks 82
blame 229
Blanchot, M. 135, 136
Blank, Arthur 43
"Blume" 114
body and voice 64–7
Boleyn, Anne 119
Borges, Jorges Luis 228
Bosch, Hieronymus 165, 166
Bosnian war 187–90
Bourgeois respectability 160
brain injury: *Amour* 23–8; madness *vs.*
    pure void 33–4; unrepresentable 22
Brechtian alienation effect 194
Brodsky, J. 122
Brolin, Josh 213
Bryant, Anita 213
burning child, dream of 29–30
Burroughs, William S. 126–7
Butler, Judith 185, 195, 197
butterfly dream 102

Caché 24
Cahiers du Cinéma 132
camera, function of pointing 100
Cameron, James 68
Camus, Albert 226
Cartesian Dualism 149
Cartesian model 150
Caruth, Cathy 43, 175, 197
casting away 76
castration anxiety 98
Catholic Church 119; *see also* papacy
Caute, David 88
Cavalcanti, Alberto 66
Cavell, Marcia 147
Celan, Paul 111–17
Chater V. 122
children: child sexual abuse 11–12;
    communication between mother and
    baby 159–60, 164–5; dream of burning
    child 29–30; infantile sexuality 9–11,
    15–17; maltreatment in post-war
    Guatemala 187; mother's neediness 180;

parental sexual abuse and incest 13–15;
    Play Room 12, 14; relationship with
    mother 165; true nature of parents/
    teachers 167
Child Sexual Behavior Inventory 11
Chion, Michel 64, 68, 69
Choang-tsu (Chinese skeptic) 102
Choreodrama 75, 88
choreographic structure 193–4
Christianity, centrality of love and
    concern 167
Christ Jesus 79, 80
cinema 53–6, 203–15; *see also* Hollywood
cinematograph 62
"civilization process" 55
claustrophobic states 166
Claustrum 166
Coetzee, J.M. 76
cognitive penetration 146
cognitive states 153
colonialism 1, 75, 77–9; *see also* touching
    and speaking
colonial period 74–8, 80–4, 86, 88–9, 91, 134
colour symbolism 162
commentary 61
communal grieving 186–7
communication: medium is part of the
    problem 161; mother and baby 159–60,
    164; through gesture 97
concentration camps 44; *see also* Holocaust
*The Cook, the Thief, his Wife and her
    Lover* 165–6
Cooper, Andrew 171
Copenhagen symposium 1
Coppola, Francis Ford 62, 63
Corpus 77
Coulthard, Lisa 20
countertransference 46, 158–9
Cowie, Elizabeth 214
Cratylian theory of communication 95
Crichton, Charles 66
critical agency 81
culture: and hysterical states 160; with
    respect to the "self" 180–2; superiority
    of 187–8; trauma, in adoption 173–4
cut finger 98–9
Cvetkovich, Ann 189

Damsio, Antonio 22
Dark Continents 80–1
das Ding 206
das Heimliche 113–14
das Unheimliche 36
Davies, Norman 161

da Vinci, Leonardo 162
Davis, Tracy 195
Davoine, Françoise 35, 43
Dayan, Daniel 204, 205
Dead of the Night 66
death 20, 26, 219–21, 222–9
death drive 36
"deferred action" 185
delayed expression of trauma 8–9
de Lestrange, Gisèle 113
Deleuzian "minor literature" 86
delusion and play-acting 166
"demetaphorization" 81
Demeure 75
depression 165
Derrida, Jacques 2, 75–7, 78
Descartes, Rene 45, 77, 144, 149, 152
desire 82–5, 118, 121–2, 178–80
destructive plasticity 21, 24–5,
    30, 35–6
Deuten 106
Diana (Princess) 80
diary 222–9
"Dice" 116
Die Familie Schroffenstein 96
digital cameras 56–7; *see also* film
    experience, paradigm shift
"disconnection," adoption 175
Disgrace 76
dissensus 137
Distinguished Service Order 40
Docudancing Griefscapes 185
dog shit 212–13
Dolar, Mladen 58, 95
Dolby technology 63
The Doll's House 166
Donne, John 118–28
"doublethink" 40
dreams: of burning child 29–30; pointing
    98–9, 102, 106; primary process 147;
    trauma 28–30
Duras, Marguerite 130–8
Dust 228
dynamic mental systems 151–5

The Ear of the Other 75
Easy Rider 64
Echo 62
"Ecstasy" 121–2, 123
Edison, Thomas Alva 62
Ego 8, 161
"The Ego and the Id" 147–9
Elias, Norbert 55
Elizabeth I (Queen) 118–19

Elizabeth (Princess Palatine) 45
Ellman, Maud 224
empiricism 150
Encore 116, 136
Entwurff 17
epilepsy 26
Epstein, Rob 207
estrangement 114
Et Dukkehjem 166
ethical violence 3
ethnic cleansing 187–90
Euclidian geometry 69
The Exorcist 66
expulsion 76
Eye/Machine 57

"The face" 232–3
"face-house experiment" 154–5
Falling out of Time 227
False Self 163
"*Familienroman*" 132
family, meaning of 182
Fanon, Frantz 82
"Fantasia" 214
fantasy of completeness *see* adopted
    women-biological fathers reunion
    experience
fantasy *vs.* reality 8–9
Farocki, Harun 57
Fassin, D. 172
"Fear of Breakdown" 8
Felman, Shoshana 2
fiction: relationship to truth 111–12; *vs.*
    truth 8–9
fictionality 23
film experience 53–70;
    see also Hollywood
Fink, Bruce 29
"The Flea" 121
Fleming, Victor 66
Fliess, W. 8
flowers 222–9
Flückiger, Barbara 63
Folman, Ari 63–4
form: annihilation of 21; destroying/erasing
    21; form of 22–4; plasticity 22
Forster, E.M. 76
Fortsein game 103
Foster, Hal 185
Foucault, Michel 60
*The Four Fundamental Concepts of
    Psychoanalysis* 130
Franco, James 207
Franko, Mark 190

Franzén, Carin 130–8
Freeman, Tabitha 171
Freud, Sigmund: aphasia 144; child sexual abuse 17; critical agency 81; death drive respresentation 36; *der Traum* and *das Trauma* 29; desire 122; difference of conscious 3; dream of burning child 29–30; dynamic mental systems 151–5; *Fortsein* game 103; hysterics and abandonment of the theory of seduction 8–9; jokes 209; meaning from mysterious data 162; mourning and melancholia 81, 224; *Nachträglichkeit* 25; pointing 98–9, 106; primary process 146–7, 150–1; problem of the image 143–56; psychic trauma 174; Schreck 28; sexuality and sexual trauma 7–8; topographical model 146; trauma 27, 174, 175; the unconscious 131, 147
Freud, the Reluctant Philosopher 150
Friedkin, William 66
"Fugue of Death" 113
function, disease of 144
Funny Games 24, 26

Gage, Phineas 21–2
Gallaccio, Anya 226
Garber, Victor 207
The Garden of Earthly Delights 165
Gaudillière, Jean-Max 35, 43
Gauker, Christopher 145
"gaze" 53–5, 69, 101
generalized seduction 11–12
Genetic Sexual Attraction 180
genocide 187–90
Ginsberg, Allen 125, 126, 127, 128
Glass, Philip 64
global warming 166
gloves 193–4
Goll, Ivan 113
Gordon, Avery F. 188, 197
Goriely, Serge 20, 26
The Grass is Singing 76–9, 81–5, 86, 88, 89
Greenaway, Peter 165–6
Green Eyes 132, 136
griefscapes 185–97; *see also* mourning
Griffith, Keith 173
Grossman, David 227
Guardian prize for literature 86

hallucinations 98–9, 104, 147
Haneke, Michael 20, 25
"haptic seeing" 57

Haus der Traume 226
healing touch 79–80
"hearing with our eyes" 70
Heath, Stephen 204
heaven/hell 165–6
Hegel, G. 96, 122
hegemonic suture 212–13
Hegemony and Socialist Strategy 211
Henry VIII (King) 119
Herman, Judith Lewis 45
Hesse, Herman 226
hierarchy and delay 62, 70
"high theory" 75
Hirsch, Emile 212
History beyond Trauma 43
Hitchcock, Alfred 66, 69, 204
Hollywood 62, 70, 99; *see also specific movie*
Holocaust 114, 125–6, 189
Holt, Robert 144
"Homage to Marguerite Duras, on 'Lol ravissement de Lol V. Stein'" 135
homosexuality 125, 126; *see also Milk*
Hopkins, Jim 154
Horgen, Peder 190
horse phobia 151
"Howl" 125, 126
Hume, D. 150, 152
hysterical states 8–9, 160

Ibsen, H. 166
identification 163, 203–4, 214–15
ideological Other 103
"Ideology and Ideological State Apparatuses" 102
images: concept of moving 57–8; metaphysics and metapsychology 146–51; psychic symptom 155–6; representation without language 143–56; and sound relationship 62
imagination 143–56
The Imagination 143
impossible 130–1, 133, 136
"improperly buried bodies" 197
indexicality 54, 56, 69
infantile sexuality 9–11, 15–17
intellectual understanding 162–3
International Committee of the Red Cross (ICRC) 188
The Interpretation of Dreams 17, 122, 144, 162

Jaws 62
Jenseits des Lustprinzip 103
Jewish community 97

Johnston, Adrian 22
jokes 34, 97, 147, 209–14
Jokes and Their Relation to the Unconscious 209
"joke-work" 206, 209
Jones, K. 176
jouissance 83, 103–6, 136–7
Joyce, Elizabeth 171–83
Jung, Carl 162–3
Jurassic Park 56

Kafka, F. 165
Kant, Immanuel 144, 151–5
Kant's Transcendental Psychology 152
Khanna, Ranjana 77, 80–1, 88
Kieslowski, K. 69, 205
Kill Your Darlings 125
Kinetoscope 62
kinship issues 182
kissing 121
Kitcher, Patricia 152, 153
Kittler, Friedrich 60
Klein, Melanie 163
koans 193
Koolhaas, Rem 61
Kristeva, Julia 61, 127, 133–5
Kubrick, Stanley 66
Kuhiwczak, Piotr 187

Lacan, Jacques: desire 118, 122, 124; destiny 83; difference of conscious 3; "irruption" of the Real 27–58; Lacanian Real 22, 137, 214; language failure 1; pointing 95, 101; the Real as impossible 130–1, 133; subjective lack 205, 206; sublimation 206; suture 214; the Thing 208; truth having a structure of fiction 75, 91, 111–12
Laclau, Ernesto 211, 213, 214
La creazione dell'uomo 94
Lambek, M. 173
Lang, Fritz 66
language; *see also* speaking: aphasia 144; and conscious thought 145; failure 1; mental image 144–6; of mourning 90–1; poetic structure 126; and pointing 99–100; representation without 143–56; taboo against English 86, 88
"language shadow" 116
Laplanche, Jean 9–12, 207, 208
latex gloves 193–4
Laub, Dori 2, 43–4

L'Autre manque 101
"Law of Association" 152
Lazarus 79
Le désir et son interprétation see Seminar VI
Le Poème 124
Les impudents 132
Lessing, Doris 74–81
Levinas 185, 195, 197
"life drives" 36
Lifton, B. 172
limiting symbolism 128
liquidity 61
listening to listening 17–18
living dead 36
living figures of death 36
"living in the Head/Breast" 165
loss: of reality 54; signifying or compensating for 69–70; unattainable love 122; unsymbolised 77
Lost Highway 66
Lost in Transmission 43
love: being in love with love 137; central to Christianity 167; denial of God's love 165; subject to 135–7
Love, Mortality and the Moving Image 90
The Lover 134–5, 137, 138
Lovers in Time or How We Didn't Get Arrested in Harare 78
Lucas, George 62, 63
Luckhurst, Roger 173
Lumiére Brothers cinematograph 62
Luna, Diego 208
Luria, Alexander 22
Lynch, David 66–7, 69

Mabey, Richard 226
Madonna (religious figure) 165
Magdalene, Mary 79, 80
Makari, George 152, 154
Malabou, Catherine 20–36, 229
The Malady of Death 135
Mandelstam (poet/essayist) 122
Man with a Movie Camera 55
Marechera, Dambudzo 74–5, 86–9
Mark (biblical) 79
Marked Woman 215
marriage 166
Mars 160
"massive psychic trauma" 41, 44
masturbation 15–17
Max-Planck Institute for Evolutionary Anthropology 100
McClintock, Anne 76

McGinn, Colin 145
McGowan, Todd 53
McMillan, Anita Schrader 186–7
meaninglessness 132
melancholia 81, 133–4, 224, 228
Meltzer, D. 163, 164
mental image and language 144–6
The Meridian 113–17
"messy text" 186
metaphysical conceit 120–1
metaphysical poetry 123
metapsychological models 143
Meynert, Theodore 154
Michelangelo (artist) 94
Milk 203–15
Miller, Jacques-Alain 2, 204, 210
Milošević, Slobodan 190, 192
Mo, Kristianne 190
Mohn and Gedächnis 115
moment of accident 24–6
"morality play," adoption 174
Morrison, Toni 190
Mossige, Terje Tjöme 190
mothers: adoptee-biological father reunion
    174–8; being needy 180; communication
    with baby 159–60, 164–5; conflict with
    231–3; relationship with 165; sexual
    abuse and incest 13–15
Mouffe, Chantal 211, 214
mourning 81, 224, 228; *see also* griefscapes
Mourning Diary 227
Mourning Sex: Performing Public Memories 196
moving images, concept of 57–8
MP3 player 59
Mr. Smith goes to Washington 215
Mulholland Drive 66–7
Mulvey, Laura 63
Murch, Walter 63, 64
murder 45
music 59–61; *see also* sound

nachträglich 8–9, 14, 17
Nachträglichkeit 25, 34
Nagra equipment 62
Naked Lunch 126, 128
The Naked Sun 79
Nancy, Jean-Luc 74
Narcissus 62
Nashville 62
naturalistic theory 153
Nature Cure 226
neediness 180
The Nest of the Singing Birds 119
neurosis 3

"new blessed ones" 34
new Messiah 165
Newton, Isaac 111
The New Wounded 20–2, 29–30, 32, 34
Nike 66
Nobus, Dany 2
"Noli me tangere" 79
"No More Sand Art" 116, 117
non-conceptual sensory experience 155
non-existing place 117
"the non-realized" 3
Norma Rae 215

object petit a 53–5, 56, 58, 67, 69
Object Relation theory 162
Oedipus/Oedipal dynamics 128, 161
O'Hare, Denis 213
"On Aphasia" 144, 145
"Only the Lonely" 67
On the Waterfront 215
The Ontology of the Accident 32
Ontology of the Accident 229
"open window," images as 58
Opsenica, Marja 190
Orbison, Roy 67
Orwell, George 40
other's perceptions 180–2
other's suffering 34–5
"other woman" feeling in adoption 180
Oudart, Jean-Pierre 204, 205
over-identification 193
overprotection 45

Palatine, Elizabeth (Princess) 45
panic states 166
papacy 80, 97; *see also* Catholic Church
paradigm shift, film experience 53–8
The Parallax View 36
pathological perverse seduction 11–12
performance, trauma and 194–7
personality 22, 167
The Pervert's Guide to Cinema 67
Petrachan conceit 119–20
Phelan, Peggy 195–6, 197
Phillips, Adam 23
phobias 166
pinching, touch screens 57
*Pirates of the Caribbean: The Curse of the Black
    Pearl* 105
plasticity 21, 22, 29–30
Plato (philosopher) 94, 95, 121
Plato's Cave, instantiation 55
play-acting 166, 180
Play Room 12, 14

The Poem 124
poetics 111–17, 126–7
pointing 94–106
Point of View 79
Poland, after communism 187
politics, familial 180–2; *see also Milk*
Pope *see* papacy
pornography 15–17
Portrait of a Black Artist in London 75, 88
post-colonial period 3, 74, 76–7, 80–1,
    88, 89
"Post-Trauma" 29–30
post-traumatic stress disorder (PTSD) 192–3
pregnancy 123
pretense and play-acting 166, 180
Pride 165
Primal Wound theory 179; *see also* adopted
    women-biological fathers reunion
    experience
primary process 146–7, 150–1
Problem of the Puer Eternus 163
process of fulfillment 229
productive imagination 153, 155
Projective Identification 163
Proposition 6 213
Protestant Church 119
Proust, Marcel 59
psyche, surviving its own
    destruction 20–36
Psychiatry journal 145
psychic symptom 155–6
Psycho 65
"Psychoanalysis, Representation and
    Neuroscience: the Freudian Unconscious
    and the Bayesian Brain" 154

Radcliffe, Daniel 125
Raeburn, Michael 85
The Raj Quartet 76
Raphael (artist) 94
The Ravishing of Lol Stein 132
reaction patterns to choreographic
    structure 193–4
reading 231
reality *vs.* fantasy 8–9
the Real: cannot be named 116;
    destructive plasticity 35; dream of
    burning child 30; fantasy covering the
    true 205; as impossible 130–1, 133;
    meeting with 114–15; poems and poetry
    116; returning in an absentee way 185;
    suture and 214; truth relationship to
    fiction 111–12; (un)representing 53–70;
    voice and body 65

Rechtman, R. 172
the Rectum 165
"reductive over-identification" 193
refreshing of images 57
Reich, Steve 64
religious superiority 187–8
remembering the dead 41–6
"rememories" 196
Renaissance era and perspective 70, 94
representing and representation:
    analyst as representative 167;
    crisis of 131–3; problem of the
    image 143; the unrepresentable
    1–4, 40–1, 46–7, 125–6, 161;
    without language 143–56
"reunion" experience, adoptee-biological
    father 171–83
Richter, Max 64
Riley, Denise 227
rituals 227
Riva, Emmanuelle 26
Rosenman, Howard 209
rugby matches 80

Sacks, Oliver 22
sadism/masochism 36
Said, Edward 1, 77
St John's Gospel 79
Saint Teresa 137
Salpêtrière hospital 25
sampling metaphor 61
Sartre, Jean Paul 61, 143–56, 208
scent as bridge 231
Schauer, Maggie 186–7
Schmidt, Michael 60
Schopenhauer, A. 154
Scott, Paul 76
scratch-video metaphor 61
Scuola di Atene 94
"seeing with our ears" 70
Self, Will 79–80, 88
"self" role, performance 179
Seltzer, Mark 173
Seminar on "The Purloined Letter" 101
Seminar VI 118, 123
Seminar VII 53
Seminar XI 3, 53, 206
sense of gesture: pointing 94–106; touching
    and speaking 74–91; (un)representing the
    real 53–70
Serious Games 57
Seven Deadly Sins 165
"Seventeen" 117
The Seventh Continent 20

sexuality and sexual trauma: child sexual abuse 11–12, 234–6; expression of 15–17; hysterics 8–9; infantile sexuality 9–11; Laplanche's theory 12–15; listening to listening 17–18; relevance of Freud's dilemma 7–8
Seymour, Jane 119
Shakespeare plays 162
Shreck 28
Sistine Chapel 94
"The Site of the Memory" 190
Six Meditations 77
"skin," body surface 68
"skin of the film" 57
Smith, Ali 226
snow 116–17
social exclusion 76
social function, jokes 213
"Solitude" 132, 136
solution in guise of a problem 156
sound 53–70
The Soundscape of Modernity 58
"sound is a modality of seeing" 61
South Africa, after apartheid 187
speaking 74–91, 99–100; *see also* language
Spielberg, Steven 56, 62
Spinella, Stephen 209
Spinoza, B. 122
Spivak, G. 88
spool game 103
Sprachgitter 114
spreading, touch screens 57
Srebrenica-Potocari Memorial and Cemetery 190
Star Wars 62
Steedman, Carolyn 228
Sterndeutung 162
still-here 114
stroke *see Amour*
Studies on Hysteria 7
Sturken, Marita 189
subjectivity and belonging 176–8
sublimation 206–10
succession of images 57
suicidal states 165
Suljagić, Emir 189
suspension 228
suture 203–15
Sveaass, Nora 186
symbolism: arbitrary nature of 161–2; limiting 128; and representation 77
symbol of void 32
Symposium 121, 136

"Take what you can, give nothing back" 105
tapping, touch screens 57
Tauber, Alfred 150, 151–2
Télévision 113
tendentious jokes 213
Terminator II 68
The Testament of Dr Mabuse 66
testimony issues 3
theory of seduction, abandonment of 8–9
therapies, focus of 167
"therapôn" 43
the Thing 148, 206
thinking *vs.* feeling 163
Thirty Years' War 45
Thompson, Emily 58
Three Colors: Blue 205
Three Essays on Sexuality 9
Time Lived, Without the Flow 227
The Times of Harvey Milk 207
"*Todesfuge*" 113, 115, 116
tone, setting with sound 58–64
"top-down" conceptual capacities 155
Torok, M. 81
touch, digital cameras 56–7
touching and speaking 74–91; *see also* language
touch screens 57
Townsend, Patricia 228
traffic light symbolism 161–2
"Transcendental Aesthetic" 153
"transcendental illusion" 152
transcendental *vs.* transcendent 153
Traum 106
The Trauma Symptom Checklist for Children 11
trauma: bodily consequences of 192–3; body locked by a lack of meaning 7–18; break-in 26–8; cerebral 21; clinical 41–7; containing influx of disturbing energy 21; culture in adoption 173–4; delayed expression 8–9; dreams 28–30; "frozen reality" of 41; griefscapes 185–97; intersubjective nature 31; as passing state 228; and performance 194–7; psychoanalytic psychodynamic approach 39–40; reaction patterns 193–4; refusal of psychic binding 23; representing the unrepresentable 39–47; trauma-*qua*-Real 28; without a subject 20–36
"Traumaculture" 173
Traumdeutung 106, 162
"The trial" 234–6

truth: defining 111–13; poetics 116;
    subjectivity and belonging 176–8;
    subject to 133–5; *vs.* fiction 8–9
tuché 27, 29–30
Tutt, Daniel 124
Two Days, One Night 215
2001: A Space Odyssey 65–6

The Unavowable Community 135–6
The Uncanny 36
Uncle Sam poster 102
"The Unconscious" 147
"Un coup de des" 116
undead ("zombies") 36
undiscovered genius 165
Unerkannt 106
"unexamined life is a Life not worth
    living" 167
unity, cognitive state 153
"unknowability" 22
unrecognizability 31–4
unrepresentable: presenting 118–28; the real
    53–70; representable and the 40–1, 46–7;
    representing 125–6, 161; thinking the 36;
    trauma and performance 194–7
unsymbolised loss 77
unthinkable, representing 36
Urbild 105

Vagrant 185
Valéry, Paul 60
van Helmholtz, Hermann 154
Van Sant, Gus 203–15
Veit-Wild, Flora 75, 88, 89–91
ventriloquism 64–7
Vertov, Dziga 55
victims being grateful 173
Vidak, Slaven 190
violent gestures 80
Virtual Reality 163, 166
viscosity 61

"vision is a modality of hearing" 61
visual agnosia 145
visual thought 143, 144
voice 54, 58, 64–7, 77
Von Franz, Marie-Louise 160, 163
von Kleist, H. 96, 100

Walkman (player) 59, 63
Walter Murch 63, 64
Waltz with Bashir 63–4
Wang, Joy 76
way out, missing 205, 206
Wenk, Dieter 60
*What Should We Do with
    Our Brain?* 21
wheelchair performer 194
"White Post Colonial Guilt" 76
The White Ribbon 20
Wilson, Emma 78, 90–1
Winnicott, D.W. 8, 163, 228
The Wizard of Oz 65
Wolfman's dream/hallucination
    98–9, 104
Women of Srebranica 197
Woods, Tiger 66
working-camps 113; *see also* Holocaust
wrestling 80
writing is nothing but advertisement
    134, 138
"*Wunsch*" 122

"you" 102, 114

Zeitgehöft 116
Zelizer, Barbie 189
Zeman, Adam 145
Zen-like *koans* 193
zero and zero-level 33, 36, 206, 210
Žižek, Slavoj 32–6, 67, 69, 204–6, 210
"zombies" (the undead) 36
Zorn, Fritz 160